THE
PICTURE BOOK
OF
PERENNIALS

A

THE
PICTURE BOOK
OF
PERENNIALS

ARNO AND IRENE NEHRLING

ARCO PUBLISHING COMPANY INC.
219 Park Avenue South, New York, N.Y. 10003

First Arco Printing, 1977

Published by Arco Publishing Company, Inc.
219 Park Avenue South, New York, N.Y. 10003
by arrangement with Hearthside Press, Inc.

Library of Congress Cataloging in Publication Data

Nehrling, Arno.
  The picture book of perennials.

  Includes index.
  1. Perennials. I. Nehrling, Irene, joint author.
II. Title.
SB434.N4 1977   645.9'32   76-46317
ISBN 0-668-04163-3 pbk.

Printed in the United States of America

Dedicated to
Dorothy Louise, Rena, Pat and Pam
and to their parents

In Appreciation

Before writing this book, we sent out about 300 question-naires to landscape architects, professional gardeners, horticultural writers and teachers, firms specializing in and selling perennials, to all state federated garden-club presidents and to the horticultural chairmen of individual garden clubs in Massachusetts. In the questionnaire we asked for comments and opinions on the negative features of perennials, since positive features are usually available from catalog descriptions. We also hoped to turn up some unhackneyed thoughts on the subject of positive features.

The response was surprisingly good and the information received added many valuable perspectives for Part I of the book. The results were well worth the time and effort involved. We have used the material we received in our descriptions of perennials from A through Z. Quotation marks have been used if a great deal of information was taken from one source. Our sincere thanks to everyone who took the time and made the effort to send along really helpful, useful information.

We are deeply indebted to Prof. Clark L. Thayer, retired head of the Department of Floriculture at the University of Massachusetts, and to Richard C. Hands of the editorial staff of *Horticulture* magazine for their all-around help and particularly for their assistance with Part I.

Our thanks to Prof. Warren D. Whitcomb, entomologist at the University of Massachusetts Waltham Field Station, for his advice on Insect and Disease Pests; to Dr. Clement G. Bowers, Maine, New York, for helpful suggestions on reducing maintenance, and to our landscape friend Harold D. Stevenson, Marshfield, Mass., for his sketches showing the use of perennials in the landscape scene.

Laura Hatton, assistant editor of *Horticulture*, helped in selecting many of the photographs and engravings. The credit for them goes to the Massachusetts Horticultural Society; to both we extend our deep and sincere thanks. Muriel C. Crossman and her competent staff in charge of the Massachusetts Horticultural Society's fine library were ever ready to be of service and are a source of dependable information. Elizabeth Higgins of the staff deserves a special "thank you."

A new book brings us the pleasure again of working with Charlotte Bowden, Marblehead, Mass., who did the line drawings which add so much to the value of the text. Paul E. Genereux, East Lynn, Mass., is responsible for most of the photography. We are grateful to both these people for their wonderful cooperation as well as to Louise Bordeau who typed the manuscript and never once complained about the copy.

We wish especially to thank our editor, Nedda Anders, for her wise counseling, complete cooperation and the endless enthusiasm she has shown in working with us on this book.

                                    Arno and Irene Nehrling
Needham Heights
Massachusetts

TABLE OF CONTENTS

Why Perennials Are Favorites

Blessed with a variety of virtues, hardy perennials have been admired and enjoyed by many generations of flower lovers. They are the spark plugs or backbone of almost any successful planting, the main feature of most American gardens. Bleeding-heart, delphinium, iris, peony and phlox, were old-time favorites and are as popular or even more widely grown and used today.

Every garden worthy of the name has some perennials. Once planted they increase in beauty and value as they mature. Fifteen or so years after purchase some perennials are still giving ample return for their space, demonstrating the durability of well-chosen varieties.

1. *Labor and money savers*—Because of their degree of permanence, perennials save the gardener both money and time. Perennials re-appear year after year with a minimum of attention; they are extremely useful for permanent effects. True, some, like the columbine, coreopsis and delphinium, are short-lived; others, like the aster and chrysanthemum, tend to die out unless the roots are dug up, divided and replanted frequently; still others, if left undisturbed, will spread and crowd out their

neighbors. However, there is a long list of perennials which if grown in congenial surroundings may be left undisturbed and will improve and increase in size and beauty with the passing years. Some, like peonies, live indefinitely.

Long-lasting plants naturally require less work; by eliminating the sowing of seeds every year, they are a real boon to the busy gardener. High maintenance can be considerably reduced by the selection of easy, permanent kinds.

Perennials are a sound investment since they increase steadily in value, multiply by dividing, and pay generous dividends of cuttings, seedlings and gifts for friends and neighbors.

2. *Infinite diversity among them*—Perennials provide widely varied flowers, foliage, form and texture and, often, fragrance. There are round, flat and cushion types; bell, trumpet and globe shapes; daisy-like forms and spike or spire-like formations. The comprehensive range of colors allows ample choice for a satisfying blend to suit any taste. Some are of relatively pure hues representing every color in the spectrum while others like the bearded iris are of indescribable blends. The gaillardia with its brilliant rich reds and yellows is a study in analogous hues.

Foliage variation in shape, hue and texture is boundless. The tall, attractive, strap-shaped leaves of the day-lily, the sword-like iris foliage and the majestic handsome growth of the peony leaves are decorative throughout the season. All shades of green and gray are represented, some have interesting autumn coloring. Many perennials present interesting foliage effects when bloom is past.

Fragrance is to be found in such old-time favorites as the lemon day-lily, lily-of-the-valley, pinks and sweet violet and many of the common roadside plants in cultivation today as bouncing-bet (saponaria) treasured only for its beautiful night-fragrant, white flowers and the richly aromatic tansy.

3. *At home in any location if wisely chosen*—The height and adaptability of perennials cover such a wide range there is a perennial to fill every need. There are tall types for the back of the border, medium ones for the center, low-growing kinds for the foreground with very low growers suitable for edgings.

There are perennials adaptable to any soil or exposure situation
—shade and heavy soil, full sun in a light, sandy location, and
moist ground.

4. *Landscape possibilities are endless*—Because of their flexi-
bility, versatility and many uses perennials lend themselves to
variations according to the taste of the individual gardener with
an awareness of their possibilities. They add charm outdoors as
well as indoors in cut bouquets. They need not be restricted to
a border. Large, bold clumps may be used effectively with
shrubs and have great landscape value. Low-growing ground
covers such as ajuga and blue phlox are effective planted under
trees and taller more rugged specimens like the globe-thistle
can add midsummer color among shrubs. Some small, low
growers make excellent rock garden plants and are effective
used in wall gardens. Many are suited to a formal style of planting, others to semi-wild or naturalized treatment where cultivation is not practical or desired. Perennials are at home beside a
pool, at the back door, along a fence or beside a patio. Many
can be effectively used in tubs, planters or boxes for the window, patio, or penthouse.

5. *Cover a long blooming period*—Perennials furnish a continuing succession of color and bloom throughout the growing season. There are eight months of the year in which some perennial subject may be flowering out of doors. With judicious
selection of spring, early summer, late summer, and fall flowering kinds, it is possible to create an ever-shifting picture. Many
as alyssum, bleeding-heart, iris and the peony bloom early in the
season long before the annuals get started. Some like the iris
and peony are at their peak for only a fraction of the season but
they contribute so much they are well worth the space and their
foliage remains decorative and an asset after the bloom is gone.
Only a few kinds bloom all season. As new plants come into
flower and old ones pass, the garden scene changes almost from
week to week. The herbaceous border need never be monotonous. There is not a fortnight in the season when some perennial does not earn for itself appreciation, and the anticipation
of the next high point of the season is almost as enjoyable as

the display itself. The first Christmas-rose may follow the last chrysanthemum by only a few weeks, to start anew the season of perennials, the coming to life and new growth of varied shoots and leaves.

6. *Companionable with other plants*—Perennials combine well with other plant material and may serve either as blenders or contrast. If not planted too closely they combine well with shrubs or hedges and are especially well adapted to the mixed border. Here they combine well with both annuals and bulbs. When bulbs have finished blooming and the leaves start to die back perennials are invaluable in concealing the dead leaves. Each perennial if wisely chosen seems to enhance its neighbors.

7. *Many new and improved varieties*—The vast number of new and improved varieties on the market today is amazing. It requires a specialist to keep up with all the new varieties of iris, hemerocallis and phlox offered in perennial catalogs, but the good commercial grower is selective and usually chooses for sale only those new varieties which are really an improvement over old favorites. Many gardeners have a sentimental attachment for some of the old-timers and enjoy growing them.

8. *Wide range of easy to grow, hardy kinds*—It is not necessary to select prima donnas if upkeep is a factor. If you choose carefully and are discriminating, you can find trouble-free favorites that are hardy, easy to grow and require a minimum of care.

Give your perennials a sound basis on which to build. If you are not an avid gardener, use perennials to create for yourself a lazy gardener's paradise, at the same time increasing the value of your property. If you are a garden enthusiast, you already know "Why Perennials Are Favorites."

Part I

The A to Z of Perennials

The A to Z of Perennials

Plants which normally live at least three years or more are known as perennials, as distinguished from annuals and biennials. A perennial may behave as an annual or biennial in a situation in which it is not at home. Although trees and shrubs are perennial in habit the term generally is applied but to herbaceous plants: those whose roots continue to live, sending up year after year new branches and flower stems which die to the ground when winter comes. The woody perennials such as trees, shrubs and some of the vines maintain a persistent trunk, stem or stems above ground. A few shrubs have semi-persistent woody stems and generally serve the same purpose as herbaceous perennials in the garden.

Plants that arise from bulbs, as daffodils and tulips, are also herbaceous perennials, but because of their different manner of growth, they are usually excluded from books and catalogs about perennials, as is the case here. However, to help the new gardener consider bulbs as part of the over-all garden maintenance and landscape picture, we have included information about them in the sections on design, the Calendar of Chores, and in pertinent references throughout.

We have tried to describe all worthwhile perennials available today either from seed or as plants. We have followed the nomenclature as in L. H. Bailey's *Manual of Cultivated Plants*, but have included some species not in that book.

Achillea Coronation Gold

ACHILLEA—Yarrow, Milfoil, Sneezewort.
This genus of the Daisy Family (Compositae) includes a common weed as well as several desirable garden subjects. Greatest failings are that they tend to spread rapidly by basal shoots and some people object to the odor. See Propagation from Seed.

A. *Millefolium*—Common White Yarrow, Milfoil. Weedy species; not desirable for the border but has given rise to: var. *rosea*, deep rose when first open, fading to a dull pink; var. Fire King, much deeper color. All 1½ feet; June-September.

A. *Ptarmica*—Sneezewort. Entire, long, narrow leaves with toothed margins. Flowers single, white. 1½-2 feet; from June on. Var. The Pearl, dull white, not fully double. 1½-2 feet; var. Perry's White, pure white, fully double. 1½-2 feet; var. Snowball, excellent double white. 15 inches.

A. *filipendulina*—(A. *Eupatorium*). Fernleaf Yarrow. Pinnately divided leaves. Yellow flowers in heavy clusters. 4-5 feet: June

to September. May require staking. May be cut, dried, and used in winter bouquets since flowers retain form and color.

A. *tomentosa*—Woolly Yarrow. Dwarf, yellow-flowered species with divided foliage, quite woolly. About 1 foot. Recommended for rock gardens in preference to borders. Tends to form dense mats and may become objectionable.

All species easily propagated by division, preferably in early spring. Seed propagation not recommended for named varieties.

ACONITUM—Aconite, Monkshood, Wolfbane.
This genus of the Buttercup Family (Ranunculaceae), includes showy, garden plants for late summer and early fall bloom. Tall, upright spikes of flowers create interesting, vertical effects used in groups in the background of the border or as specimen plants. Glossy, dark leaves, divided more or less finger-fashion, are attractive throughout the season; resemble somewhat the foliage of a close relative, the Delphinium. Showy, terminal clusters of hooded, friar's-cap or helmet-shaped flowers are largely in tones of blue, violet and purple; blue-flowered types always useful in a blue and white garden.

Aconitum Carmichaelii

Satisfactory for cut flower purposes. Avoid getting any parts of the plant in the mouth since they contain a dangerously poisonous juice.

Plants do better in partial shade and in a soil rich in humus, preferably with a pH of 5 to 6. Do not like hot summers. Taller types require staking. Seeds difficult to germinate; sow outdoors in early spring. In early fall set the tuberous roots just below the soil line, at least 2 feet from other plants. Give protection the first winter. Plants increase slowly and in general dislike being moved frequently.

Confusion exists in the nomenclature of the species, some of which are variable.

A. Anthora—Pyrenees Monkshood. Leaves divided into narrow segments. Pale yellow flowers in July and August; 1-2 feet.

A. bicolor—(*A. Napellus* var. *bicolor*). Possibly a form of *A. Carmichaelii*. Showy flowers of cloudy white edged with China blue. August; 3-4 feet.

A. Carmichaelii—(*A. Fischeri*). Excellent foliage; leaves 3-lobed, often notched. Compact spikes of lustrous, dark blue flowers. August and September; 3½ feet. Var. *Wilsonii*, violet-blue; August and September; 6-8 feet. Requires staking.

Aconitum Wilsonii

A. Henryi—May be a form of *A. Carmichaelii* and some authorities list it as *A. autumnale*. Leaves 5-lobed. Flowers usually dark blue, sometimes whitish or lilac; borne in open-branched clusters. Blooms in late summer; 4-5 feet. Requires staking.

A. Lycoctonum—See *A. Vulparia.*

A. Napellus—Common Monkshood. Variable in many respects. Leaves more finely divided than in other species. Flowers blue to violet. July and August; 4 feet. Source of the drug aconite. Var. *Sparksii* considered to be synonomous with *A. Henryi.*

A. Vulparia — (*A. Lycoctonum*) — Wolfsbane. Leaves finely divided. Flowers yellow or creamy white. From July on; 3-4 feet.

ADENOPHORA—Ladybell.
Of the 50 or more species of this genus of the Bellflower Family (Campanulaceae), few are listed in American catalogs. Seeds more commonly available than plants, chiefly from European sources. Native primarily in cold, mountainous regions, they are better sub-

Adenophora Potaninii

19

Adonis vernalis

Aegopodium Podograria

jects for the rock or alpine garden. Require much the same treatment as Campanulas. Some are dwarf, others up to 3 feet or more.

ADONIS—Pheasants-Eye.
This genus of the Crowfoot Family (Ranunculaceae) includes two perennials which are more desirable for the rock garden than the border. *A. aestivalis,* Summer Adonis, and *A. annua (A. autumnalis),* Autumn Adonis, are annuals.

A. vernalis, Spring Adonis, has numerous leaves, finely divided. Flowers terminal and solitary, yellow, 2-3 inches in diameter; April and May. Variable in height, 6-18 inches. Var. *alba,* a white-flowered form.

A. amurensis. Blooms before the leaves are fully developed. Leaves not finely divided as in previous species and less numerous. Flowers yellow to orange, up to 2 inches in diameter. April; 9-12 inches.

Good results in sun or shade. Not particular as to soil. Propagated most readily by division in spring; may be grown from seed sown in spring or autumn.

AEGOPODIUM—Goutweed, Bishops-Weed.
Extremely hardy perennial of the Parsley Family (Umbelliferae). Form most commonly

grown is *A. Podograria* var. *variegatum.* With its green and white foliage it is an excellent ground cover for either a sunny or a shady location, in good or poor soil. Must be kept under control since it spreads rapidly. In the proper location it may be cut with the lawn mower twice during the season. Dies to the ground with the first hard freeze.

When in bloom it may reach a height of 2 feet or more, but the foliage forms a good mass about 1 foot tall. Flowers small, white, produced in umbels; plants are more attractive if flowering stems are removed after blooming; one then has an even mass of foliage as with the Epimedium.

The plants spread rapidly by creeping rootstocks and are easily propagated by division in early spring. Easily grown. Seldom troubled by insects and diseases.

AETHIONEMA—Stone-Cress.
Genus of 40 or more species in the Mustard Family (Cruciferae), found chiefly in the Mediterranean region, therefore, may not be hardy in colder regions of the United States. Closely related to hardy Candytuft (Iberis) which it resembles in habit of growth and more or less evergreen foliage.

A. arnenum—Leaves narrow, about ¼ inch long, pointed tips. Flowers pink, in dense clusters, becoming raceme-like; petals of equal length, thus differing from Iberis. 4-8 inches; May-June.

A. coridifolium – Lebanon Stone-Cress. Sometimes listed as *Iberis jucunda.* Leaves slightly longer than in *A. armenum,* rounded with acute tips. Flowers pink to rose-lilac. 4-10 inches. May-June. Var. Warley Rose, blue-green foliage with pink margins. Flowers vivid rose-carmine. 12 inches, May.

A. grandiflorum – Persian Stone-Grass, Giant Stone-Cress, Persian Candytuft. Leaves grayish blue-green, silvery margins, up to 1½ inches long. Flowers soft rosy pink, in racemes, 9-11 inches; May-June.

A. pulchellum – Erect or semi-erect. Leaves blue-green, linear to oblong, rounded tips. Flowers mildly fragrant, soft rose-pink. 6-8 inches; June-July.

Recommended for rock gardens and foreground of perennial borders. Sunny location, dry, alkaline soils (add lime to acid soils), good drainage.

Propagated by seed sown in spring, by division in early spring, or by softwood stem cuttings rooted during the summer, carried over winter in pots, and planted out in spring.

Greatest objections: lack of hardiness in cold regions and winter injury when plants are not protected by snow covering.

AJUGA—Bugle-Weed.

Genus of 40 or more species in the Mint Family (Labiatae). Among the best ground covers for shade where grass will not grow. Will also grow in full sun, in good soil or poor. However, one should select species or varieties with care.

A. reptans – Species most commonly grown. Creeping type, with stolon-bearing stems which take root readily when nodes come in contact with soil. Leaves shiny green, rosette habit of growth. Flowers violet-blue, late spring and early summer; 6-10 inches, depending on character of soil. If it gets into a lawn, will almost eradicate the grass; can be cut with a lawn mower after blooming. Var. *alba,* light green foliage, white flowers. Var. *purpurea,* dark purple foliage. Var. *variegata,* leaves variegated with creamy yellow.

A. genevensis—More desirable than preceding species since it does not produce stolons. Foliage green, in rosette-like clusters. Flowers blue, in spikes. 6-10 inches; May-June. Var. Pink Spire, attractive pink flowers; 5-6 inches. Var. Bronze Beauty, bronze foliage. Var. Silver Beauty, variegated foliage; not as well known.

A. pyramidalis—Least well known of the species. Does not produce stolons. Foliage

Aethionema grandiflorum

Ajuga reptans variegata

Allium Aflatunense

Allium Ostrowskianum

green. Flowers gentian blue. 6-10 inches; early summer. Clumps increase slowly.

Most easily propagated by division of the clumps in non-stolon-bearing types, or by the rooted stolons in *A. reptans*, spring, summer or fall.

In open winters in an exposed location plants are subject to winter killing.

ALLIUM

Interesting genus of perhaps 500 species, formly included in the Lily Family (Liliaceae), now placed in Amaryllis Famly (Amaryllidaceae). Odor not objectionable unless leaves are crushed. Several species native in various parts of United States. Many species not hardy.

A. *Ostrowskianum*—possibly a variety of *A. oreophilum*, has been given quite a bit of publicity recently. Leaves blue-green. Flower stems 4-6 inches, bearing umbels of carmine-rose flowers; May-June. For edging purposes, better for rock gardens.

A. *Moly*—Leaves long, up to 1 inch wide. Flowers numerous, in an umbel, may be 3 inches in diameter, yellow. July; 18 inches.

A. *giganteum*—Leaves about 2 inches wide, 18 inches long, blue-green. Flowers in umbels, lilac to lavender-rose. June; 4 feet.

A. *senescens*—Leaves narrow, shorter than the flowering stems. Flowers in umbels, lilac, on 2 foot stems; July. Var. *glaucum*, leaves more glaucous, flowers lavender. 1 foot; July.

A. *narcissiflorum*—Leaves broad, shorter than flowering stems. Flowers large, rose, in open, drooping umbels. July; 12 niches.

Propagation by seed sown in early spring; by division or by bulblets produced on parent bulb, in fall or spring. Taller types do better in rich soils. May be injured by Thrips as are common onions.

ALSTROEMERIA

About 60 species in this genus of the Amaryllis Family (Amaryllidaceae), native in South America; more commonly listed in European catalogs. Not all are hardy in northern regions. A. *aurantiaca*, sometimes known as Peruvian-Lily, probably the most hardy species; roots somewhat tuberous and

22

brittle; leaves narrow, 3-4 inches long, with a leafy whorl under the many-flowered umbel; flowers small, lily-like, yellow to orange with brown markings. June-August; 2 feet. Var. *lutea*, yellow.

Will need winter protection in northern regions. Shady location with rich, moist soil. Propagate by division in spring or in fall after plants have died down. Seed sown in spring; seedlings should not be disturbed the first year.

Other species, if available, may be treated as tender, herbaceous perennials, lifted in the fall, stored over winter, and planted out in the spring.

ALTHAEA—Hollyhock, Marsh-Mallow.
In this genus of the Mallow Family (Malvaceae) there are forms which can be grown as annuals, biennials, or perennials.

A. *rosea*—Hollyhock, normally a biennial, frequently acts as a perennial since plants develop shoots from the base after the first season of bloom. Leaves lobed or coarsely divided. Flowers produced in the leaf axils; colors various, white, pink, rose, lavender, maroon, purple, light yellow; almost any color except blue. Most attractive in July; may become unsightly when flowers at top of spike only are in bloom. 6-9 feet. Double-flowered forms may require staking. Plant at least 18 inches apart. Properly used in the border background, or against a building when a temporary screen is desired. Propagated primarily from seed (see index); sown in June, should bloom the following year. Self-sows; little seedlings may be transplanted to desired spot. Cannot be guaranteed that named varieties will come true from seed. Extremely susceptible to Hollyhock Rust and mildew. (See section on control.)

A. *ficifolia* — Figleaf or Antwerp Hollyhock. Yellow to orange flowers. Possible that this species has been used in production of yellow flowers and deeply lobed leaves of A. *rosea* forms.

A *rosea* x *Malva sylvestris*—Bigeneric hybrid. Plants received at University of Massachusetts from U. S. Plant Introduction Station, Glendale, Md., planted out June 1, 1953; in bloom July 15. Seed from same source sown in greenhouse June 11, 1953,

Alstroemeria aurantiaca

Althaea rosea

Alyssum saxatile

Amsonia Tabernaemontana

transplanted to coldframe, began to bloom third week in August. Flowers up to 4½ inches in diameter; colors various. Continued to bloom until frost; height 5-7 feet. None of the plants survived the winter. Susceptible to Hollyhock Rust.

A. *officinalis* — Marsh-Mallow. European species which has escaped from cultivation to coastal marshy areas in North America. Leaves may or may not be lobed. Flowers pale pink or rose, small as compared with Hollyhocks; 1 inch in axillary clusters; 4 feet. Should not be confused with *Hibiscus palustris* and *H. Moscheutos,* also known as Mallows.

ALYSSUM—Madwort.
Genus of many species in the Mustard Family (Criciferae). Sweet Alyssum, annual, formerly *Alyssum maritimum,* now classified as *Lobularia maritima.* Several species desirable for rock and wall gardens and foreground of perennial borders.

A. *saxatile*—Golden-Tuft, Basket-of-Gold. Leaves gray or gray-green, entire, basal leaves up to 5 inches long, stem leaves much smaller; flowers intense yellow, in corymb-like panicles which increase in length as flowers set seed, as in the annual Candytuft (Iberis). Late April-May. May grow to 15 inches in borders; effective in wall gardens where plants assume a drooping habit. Has been said that it should never be used because of its intense color, but yet it is the most popular of all perennial Alyssums. Var. *luteum;* may be listed as *citrinum* or *sulphureum;* much paler color and therefore more pleasing to many gardeners. May; 1 foot. Var. *compactum,* same color as the species but more dwarf. Var. *flore pleno,* double-flowered form, not as attractive as the single form. Var. Apricot Gem. May; 1 foot.

A. *alpestre.* — Tufted habit of growth. Leaves small, gray, hairy; flowers small, yellow, in compact, dense racemes. Late April-May; 3-6 inches.

A. *Moellendorfianum.* — Silvery leaves, about 1 inch long; flowers yellow, may vary to white, in umbels. June; very dwarf, 4 inches.

A. *montanum.*—Leaves gray, oblong to linear; flowers in small clusters, said to be fragrant. April-May; 10-12 inches.

Best results in full sun in well-drained soils. Foliage more effective if flower stems are clipped off after blooming season. A. *saxatile* and its varieties may be used as under-plantings with early tulips. Propagation by seed sown in May, division of roots, or by softwood stem cuttings in summer.

AMSONIA.

One important species in this genus of The Dogbane Family (Apocynaceae), A. *Tabernaemontana.* Abundant foliage, leaves broadly lanceolate and remaining in good condition throughout the season. Flowers steel blue in terminal panicles; at their best in May; 3-4 feet. May be grown in full sun or in shade. Produces numerous stems from the base; plant 2½-3 feet apart. Seldom troubled by insects and diseases. Should be used more commonly. Propagated readily by division in spring or fall.

Var. *salicifolia* has narrower leaves and fewer flowers in a panicle.

Anaphalis margaritacea

ANAPHALIS—Pearl Everlasting.

One species of this genus in the Composite Family (Compositae), occasionally used in borders, rock and wild flower gardens. A. *margaritacea;* native in many parts of North America; stems and narrow leaves woolly white; flowers in rather flat pearl-white clusters, individual heads small, composed entirely of disk florets. July-September; 1½-2 feet. Does not require a rich soil. May be cut, dried and used in winter bouquets. Sometimes dyed for commercial purposes. Plants not commonly listed in the trade but may be collected in the wild.

ANCHUSA—Alkanet, Bugloss.

Genus of more than 30 species in the Borage Family (Boraginaceae), prized especially for their blue flowers.

A. *azurea,* frequently catalogued as A. *italica.* Coarse, hairy perennial. Leaves 6

Anchusa Blue Stars

Androsace lanuginosa

Anemone Pulsatilla

inches or more in length, clasping the stem. Stems branching freely and producing flowers, pink in the bud stage or on first opening, changing to a bright blue. May-June; with scattered bloom during the summer. May grow to 5 feet and require staking. Var. Dropmore, deeper blue. Var. London Royalist, an English introduction, blue-purple; 3 feet. Said not to require staking. June-July.

Species listed as A. *myosotidiflora* is correctly *Brunnera Macrophylla*.

Coarse foliage greatest objection to A. *azurea*. Propagated by seeds sown in spring or fall or by division of the clumps of fleshy roots in spring.

ANDROSACE—Rock-Jasmine.
About 85 species in this genus of the Primrose Family (Primulaceae), of which few are listed in American catalogs; grown more frequently in English, Scottish, and Swiss nurseries.

A. *sarmentosa*—Most important. Native in the Himalayas, spreads by stolons. Leaves short, in a dense, basal rosette, entire, pubescent when young; flowering stem about 5 inches. Hairy, flowers in umbels, rose, each flower about ¼ inch across; June-July. Seems to like to grow in crevices in the rock garden. Must have good drainage. Primarily plant for the rock and alpine garden enthusiast.

ANEMONE—Anemony, Windflower.
Genus of about 100 species in the Crowfoot Family (Ranunculaceae), in which the sepals have become showy and petal-like; numerous stamens add to the attractiveness of the flower; when seeds are mature, the styles become feathery (as in Clematis). Popular because of the long season of bloom obtained with various species and varieties and for their value as cut flowers.

A. *blanda* — Sapphire Anemony. Has a tuber-like rootstock. Plant with long, silky hairs. Leaves few, twice divided into threes. Flowers sky-blue, 9-14 sepals, narrow, about ½ inch long. 8 inches; early spring. Mature styles feathery and drooping.

A. coronaria—Poppy Anemony. Root-stock tuberous, very irregular, has some-what the appearance of a dry chip of wood. Short stem at the surface of the soil from which arise basal leaves, two or three times divided into narrow segments. Flowers soli-tary, terminal, on 6-18 stems, longer in some varieties grown in greenhouses; vary greatly in width, possibly 6 inches under glass, nearer to 1½-2 inches in gardens. Wide range of colors, from white through the red and blue-violet series; spring and summer. Var. The Bride, white; St. Brigid, single, semi-double, and double in variety of colors; DeCaen, single saucer-shaped flowers in various colors. In northern regions more advisable to plant tubers in spring, trusting that they will not be dried out when re-ceived by the purchaser; plant 2 inches deep. If seed is sown indoors in March and seedlings transplanted to coldframes, will start to bloom in summer and continue until freezing weather.

Anemone japonica

A. hupehensis— Japanese Anemony. Has branching stems. Basal leaves long-stemmed, 3-parted, leaflets lobed, toothed and sharply pointed. Sepals rose-pink, 5 or 6; flowers about 3 inches across; up to 3 feet. From this species Alex Cumming of Bristol Nurseries developed varieties Sept-ember Charm, silvery-pink with deeper shadings, and September Sprite, rose-pink; both 12-15 inches.

Bailey: *Manual of Cultivated Plants* (1949 edition) states: "Taller sorts grown as *A. japonica* and having 6-20 sepals should be treated as named garden hybrids or clones of *A. hybrida*." Includes such varieties as *alba*, single, white; Queen Charlotte, semi-double, pink; Whirlwind, semi-double, white; Kriemhilde, semi-double, pale pink; Marie Manchard, semi-double, white. Sept-ember-October; 3 feet or more. Prefer a soil on the neutral side rather than acid. Shelter from strong winds. Good drainage important. Seldom require staking. Full sun or partial shade.

A. Pulsatilla, (Pulsatilla vulgaris)—Euro-pean Pasque-Flower. Flowers precede the leaves; lavender to blue, or reddish-purple,

Aquilegia and Iris

2 inches or more across. Leaves softly hairy, 4-6 inches, three times divided pinnately. After flowers mature styles become feathery and attractive, may be 6-15 inches tall. Var. *alba,* white; var. *rubra,* reddish; April-May. Excellent for rock gardens.

A. *vitifolia*—Grape-leaf Anemony. Plant branched. Leaves deeply five-lobed, gray underneath as with grape foliage. Flowers pink, about 2 inches across in many-flowered clusters. August; 3 feet. Recommended for shady locations. Var. *albadura,* numerous small, white flowers, fall blooming. 30 inches. Var. *robustissima,* silvery pink, August-October; 30 inches. "May be double-planted with spring bulbs, lilies, bleeding-heart and Oriental poppies."

Other species of interest: A. *nemorosa*—European Wood anemony, flowers solitary, in various colors, 6 inches; April-May. Var. *alba-plena,* double white. A. *canadensis*—Meadow Anemony (American), white, May-August; 2 feet. A. *virginiana*—Thimbleweed (American), flowers white or greenish, May-August; 3 feet. A. *quinquefolia*—Wood Anemony (American), flowers solitary, white, sometimes tinged with purple, late April-May; 8 inches. All four species useful in wildflower gardens.

Anemonella thalictroides—Rue-Anemone, a closely related genus, roots in clusters of tubers, leaves similar to those of Thalictrum, Meadow-Rue, subtending the umbel-like cluster of small white flowers, late April-May; 6-8 inches. Wildflower garden.

Tuberous-rooted types usually propagated by seed sown when ripe or in spring; especially recommended for forms of A. *coronaria;* seed not easily scattered because of feathery character. Others propagated by division in early spring. Varieties of A. *hybrida* propagated commercially by root cuttings. Avoid windswept locations for tall types. Well-drained soil for all species. Like full sun but are shade tolerant. Black Blister Beetle, also known as Black China-Aster Beetle, especially injurious to varieties of A. *hybrida.* Various types of A. *coronaria* and A. *hybrida* excellent for cutting.

ANTHEMIS—Chamomile, Golden Marguerite.
Of all the species in this genus of the Composite Family (Compositae) A. *tinctoria* is the most important for garden purposes. Stems stiff and erect but may wilt in dry weather; leaves 2-3 times divided, with some odor; flowers single, disk and ray florets golden yellow, from late June on; 2-3 feet.

Anthemis nobilis

Anthericum Liliago

Aquilegia McKana hybrid

Aquilegia

Excellent for cutting; good keeping qualities. Propagated by division in spring; self-sows if flower heads are not removed. Var. *Kelwayi,* deeper yellow; Vars. Beauty of Grallagh, golden yellow, and Moonlight, pale yellow, of more recent introduction.

Should not be confused with the true Yellow Marguerite, Boston Daisy, supposedly a variety of the tender *Chrysanthemum frutescens.*

ANTHERICUM

One species of this genus in the Lily Family (Liliaceae), of value for garden purposes.

A. *Liliago*—St. Bernard-Lily. Frequently grown in greenhouses or as a house plant; not commonly known that it is an herbaceous perennial. Has been grown in the display garden of Waltham Field Station of the University of Massachusetts. Roots fleshy. Leaves numerous, long, narrow, arising from the crown of the plant. Flowering stems may be up to 40 inches; flowers small, about 1 inch, in a more or less open raceme; July. Positive quality, a good mass of foliage which serves as ground cover in partial shade or sun. Propagated by creeping stolons or by division.

AQUILEGIA—Columbine; sometimes incorrectly called Honeysuckle.
Genus of the Crowfoot Family (Ranunculaceae) with many species, possibly a dozen of which are of garden importance. Leaves, according to botanical terms, one to three times ternately divided, i.e., one to three times divided into threes, thus giving the plant a light, open effect; frequently of a bluish-green color; useful as a filler flower.

Structure of flower interesting since the five sepals, normally green in most plants, have become showy, taking on various colors, according to the species. Five petals prolonged backward into spurs, of varying length and form, usually with a knob at the end containing nectar. Sepals and spurs of the same color; limb (petal-like part of the spur) of a different color, usually white or yellow. In American species spurs commonly straight or flaring; in European species, hooked or curved. Doubling occurs most frequently in number of spurs; known as "hose-in-hose" type when spurs are en-

Arabis

closed one within another. Spurless types available but are not numerous.

For garden purposes three groups include most important forms; (1) Long-spurred hybrids; obtained by crossing such species as *A. caerulea* (State flower of Colorado), *formosa (californica), chrysantha, longissima,* and *Skinneri;* all are American species. Can be had in a great variety of colors, bloom from June to August, up to 4 feet. Should not require staking. Mrs. Scott Elliott hybrids still popular; McKana hybrids, awarded a bronze medal as an All-America Selection in 1955, most popular because of larger flowers, longer spurs, and excellent colors, especially in lighter tones.

(2) Short-spurred group; developed largely from European and Asiatic species, such as *A. vulgaris, glandulosa,* and *sibirica.* Double forms occur primarily in *A. vulgaris,* European Columbine; colors range from white through rose to blue and violet; May and June. Seldom above 3 feet. Not as popular as Group 1.

(3) Rock garden group; species which by habit of growth are better adapted to the rock garden than the border such as *A. canadensis* (native Eastern Columbine), *alpina, flabellata,* and its var. *nana.* Taller growing species may be used for this purpose if they fit well into the scale of the garden.

All columbines readily propagated from seed, preferably sown in the open or in a coldframe in May or June; may require 15 days or more for germination. Seedlings should be of sufficient size for transplanting to permanent location in the fall. Will self-sow if seeds are allowed to mature. Old clumps may be divided in spring. Roots are somewhat fleshy and tapering; in rich soil will penetrate deeply.

Leaves frequently become unsightly due to work of the Columbine Leaf Miner *(Phytomyza minuscula).* Crown or Root Borer, *(Papaipema purpurifascia),* also troublesome; presence may not be noticed until the plant dies when it can easily be pulled from the crown.

ARABIS—Rock-Cress.
Genus of numerous species in the Mustard
Family (Cruciferae), only a few of which are
of garden value. Much confusion exists in
catalogs in specific names. According to
Bailey, *Manual of Cultivated Plants*, *A. alpina* apparently is not common in cultivation; forms listed as *A. albida* and its varieties are correctly forms of *A. caucasica*, as
are varieties of *A. alpina*.

A. alpina—Mountain Rock-Cress. Tufted
habit of growth. Leaves hairy; lower with
wedge-shaped base, somewhat sharply
toothed; upper, sessile, more or less clasping
the stem. Flowers white in short, compact
racemes. 4-10 inches; May.

A. caucasica (A. albida)—Wall Rock-Cress.
Leaves with felt-like tomentum, obtuse,
bluntly toothed or teeth lacking near the
base. Flowers white, in short, compact racemes. 4-10 inches; April-May. Var. *flore-
pleno*, double white flowers. Var. *variegata*,
margined with creamy white.

A. procurrens (A. mollis)—Tufted plant
spreading by underground stolons. Stems
usually erect, unbranched. Leaves entire
with winged petiole, smooth above with
pubescence on margins and veins underneath; upper leaves sessile, broad, not clasping the stem. Flowers white, in racemes. 10
inches; April-May. Var. *nana*, flowers white.
6 inches; May.

A. Arendsii, a hybrid between *A. aubre-
tioides* and *A. caucasica*, may be listed in
some catalogs as *A. albida* var. *rosea;* rose.
8 inches; April-May.
Excellent plants for rock gardens, wall
gardens and for edging perennial borders
for spring bloom.
Division in spring or fall most common
method of propagation, although seeds and
softwood cuttings may be used.
Insects and diseases seldom troublesome.
Winter injury may occur in open winters
when snow cover is lacking.

ARENARIA—Sandwort.
From the Latin meaning sand, suggests the

Arenaria montana

Armeria maritima

habitat of many of the species. Well-drained soil in the rock or alpine garden since many are true alpines; not advised for the perennial border. May be used in crevices in the rock garden, in spaces between stones in a walk or between flagstones in a patio. Being natives of high altitudes where the plants would be covered with snow for a long period they may be winter-killed at lower elevations in open winters.

About 250 species in this genus of the Pink Family (Caryophyllaceae), only a few of which are available in the American trade; many more listed in the European trade. Anyone who has hiked the trails in the higher elevations of New England and other sections of eastern United States has doubtless seen *Arenaria groenlandica*, an annual species.

A. *montana* (*Alsine montana*)—Leaves narrow, about ¾ inch long; flowers white, large for this genus. May-June; 4-5 inches.

A. *verna*—Leaves narrow, flat, linear, pointed; flowers white, about ¼ inch in diameter, several on leaf-bearing stems. May; 3 inches. Var. *caespitosa* (tufted); more compact than the species; in mass forms a moss-like mat; flowers white, very small. May.

ARMERIA—Thrift, Sea-Pink.
Numerous species in this genus of the Plumbago or Leadwort Family (Plumbaginaceae), but narrowed down to a few as far as garden uses are concerned. Evergreen in most locations and developing dense tufts. Divide every three or four years.

A. *pseud-armeria*—Listed in some catalogs as A. *latifolia*. Leaves broad to oblong lanceolate, smooth with a blue-green bloom, acute, up to 10 inches long and 1 inch wide. Flowers in globular heads, up to 2 inches in diameter, white to dark rose-pink. 2 feet or less; June. Most commonly listed species of broad-leaved type. Var. Bees-Ruby, an English introduction, carmine-rose. 15-18 inches; June.

A. *maritima* (*Statice maritima*)—Sea-Pink, Sea-Thrift. A variable species. Leaves narrowly linear, acute or blunt, typically blue-green; flower stems smooth or pubescent; heads about 1 inch in diameter, purple, pink, or white. About 1 foot; May-June. Var. *alba*, white; 8 inches. Var. *Laucheana*, bright rose, May-June; 4-6 inches. Popular variety. Var. *rosea*, dark pink, from May on; 8 inches.

Because of their symmetrical habit of growth dwarf species may be used as formal edging plants. Taller forms best of the species for use as cut flowers; good keeping qualities. Excellent for the rock garden when evergreen tufts of foliage are desired. Prefer light, sandy, well-drained soils in full sun where foliage takes on better blue-green color than in shade. Flowers remain in good condition for some time. Seldom troubled by insects and diseases. Poor drainage may cause difficulty.

Propagation by seed sown in fall and by division of tufts in early fall, using care to have roots on each piece.

ARTEMISIA
Genus of about 200 species, in the Composite Family (Compositae), which include at least one annual, numerous perennials and shrubs. Most of the popular forms grown primarily for their attractive, gray-white foliage.

I. Opposite   *In a Vermont scene, a carefully planned perennial border offers varied form and abundant color. Such an assortment of material requires a high degree of maintenance.*

II. Above *For permanence, dependability and ease of culture, few hardy plants can surpass the herbaceous peonies (shown here with bearded iris). In borders with other perennials or annuals, in front of flowering shrubs, along a low fence or wall, or as an all-green hedge after flowering is past, peonies never fail to attract attention. For best results give them full sun and a well-enriched soil that has good drainage. Fall is the best time to lift and divide them and to plant new roots. Place so that the red eyes are no more than two inches below the surface of the soil. Otherwise they fail to bloom. Once established, feed them annually to keep them vigorous and healthy.*

A. *albula*—Silver King Artemisia. Stems and leaves woolly-white on both sides; lower leaves ovate or obovate, lobed, 2 inches or more in length, upper leaves narrower. Flowers in heads (as in all Composites), in racemes or open panicles, white. July; up to 4 feet or more. Grown chiefly for its gray foliage; useful in the background and for providing contrast in foliage color and texture. Frequently used in cut flower arrangements and can be dried for use in winter bouquets. Tends to spread rapidly from year to year. Should not require staking. Likes a porous, well-drained soil, preferably in sunlight. No important insects and diseases.

A. *Schmidtiana*—Leaves finely divided to the mid-rib, covered with silvery, silk-like hairs; leaves so numerous that plant forms a dense clump. Flowers white to cream. July; up to 2 feet. Var. *nana*, Silver Mound, of greater garden value than the species; characteristics similar but plant dwarf, about 8 inches with a spread of 12 inches or more. Useful as an edging plant in borders and in rock gardens as specimen plants or in small groups. Soil on the dry side in a sunny location.

A. *Stelleriana*—Beach Wormwood, Old Woman. Common above high tide line on the sandy beaches of New England and elsewhere. Leaves somewhat divided, almost pinnate, covered with white tomentum (densely woolly). Flowers yellow, midsummer; seldom over 2 feet. Not recommended for the border or rock garden; at home in pure sand.

A. *Dracunculus* — Tarragon, Estragon. Green foliage. Basal leaves divided at the tip, stem leaves linear to lanceolate, up to 4 inches long. Heads very small, greenish-white, in open panicles. June-July; 2 feet or more. Leaves used in seasonings and in making tarragon vinegar.

A. *lactiflora*—White Mugwort. Green foliage. Leaves usually divided into broad, toothed segments. Flower white, in very small heads in a more or less spike-like panicle. July; 4 feet or more. May require

Artemisia lactiflora

Artemisia Stelleriana

Aruncus sylvester

Asclepias incarnata

staking. Greatest garden value is in the foliage.

All species most frequently propagated by division in late fall (October). No important insects and diseases.

Other species of interest: *A. Abrotanum,* Southernwood, woody, with fragrant foliage; *A. tridentata,* Sage-Brush; *A. pontica,* Roman Wormwood, woody; *A. sacrorum,* Russian Wormwood, woody.

ARUNCUS—Goats-Beard.
One of the few herbaceous perennials in the Rose Family (Rosaceae). *A. sylvester* appears to be the only species listed in American trade. Plants dioecious (staminate and pistillate flowers on different plants); staminate form more showy because of numerous stamens; foliage although pinnately divided somewhat coarse; flowers small, white, borne in numerous spikes which form a large panicle, similar to that of Astilbes but much larger; June-July; strong growing, may reach height of 6-7 feet, therefore suitable for background purposes. *A. sylvester* var. *Kneiffii,* Cutleaf Goats-Beard, more finely divided foliage; flowers white; 3 feet; June-July.

ASCLEPIAS—Milkweed, Silkweed, Butterfly-Weed, Pleurisy-Root.
Genus of about 150 species; 25 listed in Gray's *Manual of Botany;* 4 in Bailey's *Manual of Cultivated Plants;* 8 in *Plant Buyer's Guide.* All characterized by having milky juice and seeds attached to tufts of hair, consequently easily carried by wind.

A. tuberosa — Butterfly-Weed, Pleurisy-Root. Most popular species for use in perennial gardens and borders. Plant rough, hairy; leaves alternate, up to 6 inches long, about 1 inch wide; flowers small, in many-flowered umbels, corolla greenish-yellow, hoods orange or yellows. June-July; 2-3 feet. Native in the eastern coastal States; has been found growing along railroad rights of way in vicinity of Amherst, Mass. Grows in poor soil, on dry, gravelly banks. Sure to attract butterflies. Excellent as a cut flower if ends of stems are seared with flame.

A. incarnata — Swamp Milkweed. Almost glabrous; leaves opposite, lanceolate, 3-6 inches long, about half as wide; flowers in umbels, corolla reddish- or rosy-purple, hoods red-purple, rarely white (var. *alba*). Late June-August; 4 feet. Does best in moist

Asperula odorata

Asphodeline lutea

to wet locations, therefore, best for the wildflower garden.

A. *syriaca, (A. Cornutii)*—Common Milkweed of roadsides and fields. Leaves oblong, entire, strongly pubescent on the lower surface; flowers small, in axillary or terminal umbels, dull pink, fragrant. July; 3-5 feet. Cut while pods are yet green, remove leaves, dry at room temperature; pods hold color well, open and hold silk and seeds indefinitely.

A. *curassavica* — Blood-Flower, native in Tropical America and has become naturalized in southern states; cannot be expected to be hardy in New England or other northern states. Desirable for greenhouse culture in a temperature of about 60 degrees. Corolla reddish-purple, hoods orange. Good cut flower if ends of stems are seared with flame to stop flow of milky juice. Propagated by seeds or softwood stem cuttings.

All milkweeds difficult to transplant or move because of nature and depth of root system; best to purchase plants from nurseries. May be grown from seeds, sown a few in a pot and seedlings transplanted to permanent location.

Good foliage and free from serious insect pests and diseases.

ASPERULA—Woodruff.
Genus of about 90 species of the Madder Family (Rubiaceae), of which A. *odorata*, Sweet Woodruff, is the only species commonly listed in American catalogs. Stems square (as in the Mint Family); leaves short and narrow, in whorls; flowers white, in loosely branched cymes; May-July; 6 inches to 1 foot. One of the popular garden herbs. Good as a ground cover in shady places and in the rock garden. Dried leaves have fragrance of hay; said to be used in flavoring wines. Propagated by the trailing, slender rootstocks and by division.

ASPHODELINE—Jacobs-Rod, Kings-Spear.
Genus of less than 20 species in the Lily Family (Liliaceae), of which A. *lutea, (Asphodelus luteus)* is most important. Produces numerous, narrow leaves at the base; stem leaves narrow and numerous; flowers in a spike 1½ feet long, yellow, fragrant, with spreading segments. Total height 2 feet or more; July.

Propagated by infrequent division since it increases slowly. Not particular as to soils.

Aster novae-angliae

ASTER—Aster, Starwort, Michaelmas Daisy. Over 600 species in this important genus of the Composite Family (Compositae), many of which are native in North America. According to the quotation from the Bible, "A prophet is not without honour save in his own country," hardy Asters were to a great extent without honor in the United States until they had been vastly improved by such nurserymen as Amos Perry, Enfield, England, and George Arends, Ronsdorf, Germany. A page of an American catalog of more than 40 years ago lists 14 species and 31 varieties, usually referred to the species from which they were derived. Now, in many catalogs, horticultural varieties are given without regard to species. Subject to a wilt disease carried over within underground parts. To control, make tip cuttings of strongest shoots in fall or spring and burn old clumps.

A. novae-angliae — New England Aster. Plant coarsely hairy, branching freely, and stems bearing many leaves, lanceolate to somewhat linear, base clasping the stem, to 5 inches or more. Heads numerous, about 2 inches across, disk yellow to orange, rays typically deep purple-blue, narrow. 5 feet or more; late August on. Var. *roseus*, pink, occurs in the wild. Barr's Pink, Lil Fardell, Mrs. Raynor, and Dr. Eckner, all pink forms, at one period popular in the United States, now more frequently listed in British and European catalogs.

A. novi-belgii—New York Aster, most important native species and has given rise to desirable horticultural forms. Variations occur in the wild; on a hiking trip in Vermont we saw white, pink, and blue within a small area. Plant smooth or slightly pubescent, leaves oblong or varying to lanceolate, up to 6 inches long, entire or toothed. Flowers in heads as in all Composites, disk yellow, ray florets varying in color. 3 feet or more; August-September.

A. Amellus—Italian Aster. Rough, hairy stems, heads clustered, up to 2 inches across, disk yellow, ray florets purple. 2 feet; July-August. One of the parents of *A. Frikartii* (other, *A. Thomsonii*), originated by Carl Frikart, Stafa, Switzerzerland; best form is Wonder of Stafa, lavender-blue, 2 feet, from July on. Popular variety.

A. hybridus var. *nanus* includes some extremely dwarf forms, known as Cushion Asters; useful for edging, foreground of the border and for the rock garden. Constance, soft pink, Lilac Time, lilac; Niobe, white. September.

George Taloumis, garden writer and lecturer, Salem, Mass. answers our questionaire:

"I like dwarf fall asters because of their small size (nine inches), which makes them ideal for edging or filler material; flower in September, a quiet month for perennials; need dividing each spring or rather it is a good idea to do it. If a supply of young plants is kept, they can be used to move into bare spots any time of the season for they move easily; pinching in early summer will make them dwarfer and delay flowering; good companion plants for early mums, add blues to the fall garden."

Dwarf Oregon Asters developed by Professor Le Roy Breithaupt, Oregon State College at Corvallis, from hybrids between *A. Douglasii*, a western species, and *A. novi-belgii*. In the true dwarf, height varies from 10-15 inches; Bonny Blue, wistaria blue; Persian Rose, rose; Snowball, white; Twinkle, claret-red, double. In the semi-dwarfs height is more than 15 inches; Pacific Amaranth, amaranth color; Twilight, violet-blue; Violet Carpet, violet-blue. August-October.

English Asters included under *A. novi-belgii*, one of the parents. Available in American trade such varieties as Ernest Ballard, rose-carmine, semi-double; Eventide, deep violet-blue, semi-double; Radar, red; Violetta, deep violet-blue, semi-double; Winston Churchill, crimson-red. Range in height 2 to 4 feet; September.

A. yunnanensis, from Yunnan Province in China. Plant pubescent, leaves obovate to lanceolate, up to 8 inches long, toothed. Heads mostly solitary, violet-blue. Var. Napsbury, orange disk, ray florets blue. 18-24 inches; May-July.

A. Farreri, also a Chinese species; leaves entire, linear or lanceolate, up to 6 inches long. Heads solitary, up to 3 inches across, disk orange, ray florets deep blue. 18 inches; from June on. Var. Berggarten, golden yellow disk, ray florets lilac-blue.

Plant listed as *Aster luteus* or *Solidaster luteus* is a bigeneric hybrid between Solidago and *Aster ptarmicoides*, White Upland Aster; leaves narrow, somewhat toothed. Ray and disk florets yellow. Heads said to have more the appearance of Goldenrod. China-Aster is *Callistephus chinensis*, an annual.

Hardy Asters provide colors lacking in other fall-blooming Composites such as Chrysanthemums, Helenium, Helianthus, Heliopsis, and Rudbeckia; a good substitute when Chrysanthemums are a problem. Tall varieties good for backgrounds but may require staking unless pinched in early summer to induce branching and lower height; others desirable for middle-ground and edging; dwarf types good in the rock garden. In general, varieties with solitary heads better for cutting than the freely-branching types. Objections: some species are weedy; frequently self-sow; some are rank growers and tend to crowd out other plants unless divided frequently; lose lower leaves due to crowding, poor light conditions, lack of air circulation or lack of water; subject to mildew. Insects seldom cause serious trouble. Not particular as to soils but too rich soils promote too rank growth.

All Asters readily propagated by division in fall or spring, preferably the latter; discard the woody center of the crown. Should be divided every second or third year. Seed sown in the spring, either for true species or to obtain new forms; should bloom the following year. Seeds of horticultural varieties do not come true to parent plant.

ASTILBE. Occasionally listed as Goats-Beard (See ARUNCUS), or Meadowsweet (See FILIPENDULA).
This genus of the Saxifrage Family (Saxifragaceae) includes plants which give best results in moist soils. In many catalogs varieties are listed without regard to the species from which they have been derived. Some of the most important species con-

Astilbe

Astrantia major

Aubrieta deltoidea

cerned are: *A. astilboides,* leaves twice divided into threes, flowers white, 2-3 feet; *A. chinensis,* leaves two or three times divided into threes, flowers white, 18 inches or more; *A. chinensis* var. *Davidii,* rose-pink with blue anthers, up to 6 feet, one parent of *A. Arendsii* hybrids, developed by George Arends, Ronsdorf, Germany; *A. japonica,* leaves two or three times divided into threes, flowers white, 1-3 feet; some varieties forced by florists derived from this species. *A. simplicifolia,* leaves three to five lobed, flowers white, 1 foot; *A. simplicifolia* var. *rosea,* flowers rose, dwarf.

Popular horticultural varieties: Deutschland, white, 30 inches; June; Fanal, most commonly listed, bronze foliage, red, 2 feet; June-July; Gladstone, an older variety, white, 30 inches; June-July; Gloriosa, deep rose, 30 inches; July; Peach Blossom, light pink, 30 inches; July; Queen Alexandra, an older variety, deep pink, 30 inches; July; Red Sentinel, 30 inches; June-July; Rhineland, bright pink, 30 inches; July; White Gloria, 30 inches; July.

All Astilbes require a moist soil, high in organic matter; if soil is light, must be watered frequently during growing and flowering season. Should be spaced 1½ to 2 feet since plants produce a mass of good foliage with the plumy panicles standing well above the leaves. May be planted near water, margins of ponds, pools, or streams; also recommended for seaside plantings. Full sun or partial shade. Excellent for arrangements if panicles are cut when half open; split stems and condition in cool place over night. Flowers better than foliage for dried arrangements. Most common pests, red spider mite, rose chafers, and Japanese beetles.

Propagation by division in spring or fall. Seed propagation not recommended for the amateur.

In late winter and early spring forced by florists for sale as house plants; if grown in porous pots, frequently placed in saucers or pans to ensure constant water supply. Such plants may be removed from pots, planted outside in April or May; will not bloom in current season but should give results in future years.

ASTRANTIA—Masterwort.
Genus of a few species in the Parsley Family (Umbelliferae), *A. major* most important. Roots dark in color, aromatic; upright, smooth herb with branching stems, leaves

palmately lobed or finely cut; flowers in simple or compound umbels, sterile and fertile in the same umbel, pink, rose, or white; bracts often showy, longer than the flowers. June-August; 2-3 feet. Suitable for planting in moist locations, also in shady spots. Propagated by seed sown in early spring (April), or by division in fall or early spring.

AUBRIETA—Rock-Cress. Sometimes given incorrectly as AUBRIETIA.
Genus of the Mustard Family (Cruciferae); *A. deltoidea*, species which has given rise to varieties commonly listed in American catalogs. Trailing habit of growth; leaves small, pubescent to hairy, entire or slightly toothed; flowers composed of four petals, about 1 inch across on stems seldom above 6 inches; colors violet to purple. From April on. Varieties: *graeca*, similar color but slightly larger flowers and a little taller; *Hendersonii*, purple; Borsch's White; *rosea*, pink. Numerous varieties available in European trade.

Excellent as an edging in the perennial border, for the rock garden and especially for the wall garden where plants assume a drooping habit of growth. Cutting back plants in midsummer should produce a second crop of bloom. Seldom troubled by insects. Prefer lighter soils and full sun. Propagated by seed sown in early summer, by division in early spring or fall, and by rooting of trailing shoots as cuttings.

BABYS-BREATH—See *Gypsophila paniculata*

BALLOON-FLOWER—See *Platycodon grandiflorum*

BAPTISIA—False or Wild Indigo.
Genus of more than a score of species in the Pea or Pulse Family (Leguminosae), native in eastern North America. *B. australis* (meaning southern, not Australia)—False Indigo. All parts of plant smooth; branching habit of growth. Leaf consisting of 3 leaflets, somewhat rounded with a short point. Flowers indigo-blue, in terminal racemes on the branches; seed pods inflated, black 1½-2 inches long. June; 2½-5 feet. Native from Vermont to North Carolina and Tennessee. Desirable for those who have difficulties with Lupines and Delphiniums. Foliage remains in good condition for the season and provides contrast with Iris and Peony foliage; turns black with drying. Black pods

Bellis perennis, Campanula Medium, Delphinium

Baptisia australis

Belamcanda chinensis

effective in dried arrangements. Taller plants may require staking. Will endure some shade. Do not require rich soil. No serious insects or diseases. Propagated by division in spring or fall. Seed may be sown outdoors after ripening and seedlings transplanted the following spring.

B. tinctoria, Wild Indigo, native from Massachusetts to Georgia and west to Minnesota. Flowers small, yellow; pods small. Better for wild areas than borders. Usually found in dry soils. 18-30 inches; July.

BASKET-OF-GOLD—See *Alyssum saxatile*.

BEE-BALM—See *Monarda didyma*.

BELAMCANDA—Blackberry-Lily, Leopard-Lily.
Genus of 2 species in the Iris Family (Iridaceae); *B. chinensis* more important. Has been known as *B. punctata, Gemmingia chinensis, Pardanthus chinensis* and *P. sinensis*. Roots rhizomatous, grows to about 4 feet with Iris-like leaves along the stem. Flowers short-lived, on short stems, 1½-2 inches across, orange with numerous, small, red spots; July-August. If dead flowers are not removed, seed pods develop which, when ripe, open and disclose the hard, black, shiny seeds, hence the name, Black-

berry-Lily. Has been said that birds sometimes mistake the cluster of seeds for black-
berries; if true, may help to explain why
the species has become naturalized in certain parts of the United States, Connecticut
to Nebraska and southward. Best results in
a sunny location, not particular as to soils,
but should be well drained because of nature
of root system. May be injured by iris borer.
In the mature condition desirable for winter
arrangements.

Propagated by seed, sown in spring, seedlings should bloom the following year; also,
by division in early spring.

BELLFLOWER—See *Campanula*

BELLIS—True or English Daisy.
Genus of about 10 species in the Composite
Family (Compositae), only one of which is
commonly available, *B. perennis*. Although
it is a perennial it is usually treated as a
biennial.

Leaves arising from a crown, forming a
tuft, spatula-shaped or somewhat obovate,
slightly toothed, pubescent, 2 inches or more
in length. Flower heads solitary, varying
from singles (one row of ray florets) to fully
double types with flat, recurved, or incurved
rays; white, pink, rose to red. May-June,
with scattering bloom during summer; 6
inches or more when in bloom. Useful as
an edging plant for beds of spring-flowering
bulbs and pansies, also, for rock gardens.
Frequently available at retail outlets where
pansy plants are sold.

Readily grown from seed which is slow
in germinating, 2-3 weeks; preferably in a
coldframe, transplanted to a frame, and put
in permanent location in early spring.
Named varieties do not come true from seed;
propagated by division in early fall, over-
wintered in a coldframe, and planted out in
early spring. Like a rich, moist soil. Will take
full sun or partial shade. Frequently in
Europe and Great Britain escapes to lawns
and becomes as prevalent as dandelions in
an American lawn.

No serious insects or diseases. Mice have
been known to cause trouble in coldframes.

BERGENIA—Has also been known as ME-
GASEA and SAXIFRAGA.
Genus of few species in the Saxifrage

Bellis perennis

Bergennia crassifolia

Boltonia asteroides

Borago laxiflora

Family (Saxifragaceae). *B. cordifolia,* and its varieties most popular; all parts of the plant smooth, leaves without cilia (hairs on the margin), large, shiny, more or less persistent through the winter. Flowers in drooping clusters, typically rose. April-May; 1 foot or more. May be taller when new foliage is fully developed. Var. *alba,* white; Var. *purpurea,* deeper color than the species.

B. crassifolia. Leaves thick, all parts of the plant smooth, margins of leaves more or less wavy-toothed. Flowers vary in color, rose, lilac, to purple, in dense, drooping clusters. April-May; under 15 inches. Var. *orbicularis,* has larger leaves and flowers are rose.

B. ligulata, least hardy of the three species in cold regions, therefore less commonly grown. Leaves smooth with cilia (hairs on the margins). Flowers white, rose, or purplish.

Hybrids of German origin are: Abendglut, deep rose; Morgenrote, pink; Silberlicht, silvery-rose. All bloom in May; 10-15 inches.

Good qualities: attractive flowers, good foliage through the season which is also useful in arrangements. Undesirable: foliage persisting over winter is frequently in unsightly condition when plants are in bloom, but new foliage develops rapidly. Useful in the herbaceous border and in the rock garden if coarse foliage effects are desired.

Division in spring or fall most satisfactory for home gardeners.

BLEEDING-HEART—See *Dicentra spectabilis*

BLUE PHLOX—See *Phlox divaricata.*

BOLTONIA
Genus of a few species, native in the United States and eastern Asia, of the Composite Family (Compositae). Asiatic species rarely listed in American catalogs.

B. asteroides. Leaves widely lanceolate, 2-5 inches long, upper leaves more narrow and shorter, margins finely toothed. Flower heads, resembling hardy Asters, in panicles, about ¾ inch across; white, violet to purple; white form most commonly grown.

Late summer and fall; frequently 8 feet in rich soil, consequently requiring staking. Because of height, suitable for backgrounds in wide borders, as a temporary screen, or in combination with shrubs. Restrain in early spring or they will crowd out neighbors.

B. latisquama. Similar to preceding species, but has larger heads with blue-violet ray florets.

Propagated by seed sown in June or July, or by division in spring. Like hardy Asters, plants should be divided frequently because of rapid increase in size of clump. No serious insects or diseases.

BORAGO
A small genus of European herbs of the borage family (Boraginaceae). The perennial *B. laxiflora* is useful in wall or rock gardens, prostrate or trailing with oblong or ovalish, rough leaves and long-stalked pale-blue, saucer-shaped flowers. It flowers from April to early autumn. If not protected by a snow covering, mulch lightly. Propagate by seeds sown in the spring or by division or cuttings. A favorite with bees.

BOUNCING-BET—See *Saponaria officinalis.*

BRUNNERA
Genus of 3 species in the Borage Family (Boraginaceae), one only being of importance for gardens and borders, *B. macrophylla.* In some catalogs may be listed as *Myosotis macrophylla* or *Anchusa myosotidiflora.* Slender, somewhat hairy plant, branching from the crown; basal leaves with long petioles, large, ovate with heart-shaped base, stem leaves smaller, upper quite narrow. Flowers small, beautiful blue, in open, panicle-like racemes. May-June; 12-18 inches. Popular because of its color and light, airy effect produced by the flowers. Makes a desirable underplanting for late-flowering Tulips, useful in the foreground of borders and in rock gardens. Excellent for shady and partially shaded locations. Being native in the Caucasus and Siberia it is hardy.

Propagated by seed sown in the fall or by division in spring. Commercially propagated in greenhouses by root cuttings.

Brunnera macrophylla

Buddleja Davidii

Callirhoe involucrata

BUDDLEJA—Name as spelled by Linnaeus, Swēdish botanist; in catalogs more frequently given as BUDDLEIA. Butterfly-Bush.
Genus of about 100 species, chiefly trees and shrubs, in the Logania Family (Loganiaceae). Included in this book since at least one species frequently behaves as a half-hardy shrub or hardy herbaceous perennial. Hardy woody species omitted.

B. Davidii (B. variabilis)—Leaves opposite, varying from ovate-lanceolate to lanceolate, up to 10 inches long, serrate margins, green above, covered with white tomentum on under surface. Flowers produced on growth of current season, typically lilac with an orange-yellow eye, fragrant, in small clusters on long, cylindrical panicles. May reach a height of 15 feet where extremely hardy; from July until frost. Var. *magnifica*, more dense panicles, larger, rosy-purple flowers with orange eye; Var. *Veitchiana*, more robust, larger flowers, mauve with orange eye; var. *Wilsonii*, rose-lilac with orange eye, drooping panicles.
Other horticultural varieties are: Empire Blue (Plant Patent 557); Fascination, orchid pink; Flaming Violet (P.P. 519); Fortune,

lilac (P.P. 206); Purple Prince, red-purple (P.P. 706); White Profusion (P.P. 786).
Winter of 1958-59 gave good test of hardiness; in Amherst, Mass., some varieties died out completely, others died back to the crown, made new growth and began to bloom in July. Best used in shrub borders or in background of herbaceous borders. Important because of long season of bloom, variety of color, fragrance, attraction for butterflies, and use as cut flowers. Give good results in a variety of soils if they are well drained. Japanese beetle doubtless the most common insect pest.
New varieties obtained from seed; best propagated from stem cuttings of semi-ripened wood (current season's growth), rooted indoors or in greenhouse.

BUGLE-WEED—See *Ajuga*.

CALLIRHOE—Poppy-Mallow.
Genus of a few species, native in North America, in the Mallow Family (Malvaceae). Species most frequently listed in American catalogs is *C. involucrata;* has also been described as *Malva involucrata* and *C. verticillata;* native from Minnesota to Texas. More or less trailing, spreading habit of growth, seldom exceeding 1 foot in height. Leaves deeply lobed or parted, 5-7 lobes. Flowers mallow-like, up to 2½ inches in diameter, varying from crimson-purple to red, rose and paler tones. All summer to October.
Most useful for rock gardens for summer and autumn color and in foreground of borders. Good for planting on dry banks. Long, fleshy roots may rot in heavy or poorly drained locations.
Grown from seed, preferably sown where the plants are to mature because of nature of root system; may also be increased by division.

CAMPANULA—Bellflower.
Genus of more than 200 species in the Bellflower Family (Campanulacea), about a dozen of which are most popular for herbaceous borders and rock gardens.

C. carpatica—Tussock Bellflower, Carpathian Bellflower. One of the most well known. Plant smooth, stems more or less spreading at the base but growing to a height of 9 inches or more. Lower leaves with long petioles, ovate, 1-1½ inches long, somewhat heart-shaped at the base, short-pointed with crenate to dentate margins. Flowers solitary, blue, up to 2 inches across. June-October; 8 inches. Var. *alba*, white; Var. Blue Carpet, deep blue, June-October; 8 inches. Var. Wedgewood, violet-blue, considered to be one of the best; flowers standing above the 6 inch mass of foliage. Var. White Wedgewood. This species and its varieties are excellent for rock and wall gardens, for edgings, foregrounds in borders, and planting along steps and paths.

C. Elatines—Adria Bellflowers. A miscellaneous group which includes var. *garganica*, frequently listed in catalogs as *C. garganica*. Plant pubescent giving foliage a grayish appearance. Lower leaves with long petioles, upper ovate, margins toothed, about 1 inch in width. Flowers numerous, small, solitary or with a few in the leaf axils, light violet-blue with white center. June; 5 inches. Effective when allowed to droop in a wall garden or over rocks in a rock garden.

C. glomerata — Plant upright, hairy to smooth, with branches, leaves rough, thick, more or less hairy; lower with long petioles, upper more or less clasping the stems. Flowers small, 1 inch or less, numerous, in dense clusters in leaf axils and terminating the stem and branches, blue; also varies to white. June; 18 inches. Var. *dahurica (superba)*, purple. June; 18 inches. Var. *aculis*, tufted habit of growth, leaves narrow, blue-violet. 6 inches.

C. lactiflora—Plant erect, having a few hairs, branching habit of growth. Basal leaves larger than the stem leaves which are sessile and toothed. Flowers in a terminal panicle or cluster, each flower about 1 inch long, pure white, but varying to pale blue forms. July-August; 4-5 feet. Pritchard's Variety, pale to deep blue; July-August; 3 feet. This species needs a very slightly acid soil, pH 5.5-6.00. Full sun or partial shade.

Campanula   Wedgewood

C. latifolia—Plant erect, vigorous. Lower leaves with long petioles, blade 5-6 inches long, toothed, rugose, and hairy; upper leaves, short petioles, more narrow and pointed. Flowers usually erect, in a terminal leafy cluster or raceme, each about 1½ inches long; purplish blue, also varies to white. June-July; 3-4 feet.

C. Medium — Canterbury Bells. Biennial species. Plant erect, with stiff hairs. Lower leaves broadly lanceolate, 6-10 inches long; upper leaves narrow, sessile, usually clasping the stem. Flowers erect or nearly so, one or more in upper leaf axils and with terminal forming an open raceme; corolla bell-shaped. Violet-blue, varying to pale violet, pink and white. June-July; up to 4 feet. Var. *calycanthema* — Cup-and-Saucer Canterbury Bell. Calyx has become showy like the corolla and forms the saucer. In the Duplex type calyx has become corolla-like, surrounding the true bell; known as the Hose-in-Hose type of doubling. Seeds of this species and variety must be sown every year to provide bloom each year; sown in May or early June plants should be large enough to bloom the following summer. In open winters the leafy plants may be killed;

Campanula lactiflora

Campanula pyramidalis Chimney Bellflower

also, injured by being frozen in ice; sometimes carried over winter in coldframes and planted out in early spring.

C. persicifolia—Peachleaf Bellflower. A favorite with many home gardeners. Plant smooth, producing many basal leaves, more or less lanceolate, with crenate, wavy margins; upper, small, narrow and few. Flowers on very short stalks, erect or nearly so, scattered, forming a loose, open raceme; blue-violet, varying to lighter tones. From July on if dead flowers are removed; 2-3 feet. Var. *alba*, white. Var. Telham Beauty, a better blue. Var. *Moerheimii*, double white. An adaptable species; will grow under a great variety of conditions, full sun, partial shade, to full shade where colors are lighter. Not particular as to soil in type or fertility. Will self-sow readily (except doubles). May become too invasive since it increases rapidly by shoots arising from the base. Good as cut flowers if ends of stems are split and seared with flame because of milky juice. Division in spring simplest method of propagation, each small unit developing into a plant of good size in one year.

C. Poscharskyana—Related to the Adria Bellflowers, but flowers are larger, corolla more deeply cut, wider than long, blue. Good species for rock and wall gardens. Much bloom during the summer. Said by some gardeners to be the best ground cover of all Campanulas.

C. Portenschlagiana—A form of *C. Elatines*. Leaves nearly circular or kidney-shaped, long petioles, blade about 1 inch wide. Flowers numerous, star-like, violet. Long season of bloom; 6-8 inches. Best adapted for use in rock gardens.

C. pyramidalis—Chimney Bellflower. Possibly more commonly grown in pots than in borders. Plants smooth, usually with a simple stem, which bears numerous branchlets on which flowers are produced, thus forming a long, narrow, raceme-like spike. Flowers white or blue. Late summer and early fall; up to 5 feet or more.

C. rapunculoides—Rover Bellflower. Well

named since the plant does like to rove. Has become naturalized in many sections. Basal leaves with long petioles, more or less heart-shaped; upper, nearly lanceolate. Flowers typically violet-blue, nodding, forming an open spike-like raceme. Good plant to keep out of borders; spreads rapidly and pieces of the fleshly roots act as root cuttings. If one is to use it, it belongs in the wildflower garden.

C. rotundifolia—Bluebell, Harebell. Naturalized in many parts of the United States. Basal leaves ovate to almost circular, frequently dying before plants bloom; stem leaves grass-like. Flowers nodding, scattered on the stem, about 1 inch long. Blue; summer; 6-20 inches, depending on the habitat. Primarily a plant for rock gardens; does well in moist locations and in ordinary soils.

All Campanulas, except named varieties, are readily propagated by seed. All forms propagated by division, frequency depending on the rate of growth; some, every third or fourth year, others less frequently.

CANDYTUFT—See *Iberis sempervirens.*

CANTERBURY BELLS—See *Campanula Medium.*

CARNATION OR CLOVE PINK—See *Dianthus caryophyllus.*

CATANANCHE—Cupids-Dart.
Genus of a few species in the Composite Family (Compositae), one perennial being most commonly listed, *C. caerulea.* Leaves tomentose, narrow to broadly lanceolate, entire or with a few teeth, crowded near the base of the stem, up to 12 inches long. Flower heads on slender stems, bearing all ray florets, strap-shaped, blue, up to 2 inches in diameter. Var. *alba*, white. Var. *bicolor*, blue edged with white. All grow to about 2 feet and bloom from June on.

Not particular as to soils. Flowers may be cut, dried, and used in winter bouquets. Fruiting heads resemble dandelions at maturity.

Plants grown from seed sown in spring should bloom the first year, hence, may be

Campanula persicifolia Peachleaf Bellflower, Peach Bells

Catananche caerulea major

Centaurea

Centranthus ruber

treated as an annual in regions where plants are not hardy. Also propagated by division.

CENTAUREA

Genus of numerous species, 500 or more, of the Composite Family (Compositae), many of which are annuals. Two perennial species more commonly grown than others; they are truly hardy.

C. montana—Mountain Bluet, sometimes known as Perennial Cornflower. Stems usually unbranched. Leaves somewhat coarse, toothed, broadly lanceolate, frequently wider, and decurrent (continuing down the stem). Flower heads solitary, on very short peduncles, outer florets much larger than those in center, up to 2½ inches in diameter. From June on; up to 2 feet. Var. *alba*, white; var. *rosea*, pink.

C. dealbata, may be known as Persian Centaurea. Leaves smooth above, woolly-white beneath, pinnately divided, basal up to 18 inches long; stem leaves much shorter. Flower heads solitary, inner florets red, outer, rose to white. June-July; up to 2 feet.

Best grown in full sun. Require no special care but *C. montana* should be divided every

third year since, with numerous stems, foliage becomes dense and crowded.

Both species propagated from seed sown in spring and by division. Light mulch over winter may be beneficial.

C. Cineraria and *C. gymnocarpa*, both known as Dusty Miller usually considered as bedding plants, and most frequently propagated by softwood stem cuttings in greenhouses.

CENTRANTHUS—Centranth.

About a dozen species in the Valerian Family (Valerianaceae), only one of which is important for garden use. *C. ruber*, also listed as *Valeriana rubra* and *C. coccinea*—Red Valerian, Jupiters-Beard. Leaves entire, grayish-green, having somewhat the appearance of a succulent. Flowers small, in dense clusters on branches, fragrant, rosy or crimson-red. June-October; 2 to 3 feet. Var. *albus*, white.

In England it might well be called a Wallflower since it will grow in rock crannies in a minimum of soil; also, in England it is said to become a nuisance in flower borders since it self-sows so freely. However this is not true in American gardens.

Prefers a dry soil and full sun. Long lasting when in bloom. Good for cutting and said to be good for use in sachets. No staking.

Seed propagation most commonly used but may also be propagated by division.

CEPHALARIA

Genus of about 30 species in the Teasel Family (Dipsaceae), one especially being used in borders, *C. tatarica*. Bailey: *Manual of Cultivated Plants* states that *C. alpina* is evidently not in cultivation, plants offered as such being *C. tatarica*. Plants give a coarse effect, even if the leaves are divided to the midrib; smooth above, petioles and under surface hairy. Flowers resemble somewhat those of Scabiosa; heads, about 2 inches in diameter, on long, naked stems, outer florets enlarged, cream to yellow. July; 3-6 feet.

Best used in the background of borders or in wildflower gardens. Not a refined plant. Native in Russia and western Asia, it should be quite hardy.

Readily propagated by seed sown in fall and by division in spring or fall.

CERASTIUM

Genus of 50 to 100 species, depending on the authority. In the Pink Family (Caryophyllaceae), *C. tomentosum (C. Columnae)* called Snow-In-Summer because of the foliage. Trailing or drooping, depending on where it is grown. Leaves grayish-tomentose, linear-lanceolate, about ¾ inch long. Flowers ½ inch or more in diameter, in open cymes, white. Late May-June; 6-9 inches when in bloom.

C. Biebersteinii—Similar to preceding, but has longer and wider leaves. Flowers larger, white. Late May-June; 6 to 9 inches.

Primarily plants for rock and wall gardens. Used in the crevices in a dry wall they droop gracefully; should not be allowed to smother other plants in the lower part of the wall. Tops may be clipped off when the main season of bloom is past. Retains foliage over winter and may become unsightly due to death of older leaves.

Propagation by seed sown in spring or late summer, by division in spring or fall, and by softwood cuttings of new growth following the blooming season.

Cephalaria alpina

Cerastium tomentosum

Ceratostigma plumbaginoides

Cheiranthus Cheiri

CERATOSTIGMA

Genus of a few species in the Leadwort Family (Plumbaginaceae), some of which are shrubby. *C. plumbaginoides*, Leadwort, only important species for use in herbaceous borders; listed in some catalogs as *Plumbago Larpentae*. Plant somewhat woody at the base, spreading widely. Leaves broad for the length (3 inches), tapering to the base, dark green turning to bronzy-red in fall, smooth except for the hairy margins. Flowers near Gentian-blue, in open to compact clusters. 8-12 inches; August-September.

Desirable for the foreground of the border but too great in width for an edging plant. Good as a ground cover. Thrives in partial shade or full sun. Well-drained soil, not necessarily rich. Like Platycodon, slow in starting into growth in spring. May winter kill in cold regions unless given a light mulch.

CHEIRANTHUS

Genus of less than a dozen species in the Mustard Family (Cruciferae), one being an old garden favorite, *C. Cheiri*, Wallflower. Leaves narrow, entire, grayish-green, closely set on the lower part of the stem and on non-flowering shoots. Flowers of 4 petals in single forms, up to 1 inch across, yellow, orange, orange-brown to reddish-brown; fragrance much like that of violets. 12-30 inches; early spring.

Used in wall gardens and borders. May not survive severe winters in the open, hence, may be necessary to over-winter young plants in coldframes. Sometimes behaves as a biennial. Excellent for late winter and spring bloom in a cool greenhouse.

Usually propagated by seed; will self-sow in some regions. Sown outdoors as late as early June, will produce some bloom in the autumn. Softwood cuttings of new growth used if desired to maintain a definite type, such as double-flowered form.

Plants listed as *C. Allionii* are correctly *Erysimum Perofskianum*, an annual, occasionally called Fairy Wallflower.

CHELONE—Turtle-Head, Shellflower.

Genus of several species, all of which are native in North America, in the Figwort

Family (Scrophulariaceae). *C. glabra*, common northern species, leaves narrow or broadly lanceolate, 2½-6 inches long, pointed, with short petioles. Flowers white or tinged with rose, about 1 inch long, lip having a white beard. 3 feet; July-September.

C. Lyonii, a more southern species, in mountainous regions; quite hardy. Leaves ovate, 3-7 inches long, with long petioles. Flowers rose-purple, about 1 inch long, lip having a yellow beard. 3 feet; July-September.

C. obliqua—also a southern species, not commonly listed. Leaves up to 8 inches, heavily veined, with petioles. Flowers deep rose, about 1 inch long. 2-3 feet; July and later. *C. obliqua* var. *alba* is said to be *C. glabra.*

Plants for partially shaded or shady locations, preferably in moist soils as in their native habitats. At their best in the wild-flower garden.

May be propagated by seed sown in spring but much more easily increased by division in spring or in fall after season of bloom.

No serious insect pests or diseases.

Chelone Lyonii

CHINESE LANTERN PLANT—See *Physalis Alkekengi.*

CHRISTMAS-ROSE—See *Helleborus niger.*

CHRYSANTHEMUM

Genus of more than 150 species, including annuals, herbaceous perennials and some with more or less woody base, in the Composite Family (Compositae). Annuals omitted from this discussion. In all species flowers are produced in heads, composed of ray florets (petal-like), which are pistillate, and tubular disk florets, pistillate and normally producing pollen.

C. arcticum (Leucanthemum arcticum)— Arctic Daisy. Plant developing into a clump. Stems simple or branching near the base. Leaves leathery, shaped like a spatula, up to 3 inches long, 3-lobed or parted, each lobe again divided; upper leaves more like bracts. Heads solitary on the branches, single, with yellow center, 2 or 3 inches in

Chrysanthemum

diameter. October; 15 inches or more. Extremely hardy but blooming too late for many regions. Several varieties available: Astrid, the first of this type to be introduced, salmon-pink; Good Morning, yellow; Igloo, white; Kristina, deep rose-pink; Peer Gynt, coppery red.

C. Balsamita—Costmary, Mint-Geranium. One of the "old fashioned" garden flowers, grown primarily for the balsam-like fragrance of the foliage; frequently included among the herbs in catalogs. Plant pubescent, stems producing many branches. Leaves oblong to oval, up to 6 inches long; basal leaves longer; all having toothed margins. Heads about 1 inch in diameter, rays white, disk yellow. August-September; 2-4 feet. Most commonly propagated by division.

C. coccineum (Pyrethrum roseum, P. hybridum) — Common Pyrethrum, Painted Daisy. Plant smooth, producing many basal, finely divided leaves. Stems erect, usually simple, sometimes forked, with few leaves. Heads large, up to 3 inches or more in diameter; rays white, pink, rose, to dark red; disk yellow. Includes types which are double (all ray florets) and the anemone form in which disk florets are elongated, forming a cushion. June-July, with some later bloom if plants are cut back after first bloom; 15-30 inches. Should be planted in groups, not as individual specimens. Excellent for cutting. At their best in full sun in fertile and well-drained soil. Insects and disease seldom cause trouble. Foliage may turn yellow. Staking unnecessary unless to prevent battering by wind and rain. May require mulching over winter in cold regions; protection desirable first winter after dividing. Propagated by seed sown in spring; seedlings blooming the following year may show variations. Division best done in late summer or early fall every third or fourth year.

C. Leucanthemum—Ox-Eye Daisy, Whiteweed. Common white daisy of fields in eastern United States. Good plant to keep out of the border since it self-sows freely; can be used in the wildflower garden.

C. maximum—Max Daisy, Shasta Daisy. Latter name misleading since the species is native in the Pyrenees Mountains; refers to Mount Shasta. Plant eventually becoming smooth. Basal leaves long, broadly lanceolate, with coarse, blunt teeth; stem leaves shorter and more narrow. Heads 3 inches in diameter, much broader in named varieties; ray white, disk yellow. June-August; 2-2½ feet. *Varieties*: Aglaya, double white, fringed; some disk florets present. Alaska, single white, yellow disk; June-July; 2 feet. Cobham Gold, creamy white, crested or cushion center pale yellow. Marconi, double frilled white, 2 feet. Mark Riegel, single white, orange-yellow disk, 2-3 feet. Mount Shasta, double white with high, crested disk. Thomas Killin, white with two rows of ray florets, ring of elongated disk florets and golden center. Wirral Pride, similar to preceding, large heads, up to 4 inches.

All Shasta Daisies are excellent for cutting. More effective in groups than as individual specimens. Height makes them suitable for the middle ground of borders. Full sun or partial shade. Drainage must be good, over winter especially. Affected by some of the insects and diseases of hardy Chrysanthemums. Propagated by seed sown in spring which may produce variations and by division in spring every third or fourth year.

C. nipponicum—Nippon Daisy. Woody at the base. Stems stiff, usually smooth. Lower leaves soon falling away; upper crowded, thick and stiff, up to 3½ inches long, with blunt teeth. Heads terminal, single, rays white, disk yellow; up to 3½ inches in diameter. September-October; 2-3 feet.

C. Parthenium (Matricaria Parthenium) — Feverfew. Bushy plant with many branches, smooth, strongly scented. Basal leaves entire, upper pinnate and the pinnae again divided. Heads about ¾ inch in diameter in clusters, rays white, disk yellow. There are rayless forms and others that are fully double. July-August; 15-30 inches. Occasionally grown in herb gardens. Var. *aureum*, yellow foliage, 12 inches; suitable for edgings and foregrounds of borders; also

Chrysanthemum   Astrid

Chrysanthemum   Teal

used in formal bedding with other foliage plants.

Feverfew not permanently hardy in cold regions. Do not require rich soils. Some varieties grown under glass by florists for sale as cut flowers.

Plants from seed sown in spring should bloom the first season. Spring division better than fall division. Softwood stem cuttings may be rooted in summer.

C. rubellum. Plants forming widely spreading clumps, leaves green, slightly pubescent on lower surface, deeply pinnately lobed, divisions coarsely toothed or lobed. Heads numerous, solitary or a few on a stem, not densely clustered, about 3 inches in diameter; rays entire, narrow, not notched at tip; disk yellow. August-September; 2-3 feet. Var. Anna Hay, salmon to salmon-pink, spread of 2-3 feet; Clara Curtis, one of the oldest and most hardy of this group, salmon pink; Jessie Cooper, bronze with yellow disk, spread of 3 feet; Royal

Command, brilliant red, 2 feet, 2½ feet across. Because of the spread of plants they should be planted at least 3 feet apart.

C. sibiricum. More commonly known as *C. coreanum,* Korean Chrysanthemum, although native in Siberia. Plant 2-3 feet high, shining, green leaves, irregularly divided. Heads single, rays white, frequently tinged with pink, disk yellow. Late October. Not attractive of itself but of importance because it has been used so much in breeding work, producing the so-called Korean hybrids and in the development of other types. Extremely hardy species but late-blooming.

C. morifolium. Previously known as *C. hortorum,* to which are now referred all types grown under glass and outdoors unless varieties are definitely referred to other species. *C. indicum* also supposed to have been involved in the development of the horticultural types described below. *C. coreanum* blood is without doubt present in many garden varieties.

53

HORTICULTURAL TYPES OF CHRYSANTHEMUMS

Single: heads daisy-like, one to several rows of ray florets (petal-like), surrounding the center composed of numerous, tubular, disk florets. Typical varieties: Apollo, orange-bronze; Daphne, soft old rose; Fred Stone, red; Gold Daisy, yellow; Louise Schling, red; North Star, white; Peachtone, soft pink; Summertime, golden yellow.

Anemone: (a) Formal: ray florets as in singles but uniform in length; disk like a cushion due to the lengthening of tubular florets; (b) Japanese: ray and disk florets irregular in arrangement and length. These types more commonly grown in greenhouses since they usually bloom too late for garden uses, at least in northern latitudes.

Spoon: varying in degree of doubleness, some disk florets present; ray florets tubular with a prolonged lip-like tip, resembling a spoon. Tyical varieties: Cardinal, red; Garnet, deeper than Cardinal; Jessamine Williams, white; Moonlight, light yellow; Yellow Spoon.

Decorative: (a) Incurved; heads semi-double to fully double, with or without disk florets; ray florets regular, curving toward the center; (b) Incurving; loose, irregular ray florets curving toward the center; (c) Reflexed; ray florets regular or irregular, recurved. Typical varieties: Abundance, bronze; Avalanche, white; Carnival, orange-bronze; Elegy, reflexed, cream white; Fascination, light lavender-pink; Flourish, orchid pink; Invader, reflexed, deep maroon; King's Ransom, golden yellow; Lee Powell, golden yellow; Moonglow, yellow; Pheasant, bronze, one of the "bird" series.

Pompon: Heads completely double or with a few disk florets, more or less globular, usually under 2 inches in diameter. Typical varieties: Blanche Litwiler, lavender-pink; Canary Wonder, light yellow; Fred R. Rockwell, orange-scarlet bronze; Masquerade, rose-lilac; Royalist, dark red; White Wonder, white.

Button Pompon: Heads very small, less than 1 inch in diameter. Typical varieties: Baby Sister, light rose; Bambino, claret; Chocolate Drop, dark red; Frisky Lad, lemon yellow; Primrose, pale yellow; Tawny Top, bronze; Watch Charm, pink to coral-rose.

Azaleamum (trademark name) and Cushion types appear to be synonomous; dwarf plants up to 1 foot or slightly more, with a spread of 2 feet or more; varieties range from single to double; early flowering, from August on. Typical varieties: Bowl of Gold, golden yellow; Bronze Queen, bronze; Dan Foley, tangerine-orange; Lipstick, red; Minnpink, rose-pink; Powder River, white; Twinkle, Fuchsia purple; Wee Willie, white.

Rayonnante: includes the spidery, plumed, and feathery forms; usually quite double with thread-like, laciniate, twisted, or drooping ray florets. Too tender and too late for border use in many regions.

Quilled: ray florets like quills, usually more or less erect. Best for greenhouse culture, such as the old variety, Petaluma.

Commercial: (a) Incurved or Standard: heads may have a few disk florets concealed by the numerous ray florets which vary in length and form but are definitely incurving. (b) Japanese Incurved or Exhibition: much like preceding but ray florets less regular in arrangement and outer ones may be recurved. (c) Reflexed; heads may have a few disk florets showing when head is fully developed; all ray florets strongly recurved. When grown in garden or border one should not expect to obtain the size attained when such types are grown in greenhouses, even if one head only is allowed to develop per stem. Typical varieties: Gaytime, reflexed, deep rose pink; Major Bowes, deep orchid pink; Mrs. H. E. Kidder, lemon yellow; Regalia, purple; Superlative, white; Westfield Bronze, bronze.

Garden or border is not complete if Chrysanthemums are lacking. By careful selection of types and varieties a long season of bloom is possible; great variety in habit of growth, form of flower, and color; Cushion varieties excellent for masses; make

Chrysanthemum maximum Shasta Daisy

Cimicifuga simplex

Clematis   Nelly Moser

fine contrasts with other late flowers such as Asters, Heleniums, and Aconitums. Some of the best cut flowers among all perennials; good foliage, long-lasting, good stems, and wonderful colors.

Success depends largely on the section of the United States where plants are being grown; winter killing in such states as South Dakota and Wisconsin, for example; come too late in the season for such states as Idaho, Utah, and Wyoming. Death of plants in early spring may be due to heaving, with dying of the roots. May lose lower leaves, in dry seasons especially. Insects: Aphis, Cyclamen Mite, Earwigs, Gall Midge, Foliar and Soil Nematodes, Red Spider Mite, Thrips. Diseases and Viruses: Aster Yellows, Mildew, Stunt, Septoria Leaf Spot, Verticillium Root Rot.

Necessary to practice pinching with many types to induce branching. Staking sometimes necessary, in particular for large-flowered varieties when they are disbudded to one head per stem.

Propagation by division in spring, every year or every other year depending on type and variety. Softwood stem cuttings in spring and early summer. Seed used to obtain new varieties; sown indoors in late winter, seedlings should bloom the first year.

CIMICIFUGA—Bugbane.
Genus of about a dozen species in the Crowfoot Family (Ranunculaceae), two of which are desirable for garden use. *C. racemosa* (*Actaea racemosa*), Black Snakeroot. A North American species. Leaves divided into threes, leaflets being once or twice divided (decompound); heaviest foliage at the base of the plant, few to no leaves on the flowering stems. Sepals petal-like and falling away. Flowers in dense, more or less drooping racemes; petals may be lacking, numerous stamens producing the attractive quality. 3-6 feet or more; July-August.

C. simplex, (*C. racemosa* var. *simplex*)— Species from Kamtschatka. Leaves much the same as in preceding species. Flowers creamy white, in dense, upright racemes. 3-5 feet; September-October. Said by some gardeners to be the best species in the genus.

C. racemosa gives better results in moist situations with partial shade and plenty of room in which to spread; excellent for wild-flower gardens. *C. simplex* better adapted to open borders. Both effective in background plantings and in front of evergreens. Useful as cut flowers.

Free from diseases and insect pests. Perhaps the name "Bugbane" applies to the plant itself as well as to its uses by humans. Propagated most commonly by division, preferably in spring. Results from sowing seed are uncertain.

CLEMATIS.

More than 200 species of woody vines and herbaceous perennials in the Crowfoot Family (Ranunculaceae), only the latter being considered in this book. Petals are lacking in all species of this genus sepals having become showy and numerous stamens add to the attractiveness of the flower. Feathery seed heads interesting in autumn.

C. heracleaefolia, (C. tubulosa)—Plant herbaceous or woody at the base, smooth. Stem striate (with many ridges), stout. Leaf consisting of 3 leaflets, large, rounded at the base, 3-6 inches, with sharply pointed teeth. Flowers polygamous (unisexual and bisexual on same plant); tubular, numerous, in axillary and terminal clusters, light blue, ¾-1 inch long; sepals reflexed. August-September; 30 inches or more. Var. *Davidiana*, plants more commonly available than the species; leaflets wedge-shaped at base; flowers dioecious (staminate and pistillate flowers on different plants), fragrant, bright blue, up to 15 in a head and few in leaf axils; August-September; 30 inches or more.

C. recta—Plant herbaceous or somewhat woody at the base, smooth. Leaves pinnate, leaflets with short stalks, 5-9, entire. Flowers numerous in a large terminal inflorescence, fragrant white. July-August; 2-3 feet. Var. *mandschurica*, stems longer and more slender; leaflets obtuse; flowers in axillary and terminal clusters, white, July. Possibly the hardier of these two species for all regions.

Lime must be added if soil is acid since

Clematis Henryi

Commelina

Convallaria majalis

Clematis prefer soils on the neutral to slightly alkaline side, gravelly or sandy. Well-drained location. Better in full sun than in shade. May require staking; rings such as are used for peonies will be helpful.

Nematodes may be injurious, also Clematis Borer and Black Blister Beetle. Leaf spot diseases may occur.

These herbaceous types best propagated by division in spring.

COLUMBINE—See *Aquilegia.*

COMMELINA—Day-Flower.
Belonging to the Spiderwort or Day-Flower Family (Commelinaceae) the genus has typical fleshy, watery-juiced stems and quickly wilts when picked. Blue flowers are short-lived. *C. erecta* and *C. diffusa* are hardy with protection over much of the country. Widely distributed from Delaware south. Both tend to sprawl and prefer moist, shady places. Often used as ground covers. *C. coelestis*, common in greenhouses, not hardy in the north. Used in blue gardens. All are easily propagated by rooting bits of their jointed stems, all spread by self-sown seeds.

CONVALLARIA
Genus of two species, in the Lily Family (Liliaceae), *C. montana* and *C. majalis*, Lily-of-the-Valley. Spreading habit of growth. "Pips", actually rootstocks, arising from long, slender, underground branches. Leaves entire, in pairs, flowering stems (scapes) arising between the leaves. Flowers white, nodding, few to many, fragrant, cup-shaped with slightly recurved lobes. 9 inches; May-June. Var. *Fortunei*, larger leaves and flowers, 12 inches; May-June. Var. *flore-pleno*, double flowers, less attractive than the single forms. Var. *rosea*, dull pink. 9 inches; May-June.

Not commonly recommended for planting in borders; spreads too rapidly and foliage may become unsightly if planted in full sun. Much better for use as a ground cover in shady locations, under trees giving high shade (limbs far above the ground), on north side of houses or other buildings. Excellent for cutting because of form and fragrance; pleasing in arrangements with a few leaves or combined with other flowers; popular in corsages. Stems may be pulled from the plant by grasping the lower part.

"Pips" which have been held in cold storage and are available from some seed and bulb stores and nurseries can be forced for winter bloom in the home, requiring three to four weeks. Planted out in the spring, they may not bloom again until the second or third year.

Occasionally red berries develop in late summer or early fall; contain a few seeds which can be used for propagation. Much more readily propagated by division in early spring before growth is far advanced, or in fall. May be left in the same location for many years; if feeding seems desirable, use a complete fertilizer, such as a 5-10-10, in early spring at rate of ¼ cup per square yard and water in immediately.

CORAL BELLS—See *Heuchera.*

COREOPSIS—Tickseed.
Genus of more than 100 species, many native to North America, in the Composite Family (Compositae). Includes both annuals and perennials, only the latter being considered here. Self-sows. Restrain in early spring or they will crowd out less robust neighbors.

C. grandiflora—Usually somewhat hairy. Branching stems. Leaves variable, upper 3-5-parted into lobes of varying form, terminal leaves 3 to 5 times as long as wide.

Flower heads on long peduncles; ray florets usually 8, 3-lobed at the tip, golden yellow; disk florets yellow. June-August; 2 feet. Var. Sunburst, double, golden yellow. June-August.

C. lanceolata—Smooth or somewhat hairy pubescent. Leaves in a few pairs or tufted near the base, broadly lanceolate to linear, entire, 2-6 inches long. Flower heads on long stems (peduncles), up to 2½ inches in diameter; ray florets about 8, 2 or 3 teeth at the tip, yellow; disk florets yellow. 1-2 feet; June-August. Var. *lanceolata* of some catalogs may be *C. grandiflora.*

C. verticillata — Thread-Leaf Coreopsis. Leaves seemingly arranged in whorls, ultimately divided into narrow segments. Flower heads on slender peduncles, about 2 inches across; ray florets entire or finely toothed, yellow; disk florets yellow. June-August; 1-3 feet.

C. auriculata. Usually pubescent, leafy at the base, spreading by stolons. Leaves long-stemmed, blade 2-5 inches long. Flower heads solitary, on long peduncles, 1½-2 inches across; ray florets toothed at the tip, orange-yellow; disk florets orange-yellow.

Coreopsis grandiflora

Delphinium, Lilies, and Phlox

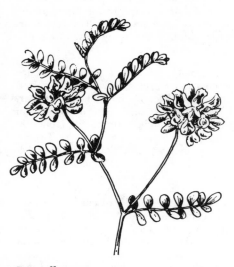

Coronilla varia

Crucianella stylosa

May-July; 18 inches. Var. *nana*, orange, May-July; 8 inches. Var. *superba*, orange. May-July; 20 inches.

A popular genus because of color, long season of bloom, and suitability of flowers for cutting. *C. auriculata* var. *nana* only form to be recommended for rock and wall gardens; others better for the mixed border. Plants may get unsightly late in the summer unless seeding heads are removed; also, may require staking when at greatest height. Leaves frequently injured by flea beetles and striped cucumber beetles. Not particular as to soils; best in sunny locations.

CORONILLA—Crown Vetch.
Genus of about 20 species in the Pea or Pulse Family (Leguminosae), only two of garden interest.

C. varia—Common Crown Vetch. Plant smooth. Leaves pinnate, 11-25 leaflets, blunt but having a pronounced tip. Flowers light rose to pinkish-white in dense umbels. Of straggling habit but may reach a height of 2 feet; all summer into fall.

C. cappadocica. (*C. iberica*), also known as Crown Vetch. Not as common in the trade as preceding species. Plant of grayish-green color because of numerous white hairs. Leaves pinnate, 9-11 leaflets. Flowers in umbels of 6-9 flowers, yellow, about 1 inch long. 1 foot; June-July.

In general Coronillas are plants to be kept out of the border because of their rampant, straggling habit of growth. Good for covering slopes and are not particular as to soil. One good quality is the long season of bloom of *C. varia*.

CRUCIANELLA
Genus of about 30 species in the Madder Family (Rubiaceae), only one species of interest to gardeners. *C. stylosa*, Crosswort. Although considered to be an annual sometimes grown as a perennial. Leaves arranged in whorls around the stem, 8 or 9, narrow, less than 1 inch long, with stiff hairs. Flowers small, 5-parted, rose, in heads terminating the stems, ½ inch across. Style prominent, protruding beyond the flower 6-9 inches; July.

Most suitable for rock gardens; rather small for use in borders.

CYMBALARIA—Kenilworth-Ivy.
Genus of several species in the Figwort Family (Scrophulariaceae), one listed in American catalogs more frequently than the others.

C. muralis—Stems smooth, trailing, rooting at the nodes when they come in contact with soil. Leaves small, alternate, usually kidney-shaped, with 3 to 7 lobes. Flowers ¼ to ⅓ inch long, lilac with yellow throat, but there may be variations in color. Indefinite in season of bloom; continuous in greenhouses. About 2 or 3 inches.

Useful where a delicate ground cover is desired, preferably in rock gardens. Is quite at home in greenhouses, under benches or on walls if the roots can obtain a foothold. Shady locations better than full sun.

CYPRESS SPURGE—See *Euphorbia Cyparissias.*

DAY-LILY—See *Hemerocallis.*

DELPHINIUM—Larkspur.
This popular genus of the Crowfoot Family (Ranunculaceae) is perhaps the cause of more pleasure and more disappointment than any other garden plant. Nothing is more handsome than a well-shaped group of one of the Pacific Hybrid Delphiniums. Included in this strain are Summer Skies, light blue with a white center or "bee"; Black Knight, dark violet; Blue Bird, medium blue with white bee; Cameliard, lavender with white bee; Galahad, pure white; Guinevere, light blue and lavender with white bee; King Arthur, dark violet with white bee; Percival, white with black bee; Astolat, pinkish with black or buff bee. These Pacific Series are now quite well stabilized, so the variation within one group —Blue Jay, for instance—is no longer great. However, it is still best to describe Blue Jay as "*shades* from medium to dark blue", in order to avoid disappointment.

To propagate: The only certain way to increase a favorite clump is to take cuttings in early spring, or divide at the same time. Seeds taken from such a favorite might produce seedlings with some variation. Seed

Cymbalaria muralis

Delphinium hybrid

sown as soon as ripe, germinates freely. Seed storage should be avoided whenever possible, but refrigerate if prompt sowing is impossible. See Propagation from Seed.

Pacific Delphinium is seldom considered long lived, but in cool areas plants may last some time, usually 2 or 3 years. They will also endure great cold during winter, as long as they are placed in perfectly-drained soil and protected from slugs by sifted coal ashes, gritty sand, or chemical repellents around the crown. Some gardeners believe that if late spikes are cut, the hollow stems will collect water and rot the crown. Perhaps it is better to allow the last stems to bend over naturally as they dry, so there will be no open channels to the crown. Do not bury crowns as plants may rot.

Good cultural practice will help these delphinium last longer. Generous liming of the soil is necessary. Place clumps far enough apart to allow air movement. Fertilize with superphosphate, but avoid high-nitrogen plant food. Begin a spray program early in the season to control various mites, aphids and leaf diseases. For the amateur, regular use of an all-purpose spray such as that used for roses is recommended. A water-soluble fertilizer is good when spikes begin to form, but late in the season fertilization is not desirable. Watering during summer droughts is important. Like most tall perennials, the Pacific Delphinium, which often exceed 6 feet when well grown, must be staked early and tied often. Each stalk should receive a stake. No more than a half dozen stalks should be left after thinning out in spring. The flowers are as handsome in bouquets as in the garden, but petals are quick to fall unless the stalk has been well conditioned after cutting. When through flowering, cut back stalks for a second flowering.

There are a number of other hybrid Delphinium strains, such as the Blackmore and Langdon and the Frank Bishop strain, the latter being shorter than most hybrids. Abroad, these strains are offered as named varieties grown from cuttings. In the United States, usually only mixed seeds or seedlings are offered, which, though inferior, are worth trying.

D. cheilanthum var. *formosum*—Garland Larkspur. Gardeners know this Delphinium as Belladonna or Bellamosum. About 3 feet tall. Often hardier than Pacific Hybrids, but it is best to keep new plants coming along by sowing seed as soon as the capsules open. Lamartine and Sapphire are deep blue forms. Cliveden Beauty is light blue. White selections are sometimes offered.

D. grandiflorum—Bouquet Larkspur, Chinese Delphinium. Less than 2 feet tall. Usually grown as a biennial. Blue Butterfly, deep blue, combines well with White Butterfly.

D. nudicaule—Red Larkspur, a seldom satisfactory American species, has been used in hybridizing, but such offspring as Pink Sensation are little better than curiosities.

DIANTHUS—Pink.

This superb genus of the Pink Family (Caryophyllaceae) has been loved as long as there have been gardens. The truly perennial species last many years in full sun, if given perfect drainage. Quality of soil should not be high. Old plantings may become clogged with grass. Then lift the clump, divide and clean it. Although it takes a great mass of any dianthus to make a show, the gray foliage makes more compact species useful for edging. Fragrance is excellent in many types. Species which normally flower once may sometimes be coaxed into a second bloom by prompt removal of faded blooms. Cut flowers are long lasting, but fragrance is greatest for the first day or two after picking. If species such as *D. plumarius* or other notably hardy types do not prove reliable in your garden, they are probably fed too much, limed too little, or not given sharp enough drainage. Also, many pinks are best left uncovered during winter. Even the best mulch seems to encourage decay of Dianthus stems. Rock chips or slate underneath the foliage of more challenging species may prove an aid in over-wintering.

Plants are easily raised from seed in most cases, but it is difficult to secure true seed of rarer species. Division is an easy way of renewing old clumps, while cuttings of favorite plants root well if taken before late summer

Dianthus   Coral Gem

(stems become rather woody). The roots of most Dianthus are long and rangy, so it is always best to move the plants when they are young, before roots have traveled far. Plants are notably pest free. Fermate may be needed for leaf spot on some types.

Dianthus Allwoodii—One of the most famous crosses made by the English firm of Allwood, using *D. plumarius* and the perpetual flowering carnation, *D. caryophyllus*. The use of the latter species naturally caused the hybrid to be less hardy than *D. plumarius*, but it is nevertheless worth trying, particularly if named clones are planted. About 1 foot. Blooms repeatedly from spring on. Var. *alpinus*, dwarf and fragrant, ranges from white to rose red. Useful as a rockery or edging plant.

D. alpinus—This true Alpine makes a fine rose-pink mound in late May when well grown. Like many Alpines, it suffers in lowland summer heat. Provide some shade. In areas with little snow, this pink requires protection. An inverted berry basket may prove best.

D. arenarius—Fragrant white to rose-pink flowers. About 3-4 inches. Hardy.

D. barbatus—Sweet William. Rarely perennial, but volunteer seedlings common. Little seedlings you wish to save may be transplanted to the spot where wanted. Various strains from 6 inches to more than 2 feet. A variety of colors and bicolors. Among showiest of the genus.

D. carthusianorum—Useful where a tall pink is desirable. 2 feet. Rose-pink shades. Early summer. Hardy.

Dicentra formosa

D. Caryophyllus—Carnation, Clove Pink, Picotee, Grenadine. Not hardy, but long blooming period makes them well worth growing. The Chaband carnation sown in late February will bloom from July to November in New England. Few other garden plants offer as much bloom or as fine a fragrance. Many strains, including greenhouse types. About 2 feet. Sprawls if unsupported. Calyx tends to split in these double forms, although breeders are making progress in improving this.

D. deltoides—Maiden Pink. Small, numerous rose-pink flowers. 8 inches or more. A favorite rockery plant. Charming rambling habit. Easy from seed.

D. gratianopolitanus — Cheddar Pink. Often listed as *D. caesius*. Divide regularly to keep vigorous. Pink flowers in spring highly fragrant. Rockery.

D. Knappi—Yellow. Some think very well of its habit. Less need for staking, even though it may approach 2 feet in proper gritty soil.

D. neglectus—Various shades of rose with light tan on reverse of petals. 6 inches; June.

D. plumarius—Cottage Pink. Centuries in cultivation, still worth growing. Shades of rose and pink look poor beside modern Dianthus hybrids, but the fragrance and charm of this Pink are great. A foot tall. Many improved strains in clear, clean colors. Early summer.

DICENTRA

Including some of the most charming plants in cultivation, this genus of the Fumitory Family (Fumariaceae) is very popular. The Fringed Bleeding-Heart is common in old gardens, where it spreads freely, largely from self-sown seedlings. Finely cut leaves of this plant are more appealing than the abundant rose-pink flowers. It will endure in heavy shade in competition with tree and shrub roots. Tall Bleeding-Heart is showy in bloom, but dies down quickly in most gardens and leaves a gap.

D. Cucullaria — Dutchmans-Breeches. A North American wildflower. White flowers with yellow tips and pink tinges. Early spring. Better in cool, moist woodland gardens than open borders. Variable in height, depending upon location.

D. eximia—Fringed Bleeding-Heart. Another native species. Long flowering. Few troubles, though sometimes attacked by aphids. Best grown where volunteer seedlings will not be a problem. Seedlings, not always easy to move. Many selected forms are offered. The hybrid Bountiful blooms well in sun, but its reddish blooms are not durable in all locations. A white variety is inclined to be a miff. About 1 foot tall.

D. formosa — Western Bleeding-Heart. Often sold for *D. eximia*, it may prove troublesome because of its spreading nature. Does best in shade, 1 foot. Like *D. eximia*, it blooms all summer.

D. spectabilis — Bleeding-Heart. Swiftly passing splendor. Rises quickly in early spring, unfurls its graceful, arching stems studded with heart-like blooms, then dies back by summer in all but the most favored shady locations. In bloom it makes a broad plant well over 2 feet tall even when casu-

III. Opposite *Pink astilbe, pink phlox, blue delphinium and whit* snakeroot (Cimicifuga racemosa) *white campanula and double feverfet* (Chrysanthemum Parthenium) *photographed in early July.*

ally grown, hence, when dried back, leaves
a large gap. Yet it is hard to plant camouflage too near for fear of damaging this
Bleeding-Heart's thick, fleshy root. Useful as
a cut flower.

DICTAMNUS—Dittany, Fraxinella.
This genus of the Rue Family (Rutaceae)
also has the name Gas-Plant, because under
ideal conditions oil given off by the plant
may be ignited. Although long-lasting when
established, it is slow to amount to much
when first planted and is difficult to move
except in seedling size. An old plant will
need a large area to look its best, but the
clean leaves are always appealing. Neither
the pink nor white form last long in bloom
during July. Flowers are not of greatest
value when cut, but seed pods are decorative in dried arrangements. Unlike most
large plants, it requires no staking. Plant in
sunny location in well-drained soil. Many
find the aromatic foliage pleasant. Seeds require frost to germinate.

D. albus (D. Fraxinella). A variable species. 3 feet. Var. *caucasicus* is a larger type.
Var. *ruber* is rose-colored.

DIGITALIS—Foxglove.
A genus of the Figwort Family (Scrophulariaceae), Digitalis is often more biennial
than perennial, but many species self-sow
freely. Finest and healthiest in moist, partly
shaded gardens. Pests and diseases sometimes distort the stem and disfigure foliage,
especially when plants are in full sun. Tall
varieties are best staked, but often are strong
enough to stand alone. Newer strains are
much preferred over species, being raised
from seed sown in summer. Evergreen foliage needs light, airy protection in winter.

D. grandiflora—Yellow Foxglove. Often
listed as *D. ambigua*, 2 feet or more. Self-
sows. Worthwhile for its shorter stature.
June. Repeats bloom.

D. mertonensis—A tetraphoid cross between *D. ambigua* and *D. purpurea*. Pink
flowers are good size, very well liked by
some gardeners. 2-3 feet.

Digitalis

Dictamnus albus

*. Opposite Attracting attention in the foreground is the charming
ngle, pink peony (L'Etincelante) planted with pink pyrethrum, clumps
dainty coral bells, oriental poppies and irises.*

Dodecatheon

Doronicum

D. purpurea—Common Foxglove. This familiar biennial may prove disappointing with its rose-colored blooms suspended downward on one side of the 3 or 4 foot spike. Recent Excelsior strain has upright blooms held around the stem in a variety of clear colors. Many seed houses offer selected strains that are worth trying. White ones are excellent in dappled shade.

DODECATHEON—Shooting Star.
This genus of the Primrose Family (Primulaceae) has sprightly reflected flowers suggestive of those of its close relative Cyclamen. These attractive American plants should be more widely used in moist partly shaded gardens. Like many spring-blooming wildflowers, their tops die back as summer approaches. Transplant when dormant into humusy soil and leave a foot between plants. Sow seed as soon as it is ripe.

D. Hendersonii—(D. latifolium). Rose-purple. About 18 inches.

D. Meadia—Variable in color, pink shades common. 2 feet.

D. pulchellum — (D. paucifolium) — Rose with yellow basal markings. Averages 1 foot.

DORONICUM—Leopards-Bane.
An early-blooming genus of the Composite Family (Compositae), Doronicum would be more widely appreciated if it did not have precisely the color of dandelions. In any case, the long stems make for good cut flowers. Clumps are easily split into many plants after flowering, but the divisions do not establish quickly unless well watered and shaded. Many species self sow too readily, as is typical of composites. Handsome dark green leaves seldom retain their beauty during summer. There is great difference in the charm of smaller types and the coarseness of larger ones.

D. caucasicum. A spreader by stolons. Madam Mason is best known form. 2 inch flowers borne singly on 1½ foot stems may be smaller the second year. Var. *magnificum* is larger flowered and stronger growing.

D. Pardalianches. Also stoloniferous. Flowers carried in clusters, so blooming period is somewhat longer than other Doronicums. 3 feet.

D. plantagineum—More of a tuberous root than the above species. Also stoloniferous. One of the largest, with 3 inch on four foot stems.

DRACOCEPHALUM—Dragonhead.
This genus of the Mint Family (Labiatae) does well in any soil as long as drainage is good; it is truly hardy. Flowers last longer in a lightly shaded location. Plants are easily increased by division after flowering or by cuttings taken in spring. There are a number of species, but the one below is best known.

D. Ruyschianum. Quite attractive for a member of the Mint Family. Blue. Midsummer; 2 feet.

DUSTY MILLER—See *Centaurea Cineraria*.

DUTCHMANS-BREECHES—See *Dicentra Cucullaria.*

ECHINACEA—Purple Coneflower.
This American wildflower, a genus of the Composite Family (Compositae) has curious cone-shaped central disks and rosy-purple rays which typically hang downward. Suitable for a wild or pasture garden, but not the best choice for a border. The late and long summer blooming period is an asset, however, and selected forms are better than the species.

E. purpurea—Sometimes listed as a rudbeckia. Averages about 3 feet in gardens, but may grow taller. Strong stems need staking only in exposed locations. Useful as a cut flower. A selection, The King, has better colored flowers and large horizontal rays. White forms often have a greenish cast which, like their drooping rays, may or may not be considered attractive. Species easy from seed. Selected forms can be increased by division after flowering.

ECHINOPS—Globe-Thistle.
This genus of the Composite Family (Compositae) contains many species, only a few of which are often found in gardens. In spite of its stiff habit and spiny foliage, this genus always draws attention when its spherical heads turn steel blue in late summer. Easily divided in spring or after flowering, but plants should only be handled by the roots. Foliage brushing against the skin repeatedly may cause discomfort for 2 or 3 days. The heads last a long while both in the garden and bouquets. Flowers and leaves dry well. The plant is not invasive and will grow in light soil. Small divisions become established much more easily than large clumps. Few pests or diseases are troublesome except for aphids occasionally. It is a favorite bee plant. Staking is advisable in windy gardens. Requires grouping with lower plants to reduce ungainliness and conceal lower foliage which usually deteriorates.

E. exaltatus—The forms listed as *E. sphaerocephalus* and *E. Ritro* are botanically included within this species. Better grown on lean soil to keep the height down. Steel blue flowers through late summer. The selection Taplan Blue has larger, bluer flowers.

E. humilis var. *nivalis*. A 3 foot white form seldom as hardy as the blue kinds.

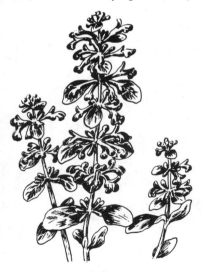

Dracocephalum nutans

Echinacea

Echinops

Epilobium angustifolium

ENGLISH DAISY—See *Bellis perennis.*

EPILOBIUM—Willow Herb.
A large genus of the Evening Primrose Family (Onagraceae). Some species are self-sowing weeds, especially *E. angustifolium.*

E. Dodonaei is better behaved, a useful reddish-flowered rock plant blooming in summer.

E. rosmarinifolium is taller, growing 2 feet tall or more. Pink flowers through much of the summer. Raised from seed.

EPIMEDIUM—Bishops-Hat, Barrenwort.
Although this genus of the Barberry Family (Berberidaceae) has been appearing in books since the time of Dioscorides, physician in the Legions of Nero, it has not been widely accepted as a garden plant. This is strange, for it forms a beautiful slow-spreading ground cover in the worst soil, even in heavy shade. Its charming flowers are among the most pleasingly shaped of all cultivated plants and may be enjoyed in a variety of colors. However, it is best alone, without competition from taller material. The long attractive varicolored foliage is not troubled

by pests, but it should be cut back in late winter or early spring. Increase by division.

E. grandiflorum. Flowers about 1 inch with sepals red and violet, long-spurred petals white. About 1 foot; June.

E. pinnatum. Yellow with rose-red petals. Material offered in catalogs is var. *colchicum,* slightly different in leaf pattern. About 1 foot, a little later coming into bloom than *E. grandiflorum.*

E. rubrum. Unusually attractive leaves in fall and in young stage. Sepals crimson, petals cream, touched rose-red. Blossoms more numerous on each stem than other Epimediums. 1 foot.

E. versicolor var. *sulphureum.* A hybrid, like *E. rubrum,* sepals pale yellow, petals brighter yellow. 1 foot; May.

E. Youngianum var. *niveum.* A bit shorter than those above. Bronze foliage sets off white flowers well. April-early May.

EREMURUS—Desert Candle.
When well grown, the taller species of this genus of the Lily Family (Liliaceae) can be as striking as Pacific Delphinium, with some-

what more lightness and grace. They are not easy to place except in large gardens, and the spreading, fleshy root, so likely to be injured in handling, is not easy to establish. Fall moving and nearly foot-deep planting in well-drained, limed soil is best. Slugs may be discouraged by placing Eremurus on a bed of sand and adding Chlordane dust. Areas with wet springs followed by cold are not good for these perennials, for early shoots may be nipped, as is the case with some Lilies. An airy mulch offers protection. Though very tall, in most cases, the stems are sturdy enough to hold themselves without support except in windy gardens. Propagation by seed is slow but successfully grown old plants profit from division, so a stock may be eventually built up.

E. himalaicus. One of the largest, to 8 feet tall. Sometimes curiously described in garden writings as less than half this height, which may be due to unsatisfactory cultural practices. White. Blooms in early summer, a remarkable feat for a tall plant.

E. robustus. Can attain 10 feet. Attractive pink flowers. June.

E. stenophyllus var. *Bungei.* Usually listed simply as *E. Bungei.* Bright yellow flowers with orange-red anthers. Although sometimes referred to as a "dwarf" in the genus, 4 foot stems are not uncommon. June-July.

ERIGERON—Fleabane.
Like so many members of the Composite Family (Compositae), this plant has developed something of a reputation as a weed. This is rather unfair, for these plants are not troublesome if kept from self-sowing. Daisy-like flowers appear over a long period from June to late summer, varying somewhat among hybrids in flowering time. Fleabane may be divided early in the year, or after flowering, which of course is the only way, other than taking cuttings, of increasing a favorite hybrid.

E. aurantiacus — Double Orange Daisy. Useful for its 10 inch height, though its strong yellow color is not everyone's favorite. Late June. Varies considerably, but no form lives long.

E. compositus. Also good for its height—usually less than the above. White to bluish flowers through summer.

E. Coulteri. White to purple. About 1½

Eremurus himalaicus

Epimedium pinnatum

Erigeron speciosus

Erodium chrysanthum

feet tall. Worthwhile for gardeners who appreciate mauve tints. Summer.

E. glabellus. Light blue, an agreeable shade. Variable in height, average about a foot; summer.

E. speciosus. Other species such as *E. glaucous* and *E. multiradiatus* are listed in seed catalogs, but selections of *E. speciosus* and hybrids of uncertain parentage are better garden plants, with sturdier nature as well as larger better-colored flowers. The American gardener should discover such introductions as pink Gaiety and Vanity, mauve Elsie and Festivity. Large harmoniously grouped plantings are especially attractive.

ERODIUM—Heronsbill.
This genus of the Geranium Family (Geraniaceae) may prove interesting to gardeners familiar with the Geranium (Cranesbill) and the Pelargonium (Storksbill). The common names derive from the resemblance of the seed pods of the genera to the beaks of these birds. Like their relatives, Erodiums are easily grown in well-limed, well-drained soil in full sun. They are raised easily from seed.

E. absinthioides var. *amanum.* Gray foliage, white flowers, through much of the summer; six inches.

E. chamaedryoides var. *roseum.* Pink, red-veined flowers suggesting *Geranium sanguineum* var. *prostratum* (*G. lancastriense*). Blooms through much of the summer; 2 inches.

E. Manescavii. A less than satisfactory purplish-rose shade. A foot or somewhat taller. Another long bloomer.

ERYNGIUM—Eryngo, Sea Holly.
It is unfortunate that this member of the Parsley Family (Umbelliferae) has not become more popular, for it has uniquely-formed blossoms, holds its color for a long time and does well on average soil, as long as drainage is good. Difference in foliage between species is an interesting feature. They last as well cut as they do in the garden,

and should be high on the dried arranger's list of material. Easy from seeds, root cuttings, or divisions early in the spring. Staking is usually necessary for taller species.

E. alpinum. Highly desirable, seldom exceeding 2 feet. Especially attractive foliage. Steel blue. Midsummer.

E. amethystinum, 1½ feet, flowers and stems blue.

E. Bourgartii. Strong-growing. 1½ feet or smaller. Grayish leaves. Bluish flowers have unusually attractive bracts. Stems are also blue-covered.

E. giganteum. Striking, but rather tall for general use. 3 feet or more. Bluish stems and leaves as well as flowers. Flowers once, then dies, but self-sows readily. Late summer.

E. Oliverianum. A very fine hybrid with highly cut frequently blue leaves. Many deep blue selections offer best colors in the genus. 3 feet; late summer.

E. planum. Less tall plant with highly cut leaves. Good branching produces abundant blooms. 2-3 feet; midsummer. Color is inferior.

ERYSIMUM—Blister Cress.
Although the best known species of this genus of the Mustard Family (Cruciferae) are biennial, they are enormously popular.

E. asperum. Sown early in the year, this plant will bear brilliant orange flowers the first summer. More often sown in late summer for flowering the next spring, at which time it makes *Alyssum saxatile* look pale by comparison. Related to Wallflowers, sometimes listed as *Cheiranthus Allionii.* 1½-2 feet tall. Can be quite bushy if well grown and given ample space. Best sown in place or moved when young. It blooms a month or more.

EUPATORIUM—Thoroughwort, Boneset.
An enormous genus of the Composite Family (Compositae), a few species of which are familiar American wildflowers. Although these are stunning when they cover mead-

Eryngium amethystinum

Erysimum asperum

Eupatorium coelestinum

Euphorbia Wulfenii

ows, they are hardly suitable for the formal border. Restrain by digging up every couple of years. Yet their late-flowering period is a strong point in their favor. Easily divided early in the spring or raised from seed. Some gardeners find it subject to blight, but if it is kept growing lustily in moist soil, it should avoid this trouble. The flowers have none of the daisy-like appearance of most Composites, so may be used by arrangers who prefer a more airy-looking bloom. Most well-known species may be dried by hanging flowers upside down in a shed just as the heads are about to open.

E. cannabinum. A European species. Rose-purple. Var. *plenum* is commonly offered. 4-5 feet; midsummer.

E. coelestinum — Mist-Flower. The common name Hardy Ageratum is most unsuitable for this species, for gardeners accustomed to the compact habit and clean color of improved annual ageratum may be disappointed with this Eupatorium. Plants can exceed 2 feet in rich soil. Like most other species, this is coarse-looking and planted only because it is useful for cutting and as a late-summer garden plant. Color is more purple than blue. Spreads very much, so best kept away from choice plants.

E. purpureum—Joe-Pye Weed. Most familiar of the genus. Rose-colored. Late summer. Belongs in every wild garden, but not elsewhere.

E. rugosum — (*E. ageratoides*). White Snakeroot. The common name is usually associated with Cimicifuga, though *C. racemosa* is properly Black Snakeroot. Occasionally found wild in association with *E. purpureum*, though usually in lesser numbers. About 3 feet. White.

EUPHORBIA—Spurge.
This genus of the Spurge Family (Euphorbiaceae) contains a few desirable perennials as well as some which spread terribly. They are usually easy to raise from seed, but should be put in their final places when quite young. Old plants resent transplanting.

E. corollata—Flowering Spurge. Small white flowers similar to Gypsophila in midsummer. Reddish leaves in fall. Hardy. 2 feet.

E. Cyparissias—Cypress Spurge. Has attractive bracts, but unimportant flowers, as is the usual case with Euphorbias. A useful ground cover in arid corners where its invasive nature will not be a problem. Yellowish-green. A foot or less; May.

E. epithymoides—Commonly offered as *E. polychroma*. About 1½ feet. In flower, its yellow bracts cannot compete with *Alyssum saxatile*, if that perennial is present in quantity. Neat habit and clean foliage, reddening in fall.

E. Griffithi. A recently introduced species. Yellow. 1½ feet. Attractive foliage. Late spring.

E. Myrsinites. Low grower with yellow bracts. A traditional wall plant. Difficult to confine. Semi-evergreen. 6 inches; June.

E. sikkimensis. Foliage has possibly the best red coloring in spring of any Euphorbia, like ruby glass in sunlight. Yellow bracts through much of the summer. 3 feet.

E. Wulfenii. Another 3 foot species. Unusual blue-green leaves. Yellow bracts. Good cut flower. May.

EVERLASTINGS—See *Anaphalis*.

FILIPENDULA—Meadowsweet.
A tall genus of the Rose Family (Rosaceae). Filipendula has attractive fern-like foliage which usually remains in good condition throughout the growing season, and is as good in arrangements as the white fluffy flowers. Its appearance suffers during dry periods, however. Freedom from pests and diseases is a good feature. The former name Spiraea is used in some lists. Division in spring is the usual method of propagation.

F. hexapetala—Dropwort. Prefers full sun and dry soil in contrast to most other *Filipendulas*. 1½ foot height better than the giant species. White flowers. June. Double form particularly desirable.

F. purpurea—Not dependable without mulching in extreme winters. 3 feet. Rose-pink. July. Must have moisture.

F. rubra—Queen of the Prairie. Pink flowers. June. 5 foot height hard to place in small gardens. Selected large-flowered peach-colored forms are grown.

F. Ulmaria—Queen of the Meadow. Both single and double forms available. 4 feet. White. June.

Fragaria vesca

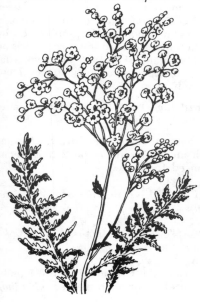

Filipendula hexapetala

Gaillardia   Sun God

FLAX—See *Linum narbonnense.*

FLEABANE—See *Erigeron.*

FLEECE-VINE—See *Polygonum Aubertii.*

FORGET-ME-NOT—See *Myosotis.*

FOXGLOVE—See *Digitalis.*

FRAGARIA—Strawberry
This well-known genus of the Rose Family (Rosaceae) is sometimes recommended as an edging plant. But the foliage seldom remains clean-looking enough to be enjoyed at close quarters. Also, abundant runners must be contained. Those who wish the foliage was better might try some of the herbaceous Potentillas, which are similar, but cleaner.

GAILLARDIA.
This genus of the Composite Family (Compositae) is admired for its long display of bright flowers. Pick often for long bloom. Many types sprawl unless staked early, and the best of the Gaillardias are *seldom very hardy.* Replacements are easily grown from seed or from shoots produced at the base of parent plants. (See Propagation.) They are largely pest free. Compact forms are preferred, and there are many newer hybrids which have better colors, more varied ray structure and sturdier habits than species. Light, well-drained soil in full sun is preferred. This is a good genus with which to practice taking root cuttings, especially useful for increasing named varieties which seldom come true from seed.

G. aristata. The parent of most improved clones offered. Burgundy is a deep red, 2 feet tall. Goblin is a foot tall dwarf. Sun God is all yellow, 2 feet tall. There are many others, a number with the typical red and yellow rays one associates with the genus.

GALEGA.
This genus of the Pea Family (Leguminosae) contains one species found in gardens, *G. officinalis,* Goats-Rue. Rose-purple pea-like flowers in June; 3 feet. Needs camouflage after flowering. A white form is available. Easily increased by seed or division.

GALIUM—Bedstraw.
A large genus of the Madder Family (Rubiaceae), many species of which have been long in cultivation. Most of the commonly grown ones are similar to Gypsophila. Easily grown in full sun, started from seed. Division in early spring. Flowers are somewhat fragrant, and are useful in bouquets if cut before fully open.

G. aristatum—False Babys-Breath. White. Midsummer; 2½ feet.

G. verum — Yellow Bedstraw. Blooms through much of summer on 2 foot stems. Pronounced fragrance.

GARDEN HELIOTROPE — See *Valeriana officinalis.*

GAS-PLANT—See *Dictamnus.*

GAURA.
This genus of the Evening Primrose Family (Onagraceae) is not often planted. *G. Lind-*

heimeri is raised from seed or cuttings. It is readily grown in full sun in light soil, but is not dependably hardy in the North. Light rose flowers much of the summer; 3½ feet.

GAYFEATHER—See *Liatris*.

GENTIANA—Gentian.
This genus of the Gentian Family (Gentianaceae) contains a number of challenging rock garden species and a few suitable for more general use. Only the latter are included below. Propagation from seed is surprisingly successful if the seed is fresh, and if seedlings are not permitted to dry out. Planting in humusy soil and partial shade is recommended.

G. *Andrewsii*—Closed Gentian. One of the easier species in most gardens. Deep blue. 18 inches; July. Not one of the more showy Gentians.

G. *asclepiadea*—Willow Gentian. Highly variable from seed—light blue to deep violet. Rich, moist soil and shade are essential. A fine plant 2 feet tall; late summer. Division of best-colored plants is possible in early spring.

Galega officinalis

Galium aristatum

Gaura Lindheimeri

G. septemfida. Blue flowers open in June. Long-flowering. A foot tall or less. Another Gentian which may be divided early in the spring.

GERANIUM—Cranesbill.
This genus of the Geranium Family (Geraniaceae) contains a number of hardy perennials, in contrast to the bedding or pot geraniums which belong to the genus Pelargonium. Very few of the common Geraniums are choice plants, but some are good in rockeries or edgings. Division after flowering is the easiest form of propagation.

G. grandiflorium. Very hardy and rather a spreader. About a foot tall. Blue with red veins. Var. *alpinum* forms a smaller plant with larger flowers. Late spring, early summer. Red fall foliage.

G. ibericum. A tall geranium, to 2 feet. Violet. Midsummer.

G. platypetalum. Larger blooms of a better purple shade than *G. ibericum.* Blooms over the same period.

G. sanguineum. A rose-purple Geranium common in old gardens. Hardy under shrubs in poor soil. Forms a mound a foot or slightly taller. Will live in one spot for years, but must be lifted when clogged with grass. Var. *prostratum,* still known as *G. lancastriense* by gardeners, is more compact with fine pale pink, red-veined flowers through summer.

G. Wallichianum. The form Buxton's Blue is more restrained than many geraniums. Finely cut leaves. Blue-violet flowers with pale purple veins. White-centered. Blooms late summer and fall; less than 1 foot.

GERBERA.
Although the genus of the Composite Family (Compositae) is seldom hardy in the North, its usefulness in southern gardens makes it worth including here.

G. Jamesonii—Transvaal Daisy. 18 inch tall daisy-like flowers now available in an assortment of colors, largely warm hues. Raised from seed.

GEUM—Avens.
This genus of the Rose Family (Rosaceae) has never been very popular in this country, despite the brilliant colors of many selections. 2 foot tall stems rise from a basal rosette of leaves. Geums require reasonably good soil and an evenly moist situation, particularly if they are to repeat bloom after the first early summer flowering. A few species are offered, but selections of *G. chiloense* are more commonly used in gardens. Both red Mrs. Bradshaw and yellow Lady Stratheden are very easy from seed, but they are inclined to suffer during winter unless placed in well-drained locations and covered with a perfect airy mulch. Despite their defects, these will continue to be planted until such newer, reliable clones as orange Princess Juliana, Fire Opal and Wilton Ruby are generally available.

GLOBE-FLOWER—See *Trollius europaeus.*

GLOBE-THISTLE—See *Echinops.*

GOLDEN-GLOW—See *Rudbeckia laciniata hortensis.*

GOLDEN MARGUERITE—See *Anthemis.*

Gentiana septemfida

GYPSOPHILA

This genus of the Pink Family (Caryophyllaceae) contains the well-known Babys-Breath, a favorite for generations. The misty appearance of the perennial relieves the heavy appearance of more solid-looking plants, and has been traditionally used to cover gaps left by the withering of poppies, *Dicentra spectabilis* and other early bloomers. Species are easy from seed sown in the summer to flower the next year. Propagation of named clones is usually done by grafting onto the roots of species. Seedling plants can be safely moved only in early spring before growth begins. Old plants should be left alone. Place in a fertile well-drained, limy soil. They are very likely to be partly thrown out of the ground during winter unless mulched after the ground is frozen. As a cut flower, Gypsophila was more popular in old-fashioned bouquets, but it still is good if used judiciously. The more you pick, the more it blooms. It dries well if cut before the numerous small blossoms are fully open. Dwarf forms are especially useful. The colored forms may appear a less definite pink than one might hope for. Like other perennials that last for years, Gypsophila may in time become clogged with weeds.

Geum Red Wings

Gerbera Jamesonii

ranium sanguineum

Hedera Helix

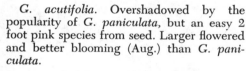

Gypsophila Oldhamiana

G. *acutifolia*. Overshadowed by the popularity of G. *paniculata*, but an easy 2 foot pink species from seed. Larger flowered and better blooming (Aug.) than G. *paniculata*.

G. *Oldhamiana*—One of the best perennials for late summer and fall, yet seldom planted. Reaches 3 feet, sprawls, looking better this way than staked, if space can be allotted. Pinkish flowers appear into October. Easy from seed.

G. *paniculata*. Best known species. 3 feet. White. July and August. Not the best choice for the small garden, as smaller species have similar effect in half the space. Bristol Fairy is the best known double form. Like many perennials, repeat bloom may occur if first flowers are promptly cut after fading.

G. *repens*. A low grower more difficult to keep weed free than upright species, nevertheless a wise choice for the small border or rockery. Var. *rosea* is easy from seed. Rosy Veil is another pinkish form, but with more upright habit.

HEDERA—Ivy.
This familiar genus of the Aralia Family (Araliaceae) is, of course, a woody plant rather than an herbaceous one. It is included here because of its value in clothing difficult areas where few herbaceous perennials thrive. H. *Helix*—English Ivy, is available in many types, varying in hardiness as well as leaf form. An easy plant from cuttings or layers. Southern gardeners can use many of the unusual sorts, but Northerners are advised to select clones which look well after winter. Few qualify, especially if the planting is in sun. One of the best introductions is called 238th Street. It holds green color all winter and makes new growth very early in the spring. This ivy spreads laterally and produces attractive flowers and fruit when young.

HELENIUM—Sneezeweed.
This coarse, late-blooming genus of the Composite Family (Compositae) is not very popular. Though not the most graceful perennial, the plant has enough to offer, with its abundance of yellow, wine or mahogany

blooms borne at a time when perennial bloom is scant. The tall, heavy stems are best staked, or may snap at the base. Abundant basal rosettes can be divided early in the spring. Helenium will grow anywhere, but is best in loam with some substance. Tall varieties may be pinched back about six weeks before blooming to encourage branching and reduce height, as is often done with fall asters and summer phlox. The more you pick, the more they bloom.

H. autumnale. Most introductions have come from this North American wildflower and range from 3 to 4 feet tall. Riverton Beauty is yellow with dark central marking. Riverton Gem is red and yellow. Moerheim Beauty is maroon. Many others display similar warm colors in various combinations. Of these, Bruno, especially good, offers dark red blooms on 2½ foot stems that require no staking.

HELIANTHEMUM—Sun-Rose.

This genus of the Rock Rose Family (Cistaceae) seldom looks its best in rockeries and edgings if neglected. It is not herbaceous, having woody stems. Unless these are clipped after flowering plants become stringy and unattractive. A well-drained

position in full sun is necessary. Seed germinates easily, but seedlings develop slowly. Transplant to permanent location when young, as older plants do not move well. Desirable seedlings or named varieties can be propagated by cuttings, taken with a heel in August. Almost any shade on the warm side of the color wheel is available, but rousing reds usually attract the most attention. All bloom through much of the summer. They are evergreen, so require winter protection.

HELIANTHUS—Sunflower.

A few species of this genus of the Composite Family (Compositae) are suitable in the large border, but they are hardly top-rated perennials. They are tall and usually coarse, but some of this appearance can be disguised by grouping them behind tall asters or chrysanthemums. Easily divided early in the year, a chore best done every other year or so, as Helianthus soon uses up soil nutrients. Spray early with fungicide to control mildew. Restrain rambunctious plants early in the spring.

H. decapetalus—Thinleaf Sunflower. Better branched than many sunflowers. 2½ inch yellow flowers, mid to late summer; 4 feet.

Helinium autumnale superbum

Helianthemum nummularium

Helianthus decapetalus

Heliopsis scabra

Var. *multiflorus*, usually offered in several selections, is probably the best for garden use.

H. salicifolius. Attractive willow-like foliage. Deep yellow. 7 feet; September. The clump should be loosely roped, or will sprawl in autumn rains.

HELIOPSIS.
This genus of the Composite Family (Compositae) is similar in flower appearance to a large coreopsis and in cultural needs to Helianthus. Not as tall as Helianthus, Heliopsis is easier to place. Division every second or third spring is recommended. See also Propagation from Seed. Well spaced in full sun, given good garden soil, newer Heliopsis introductions can be most attractive. Attention to fertilizing and watering is necessary if better forms are to perform well.

H. scabra — Semi-double, orange-yellow flowers in many recent selections. Orange King is a preferred type, in that staking is not required. Self-sows freely, so faded flowers should be promptly removed. There are a number of selections which vary in their shade of yellow and degree of doubleness. Few are available in the United States.

HELLEBORUS.
There is some question whether this genus of the Crowfoot Family (Ranunculaceae) is much more than a curiosity. If its species did not bloom in winter or early spring, doubtless it would be discarded as a nuisance. Humusy rich soil with an even supply of moisture is needed for best results, while the flowers are seldom satisfactory unless protected by sash. Grown in the open, Helleborus may suffer the discoloration common to many evergreen plants. The plants resent disturbance, and should be placed in their permanent position when young. Propagation from seed is not difficult, but slow. Self-sowing sometimes occurs. The flowers last for weeks outdoors. When cut, the ends should be burned. Slug bait should be kept around plants, and fungicide spray may be necessary to keep foliage clean. Roots are poisonous.

H. foetidus. A large species generally easier to grow in a variety of soils than *H. niger.* As its name suggests, this Hellebore is strong smelling. Handsome divided leaves. Flowers green tipped rose-purple. Later flowering than *H. niger.*

H. niger. The white species. In greatest demand. Optimistically called Christmas Rose, although it may not celebrate with bloom until the New Year. Over a foot tall well grown. Variable, some seedlings may have pinkish flowers. Short-stemmed blooms may be buried in leaves, so the longer stemmed Var. *altifolius* is preferred, if the true variety can be obtained. The crowns of young plants must be shaded with mulch. Foliage of old plants should be kept in good condition to continue this shading.

H. orientalis — Lenten Rose. Variable in color, white to rose and purplish. Often easier to grow than *H. niger,* and with branching flower stems. Later flowering. Large plants nearly 2 feet tall and bushy.

Helleborus niger

HEMEROCALLIS—Day-Lily.

Few perennials have increased in popularity so swiftly as has this genus of the Lily Family (Liliaceae). This is due to the hardiness of the plant as well as the improvement made in flower color and form, in extending the blooming period, and in variation of height. If ever there was a perennial with "architectural" value even when out of bloom, this is it. Handsome arching foliage is attractive all year except in a few regions where there may be some yellowing. Prejudice remaining against the genus is largely due to the commoness of *H. fulva,* but the modern Day-Lily is far more lovely and often as hardy. Occasionally weak clones are seen in collections, but they are the exceptions. There are no serious pests, though slugs and cutworms may give some trouble. Plants are usually divided after they flower, but they can be easily moved at any time. Full sun or partial shade suits them, the latter being preferred for pink or pastel colors which often fade in hot sun. Removal of withered flowers improves ap-

Hemerocallis

Hepatica acutiloba

Hesperis matronalis

pearance. Most Day-Lilies will bloom somewhat in deep shade, though not as well as in sun, and stems will tip awkwardly toward the light. Especially attractive are fine light yellow, nearly white, hybrids. Crimsons have also been greatly improved. Among medium yellows, Hyperion remains popular, though it is no longer the top member of its class. It is pointless to list selections here, for hundreds are fully described in specialist catalogs. Varieties with ruffled or twisted petals, bicolors or very early- or late-blooming periods may prove especially desirable. July remains the big month for Day-Lily bloom, at which time you should visit a good planting or show and make your selections. Most plants need 2 or 3 feet around them, or they will swallow less robust perennials. Although not naturally long-lasting as cut flowers, a few of the large-petalled, beautifully colored introductions make a pleasing arrangement. Look for well-branched varieties which carry many buds, so that though each bloom lasts but a day, flower production may continue for weeks. Some have good fragrance. Evergreen types are preferred in the South, and new non-fading types are especially useful there also. This perennial is easily grown throughout the United States.

Many who answered our questionnaire were most enthusiastic about hemerocallis for the perennial garden. Edwin F. Steffek, of *Horticulture* magazine, urged gardeners to try new varieties, infinitely better than the old wild ones. Mrs. Daniel Mann, President, the Garden Club Federation of Maine, reports that they are her favorites. Mrs. Percy Merry, Past President Needham (Mass.) Garden Club, comments: "Hemerocallis has taken over the old midsummer slump of the perennial border. Will grow in full sun or semi-shade. Non-fading and longer-lasting varieties now being produced. Great variety in form and color. Pale yellow, approaching white through all shades of yellow and orange, pale pink to deepest red, polychrome and eyed varieties, also lavender and purples. All dormant varieties reliably hardy in north and many evergreens, which are preferred in the south, due to foliage remaining green throughout the year."

H. flava—Common Yellow Day-Lily, Lemon-Lily. Long in cultivation, it is still a handsome plant in May and early June. Completely hardy, and can be left for years without dividing. The attempt to assign it the name *H. lilio-asphodelus* will be deplored by old-time gardeners.

H. fulva—Common Orange Day-Lily. The charitable common name Tawny Day-Lily is misleading for a flower which is really a hard orange. Always pleasant to see this romping along roadsides, but should be detoured around gardens. It is much too large a plant, spreads much too rapidly. The double Kwanso has a curious-looking flower with the same strong color. There is something sad and lovely about these old orange Day-Lilies grouped around a cellar hole, but something even sadder when they are in the yard of a conscious gardener.

HEPATICA—Liverleaf.
This wide-ranging North American wildflower, a genus of the Crowfoot Family (Ranunculaceae), is best known in the species *H. americana*, which bears 5 inch blue or nearly white flowers in early spring. Attractive leaves remain in good condition all year, a noteworthy feature for a woodland wildflower. Shade and humusy soil is necessary. Easy to grow, but slow from seed. Increase by division in the fall.

HESPERIS—Rocket.
This old-fashioned plant, a genus of the Mustard Family (Cruciferae) has been grown for generations, lasting by self-sowing. The parent plant is seldom long lived.

H. matronalis—Dames Violet or Sweet Rocket. Flowers vary from white to shades of purple. Double forms are sometimes offered. 2-3 feet; June. Useful for cutting and quite appropriate in old-fashioned gardens in spite of its weediness.

HEUCHERA—Alum Root.
This genus of the Saxifrage Family (Saxifragaceae) contains the Coral Bells, one of the finest perennials in cultivation. Graceful, hardy, easily grown in a variety of locations,

Heuchera sanguinea

Heucherella tiarelloides

Hibiscus

providers of abundant divisions, evergreen, useful for edging. The list of virtues is endless. They are sometimes criticized for not making enough of a "show"; their numerous, small flowers not appearing too bold from a distance. This is absurd, for if properly massed there will be "show" enough for anyone, without that heaviness of large-flowered perennials. Coral colors remain very poular. Flower stems are wand-like, held two feet or so above the basal leaves. Occasionally there is a toppled stem, but usually no staking is required. Many shorter clones are available—crimson varieties are usually quite compact, and as vigorous as older forms, as long as they are divided every 2 or 3 years in early spring. Cream to white selections are available, but may pass out of bloom rapidly, in contrast to most other kinds which bloom, usually at diminishing rate, all summer. Foliage is probably of greater value in arrangements than are flowers. This is a favorite plant of hummingbirds. In mild climates, evergreen foliage is fine in winter. To the North, leaves brown in open winter, and roots heave in thaws unless mulched. Divide every three or four years for best results. Set 1½" below soil line.

H. sanguinea—The type has good-sized blooms, for a Heuchera, but they are sparsely grouped on the stem. Hybrid *H. brizoides* has an abundance of small blossoms on long stems. Much crossing has been done between these two species, so that one might build up a very large collection of Heucheras. Groupings which blend from white to coral and pink to red are always handsome. Red Spangles is a long-blooming red, shorter than most, being under 2 feet. Often cited Pluie de Feu and Rosamundi have been replaced by newer introductions which flower more freely and branch better. Unfortunately, such ones as Coral Cloud, Rhapsody and Orphee are not widely offered in the United States.

HEUCHERELLA

A genus of the Saxifrage Family (Saxifragaceae) which includes hybrids between Heuchera and Tiarella. *H. tiarelloides*, Bridget Bloom, most commonly offered, is 1½ feet tall with deep pink flowers intermittently displayed through summer. Flower structure is botanically different from Heuchera, but garden effect is similar. Culture is easy in any good garden soil.

HIBISCUS—Rose Mallow.
This showy genus of the Mallow Family (Malvaceae) is admired by those who enjoy large, colorful flowers. Blooms appear mid to late summer. Tropical in appearance, but those noted below are completely hardy. Platter-size red forms attract most attention, but various shades of pink are also striking. Cool-looking white Hibiscus are badly disfigured by Japanese beetles. Other colors often attacked, also. Unless moisture is available, leaves wilt when maximum height is reached, this period arriving at the time of summer drought. Unless seed heads are promptly removed, self-sowing may be a problem. These pods are useful in dried arrangements. Division in early spring is possible, but the chore is as wearing as digging a large shrub—the roots probe deeply to find moisture and nutrients and to support the great top growth, which seldom needs staking. They are best placed apart from less robust border plants. Species are of little value, except for *H. palustris* which flourishes as well in moist gardens as it does in salt and inland marshes. Rose-pink 6 inch flowers. Varies from 3-8 feet, depending on moisture available. *H. Moscheutos*

has narrower leaves and white red-centered flowers. It forms a larger plant. Many hybrids have been produced by crossing and selecting. Poinsettia is bright red; Mrs. William H. Allen is a finer pink than *H. palustris*. There are many others. Massive when well grown.

HOLLYHOCK—See *Althaea rosea.*

HOSTA—Plantain-Lily.
This genus of the Lily Family (Liliaceae) provides one of the best ranges of foliage form among herbaceous plants. It is a reliably hardy perennial. Species names have been subject to frequent revision. Not all nurserymen are entirely up-to-date on Hosta nomenclature, so the gardener is advised to pay more attention to catalog descriptions of foliage shape and color than to names, a policy which will help him avoid duplications. Flowers are usually white or bluish-purple. Variegated forms differ in the amount of white in the leaf, depending on exposure and season. Most are easy to grow in light to moderate shade in a variety of soils, though they do best in moist, humusy gardens. Readily divided in spring or after

Hosta plantaginea

Hosta Fortunei marginata-alba

Hypericum calycinum

flowering. Leaves sometimes insect damaged. Use chlordane for slugs and earwigs. They rarely object to poor air circulation, and are especially useful in city gardens. Foliage good in arrangements.

H. decorata—Blunt Plantain-Lily. Purple flowers bloom just above the 2 foot tall mass of oval, white-margined leaves. Usually offered as the Thomas Hogg Variety.

H. Fortunei—Tall Cluster Plantain-Lily. Available in many varieties. 2 feet. Lavender flowers in May. Light green leaves about twice as long as wide. Leaves of desirable varieties may be heart-shaped, white- or yellow-edged or greatly oversized.

H. glauca—Short Cluster Plantain-Lily— Blue Leaved Plantain-Lily. One of the most handsome of all foliage plants. Large bluish with ridged texture. Unimportant white flowers. Often called *Funkia Sieboldiana.*

H. lancifolia — Narrow-Leaved Plantain-Lily. The common name adequately describes the deep green foliage. Light purple blooms in August; 2 feet tall. Yellow and white variegated forms are offered. The fall flowering var. *tardifolia,* now often treated

as a separate species, is a useful garden plant no matter what its botanical standing.

H. plantaginea — Fragrant Plantain-Lily. The most sweetly scented of all Hostas. Common in old gardens. Large, white blossoms high above medium to light green leaves in late summer. Offered under such names as *H. subcordata* and *H. grandiflora,* but always recognized best as the Fragrant Plantain-Lily.

H. undulata—Wavy-Leaved Plantain-Lily. Again the common name is self-explanatory. Variegated oval leaves. Over 2 feet tall. Lavender flowers; July.

H. ventricosa — Blue Plantain-Lily. Long dark green foliage. Flowers less lavender, more nearly blue than most Hostas, rise 2½ feet in midsummer. Also a variegated form.

HYPERICUM—St. Johnswort.
This genus of the St. Johnswort Family (Hypericaceae) includes a number of commercially available perennials and small shrubs, a few of which are so outstanding as to eclipse most of the others. Easy to grow in full sun if given good drainage, the Hypericums are noted for their long display of deep yellow blooms through much of the summer. They are increased by seed or cuttings.

H. calycinum—A small evergreen to semi-evergreen shrub spreading by stolons. 2 feet. A long display of large, yellow flowers. Useful as a ground cover.

H. patulum. The most useful member of the group, especially its varieties *Henryi* and *Hidcote,* both attaining 3 feet. Var. *Forrestii* is larger flowered and somewhat more compact. All are best treated as cutback shrubs in the North. There are few perennials or small shrubs which provide so generous a display of yellow flowers, except perhaps *Potentilla fruticosa* and its forms, which are smaller flowered.

HYSSOPUS—Hysop.
This long cultivated genus of the Mint Family (Labiatae) contains one species, *H.*

86

officinalis which is sometimes included in the herb garden, but is not an especially ornamental plant. Purplish-blue flowers in fall. A pinkish form is also available as well as a white. Seed or cuttings. Full sun. Perfectly drained soil helps in over-wintering, but heavy spring pruning is usually necessary in any case. In the North it is probably better brought inside, as is Rosemary. About 1½ feet tall.

IBERIS—Candytuft.

This familiar genus of the Mustard Family (Cruciferae) is useful as a year-round edging plant, although its evergreen foliage often suffers in open northern winters. *I. sempervirens* is easy from seed, but preferred selected forms are increased by cuttings taken from new growth, preferably with a heel, made after flowering. Divisions do not always establish well. The chalk-white flowers may glare unpleasantly in spring sun, in contrast to softer Arabis, the double form of which blooms about the same time. Old plants may become massive, spreading to cover smaller plants. Generally pest-free, though red spider, a problem in a few areas, must be controlled with a miticide. Light trimming after blooming keeps plants neater and more vigorous. Unless this is done, some kinds may self-sow weedily.

I. saxatilis—A 3 inch plant for the rock garden, but of no value in the border.

I. sempervirens—Species most commonly grown. Little Gem is seldom much over 6 inches tall, remains compact with less attention than taller selections; May. Purity blooms at the same time, but is larger. Repeat bloomers offered as either Autumn Snow or Christmas Snow are probably identical. The form Snowflakes, possibly springing from another obscure species, is admired for its unusually large flowers.

ICELAND POPPY—See *Papaver nudicaule*.

INCARVILLEA.

This genus of the Bignonia Family (Bignoniaceae) often is given the name Hardy Gloxinia, indicating somewhat of a similarity in flower to the popular Gesneriad. They

Hyssopus

Iberis sempervirens with Bleeding-Heart

Incarvillea Delavayi

are increased from seed, but young plants are best moved only early in the spring. Heavy roots require light but fertile, well-drained soil. Division of old roots is possible, but not always certain to succeed. Slug bait should be placed about when the plants are actually growing. Though not usually considered the hardiest of perennials, they may prove quite dependable even in the North, if given light covering.

I. Delavayi. Large rose-purple to reddish flowers early summer, many on a branch; 1½ feet. An excellent perennial when well grown.

I. compacta grandiflora. Somewhat larger, lighter flowers with a cream-colored throat blotch. A more compact plant than the above, blooming over the same period. Usually offered as *I. grandiflora. I. c. brevipes* has blossoms of as good a crimson as one can expect in the genus.

INULA

This seldom-planted genus of the Composite Family (Compositae) displays the stiffness common in so many genera of this family. 3 inch daisy-type flowers. Increased from seed or early spring divisions. Moisture must be available throughout the growing season.

I. ensifolia. One of the better species for small gardens. Less than a foot tall; small yellow flowers late summer and early fall.

I. glandulosa. Fringed yellow flowers are unusually attractive for the genus. 2 feet; midsummer.

I. Helenium—Elecampane. An immense 6 foot plant of little garden value, but striking in a large wild garden.

I. Royleana—4 inch orange-yellow flowers on 2 foot stems; late summer, early fall.

IRIS—Fleur-de-lis.

It is a pity that most gardeners think only of tall "German" Iris when this genus of the Iris Family (Iridaceae) is mentioned. Although these handsome May-blooming favorites are among the most dependably hardy of perennials, there are scores of other excellent iris species. By using many of these, from the charming *I. pumila* and *I. cristata* of spring to the *I. sibirica* of summer, gardeners can enjoy not only a longer blooming period, but greater variety of height and flower form. A very brief summary such as given below can only suggest the value of a genus on which lifetimes of study have been spent. The genus is divided into the bulbous and rhizomatous. The bulbous group containing the excellent *I. reticulata* and *I. histroides major* is only mentioned here. The rhizomatous group is split into smaller divisions based either on conspicuous or obscure botanical features. Gardeners are usually more interested in blooming time, height and color of various Iris, so these factors are the basis of the following brief list. In such a large genus it is unwise to offer gereralizations about cultural practices. However, most Iris profit by being planted shallowly (but in broad holes) in well drained soil, although a few, such as the Japanese Iris, especially, require an even moisture supply when actively growing. Even the very hardy Tall Bearded Iris may suffer in wet or icy winters unless planted in slightly raised beds or on slopes. Most Iris are easily divided after flowering, and should be so split at regular intervals, perhaps three or four years on the average, to keep the plants from deteriorating and to clean the rhizome of borers or other pests. Iris borer is often a serious pest. References commonly suggest that the leaves should be squeezed when streaked with a watery residue, but this is hardly practical if the planting is large. Regular spraying in spring with DDT or a newer insecticide will afford some protection but sanitation measures must accompany such chemical treatment. Some pests are almost certain to be missed even in the most rigid schedule. These may be destroyed by cleaning the rhizomes when dividing and by burning foliage in the fall. Tall German Iris usually require staking; newer, more compact varieties seldom do. Many Iris make lovely, if not very long-lived flower arrangements, and often have a distinctive fragrance. Although division is the common method of increase, seed sowing may prove the only means of developing a collection of rarer species. The frequent criticism that Iris has a short blooming season usually springs from limited experience with two or three species. The flowering period of a species may indeed be brief, as is the case with so many lovely plants; but the genus itself distributes its bloom throughout the growing season. This summary is given roughly in the order of bloom:

I. Chamaeiris—A large color range—shades of blue and yellow as well as white. Beard usually contrasting color. Commercially much confused with *I. pumila*, which has a very short or completely lacking flower stem. April or early May; 8 inches.

I. pumila. Colors similar to the above. One of the fastest-increasing Iris. Must be divided often. Place in rockery or front of the border. 5 inches; April. Numerous named varieties, a few of which rival the colors of Tall Bearded Iris.

I. cristata. One of the most delightful American wildflowers. Light lavender with

Inula ensifolia

an orange crest. May. Flower stem only an inch high. Vigorous in spite of its size, acting as a ground cover in some locations. Divide often. A white form is usually less robust.

I. germanica—German Iris. Of course this is not a species, but the result of much hybridization. Many new flower forms are offered with pronounced "horns" and flounces. The beard is often a conspicuous feature of the flower, especially when of a contrasting color. May and June. Several iris specialists list hundreds of species, so it is impractical to suggest many varieties here. When reading catalogs, check height as well as color. Older, less expensive varieties may provide a satisfactory show. Blue Rhythm is a satisfactory bright blue, Sable Night a favorite dark purple. Many of the best pinks and multi-colors should be seen in gardens or at shows to be appreciated. The so-called Intermediate Iris usually include Tall Bearded Iris in their parentage, as well as dwarf species. They are generally shorter than the Tall Bearded and somewhat early flowering.

I. sibirica. Like the preceding, this iris does better in moist gardens. White, blue, or dark red beardless flowers carried on 3 foot

Iris

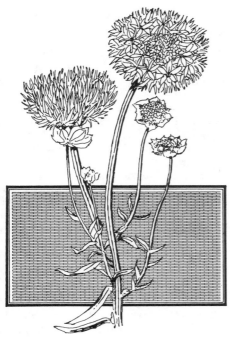

Jasione perennis

stems; June. Caesar's Brother is a superior, deep purple.

I. Kaempferi—Japanese Iris. Montague Free once crisply observed that "names of the garden forms are in a mess." This is due to confused and generally unfortunate attempts to transliterate Japanese names, much as is done with some peonies and Japanese cherries. The result is that one variety may have 2, 3 or more names. Therefore, when ordering, pay more attention to descriptions than names. All have flat flowers, a form which may or may not be appealing. In moist spots they may make massive plants 4 feet tall in bloom; July.

I. orientalis—White and yellow flowers. July. Blue forms difficult to locate. Also may be listed as *I. ochroleuca*. 4 feet. A beardless iris.

I. dichotoma—Useful for its August blooming period. Variable small flowers, white and purple shades. Beardless. 3½ feet or somewhat less. Not a very hardy species, it is better grown in the South.

Edwin F. Steffek, editor of *Horticulture* magazine says: "As with hemerocallis, too few gardeners have the newer and far superior varieties, being content with 50- to 70-year-old kinds. Also fail to take advantage of long season and variety of forms provided by Japanese, Siberian and dwarf irises. Bearded iris especially must be sprayed in spring, if borer is present. Properly selected, iris can furnish a very long season of bloom. All iris groups are among finest of garden perennials."

IVY—See *Hedera*.

JASIONE.
This attractive but seldom seen genus of the Bellflower Family (Campanulaceae) has only one commonly available species. *J. perennis* is not long lived, particularly in heavy, wet soil. But replacements are easily raised from seed. The lavender blue flowers which resemble those of a Centaurea, are borne on foot-long stems through much of the summer. Staking usually necessary for best appearance. Excellent, long-lasting cut flower.

KNIPHOFIA

Still widely known as Tritoma by many gardeners, this genus of the Lily Family (Liliaceae) is also called Red Hot Poker or Torch Lily. This startling African plant is not reliably hardy in the North, where it is best stored inside. In moderate climates the crown may be protected by drawing up the dark green long leaves and tying them. Most common are bright orange forms close to the species *K. Uvaria*. Yellow and cream hybrids are somewhat easier to place in the garden, but they are all stiff-looking with their poker-like flowers. Variable from seed. Easy to make spring divisions. Light soil best. Generous summer watering and phosphate fertilizer encourages abundant, prolonged bloom. Best in sun. Long-lasting cut flower for unusual arrangements. Pest- and disease-free. Most are about 2 feet tall. *K. galpini* is an attractive dwarf, but not very hardy. Taller species such as 4 foot *K. caulescens* are seldom useful in the small garden.

Kniphofia Uvaria

LACE-VINE—See *Polygonum Aubertii*.

LAMIUM—Dead Nettle.

This easily grown genus of the Mint Family (Labiatae) makes a satisfactory ground cover in moist, shaded areas. Both white and rose-purple forms available. Long flowering—most of summer—in proper location. Too much of a spreader for use near choice plants. Easily divided at any time. Leaves have central white stripes. Somewhat useful as cut flower.

LARKSPUR—See *Delphinium*.

LATHYRUS—Everlasting Pea.

This hardy genus of the Pea Family (Leguminosae) is best known among growers of perennials for the species *L. latifolius*, which bears rose-colored blossoms abundantly in midsummer. 6 foot climbing stems are hard to place, except as cover for an old fence or stump. White and pink forms are available. Seed or root division in early spring. Easy in any soil.

LAVANDULA—Lavender.

This fragrant genus of the Mint Family (La-

Lamium maculatum

Lathyrus latifolius

Lavandula Spica (bottom)

biatae) is one of the best known of all herbs. Thin, purple flowers in July are not striking, but gray foliage makes a useful garden feature. Dwarf forms are good edgers. A woody evergreen rather than an herbaceous plant, likely to be injured in open northern winters. Perfectly drained limy soil is imperative. Seed germinates erratically, but 1 inch tip cuttings or heel cuttings root well after flowering period. A favorite for drying.

L. officinalis. Also listed as *L. Spica* and *L. vera.* Reaches 3 feet. Trim after flowering. Dwarf forms Munstead, Hidcote and others are preferred for edging.

LEONTOPODIUM—Edelweiss.
This curious alpine, genus of the Composite Family (Compositae) is more common in its native region than legend would lead one to suspect. The true flowers of *L. alpinum* are small, but woolly bracts are conspicuous in late spring; 6 inches. A curiosity for the rock garden, but it is surpassed for appearance by a score of less legendary alpines.

LIATRIS—Blazing Star, Kansas Gayfeather. This stiff genus of the Composite Family (Compositae) is useful as a late summer accent. Opens at the top of the stem and blooms downward, which makes spent florets especially conspicuous. Well-drained soil, full sun preferred. Less reliable or choice species are best dug and stored in sand over winter. Division easy in spring. Also raised from seed. Staking needed for all but shortest kinds. A popular cut flower. Easily dried. Pest- and disease-free.

L. punctata. Purple. About 2 feet; mid to late summer.

L. pycnostachya. A taller species over 3 feet. Purple or white forms available. Best dug and stored during winter.

L. scariosa. The variety September Glory, purple, indicates flowering time. 3 feet average. White. Spire is especially attractive.

L. spicata. Purple forms most common. 2 or 3 feet, but variable in height.

LIGULARIA
This genus of the Composite Family (Compositae), formerly included under Senecio

has never been very popular in the United States. Large leaves and yellow to orange flowers are at their best in moist soil. Raised by seed or division in spring.

L. clivorum. 4-5 feet, many varieties. Othello has leaves touched with purple. Orange 'flowers. Orange Queen is larger flowered.

L. Kaempferi. Spreads underground so must not be placed near choice plants. 2 feet. Var. *aureo-maculata*, admired for its leaves variegated white, rose-pink and yellow, is not reliably hardy.

LILIUM—Lily.
Although this handsome genus is bulbous rather than herbaceous, it is included in this list because of its special value in the border. It would be difficult to imagine a perennial garden wtihout at least a few Lilies, which provide with their reflexed, trumpet, cup-like or saucer-shaped flowers, a most attractive display. They vary greatly in height and flowering time from the 2 foot *L. rubellum* of May to the 6 foot size attained in August by *L. Henryi* and its offspring, such as the Aurelian Hybrids. Only general cultural suggestions can be offered for this genus con-

Leontopodium alpinum

Ligularia clivorum

Liatris scariosa

taining species from very different areas of
the world. Like most bulbous plants, Lilies
require a perfectly drained soil. Many failures blamed on severe winters or disease are
due to placement in heavy, poorly drained
soils. Also see Mosaic Virus. A slope or
raised bed is almost always the preferred
location. However, adequate moisture must
be present, especially when the stem is
growing swiftly and forming buds. Without
this moisture, the plant will attain only a
fraction of its normal size. Generous amounts
of peat moss should be worked into the soil
at planting time (except for Madonna Lilies)
in addition to bonemeal. Dried manure is
useful, especially if it is placed well below
the bulb, so roots can reach for reserve nutrients as the years pass. Some old-school
gardeners prefer to place the bulbs on a
layer of sand or to tip the bulbs on their
sides so water will not settle between the
scales. Many others feel these measures are
unnecessary if the soil is properly drained.
Unlike many bulbs, Lilies have a brief dor-
mancy period, or none at all, so should not
be left out of the ground any longer than is
necessary. If bulbs are to arrive during cold
weather, as will be the case with late ma-
turers such as *L. speciosum* and its varieties,
a position must be mulched and kept frost-
free so the bulbs may be planted as soon as
they arrive. The Madonna Lily, *L. candidum* is moved in August or September,
planted only slightly below the surface, and
allowed to make a basal rosette of leaves before cold weather. Most other Lilies may be
planted about 5 or 6 inches deep and 2 feet
apart in the fall, and will form roots along
the underground stem as well as at the bulb
base. As is the case with most bulbs, good
bloom the first year is almost certain if superior stock has been purchased. Modern
Lilies are far more disease-free than the im-
ported, poorly-handled material familiar to
an older generation of gardeners. The gardener's task is to keep the Lily plant growing well so bulbs are kept vigorous and able
to bloom in the future. The longer the foliage is kept green and healthy, the better will
be the next year's bloom. A complete fertilizer applied in spring or early summer, followed by regular watering, is desirable.

Spraying with a combination insecticide-
fungicide is good insurance, but if a plant
is seriously attacked by disease it should be
removed at once. Lilies are a desirable, fragrant cut flower, but as few leaves as possible should be removed to prevent deterioration of the bulbs. Situations in deep
shade, or in competition with tree or large
shrub roots should be avoided, for stems will
be weak and prone to attack. However, light
shade may be desirable, especially to retain
the pastel shades of certain modern Lilies.
Staking is always desirable for taller specimens, but the stakes must be placed with
care so that the bulbs are not pierced. A
mulch, too, is highly desirable. E. H. Wilson
once remarked that Lilies are commonly
found in the wild in association with small
shrubs and herbaceous plants, so that the
Lily shoots are protected from frost in spring
and from parching sun in summer. This condition is best duplicated in the garden by a
ground cover or a light airy mulch, such as
ground sugar cane, buckwheat hulls or compost.

Propagation is by division of old clumps
in early spring before growth begins; by
sowing stem-produced bulbils of such species as the Tiger Lily in late summer; by
removing bulb scales during the period when
the plant is most nearly dormant; and rais-
ing plants from seed, which, for some species such as *L. regale*, *L. formosanum* and
L. pumilum (L. tenuifolium), is very easy,
with blooms in some cases appearing only a
year or two after sowing.

L. auratum—Goldband Lily. Large, fragrant white flowers with gold bands and
reddish-mahogany spots. Can reach 6 feet;
August. Var. *platyphyllum* is larger, with
spotting concentrated in the flower's central
portion. Var. *virginale* is unspotted, but the
gold bands remain. The Red Band Strain is
vigorous, with the gold bands replaced by
red ones.

Aurelian Hybrids, one of the better known
strains, contains several Lilies in its parentage, including the 6 foot tall *L. Henryi*.
Technically this is a grex, a term derived
from the Latin, meaning a flock. In the Aurelian "flock" there will be some differences

between individual members. The Aurelians produce yellow to orange flowers in August.

L. candidum—Madonna Lily. Variable in behavior, from being most unreliable to almost indestructible. Subject to botrytis disease. Cascade Strain more vigorous. 3 foot fragrant white flowers; late June-early July.

Emerald Strain. White, flushed green when buds open. Less need for staking.

L. formosanum—Trumpets white with purplish tints. Variable in height, young plants blooming at less than 2 feet. Disease-prone, seldom long lived.

Golden Chalice Hybrids. Lemon to orange flowers in June; 3 feet or more. Vigorous, resistant to dryness.

L. Hansonii—Japanese Turkscap Lily. Orange, spotted. 3 feet; late June-early July. Like *L. regale*, it appears in early spring, needs frost protection.

L. Henryi. Reflexed orange-yellow flowers on average 6 foot stems; August. Best in light shade. A hardy parent of many modern Lilies.

L. pumilum—Coral Lily. A handsome small-flowered scarlet lily. About 2 feet; June. Short lived.

Mid-Century Hybrids. Compact 2-3 foot plants need no staking. A variety of named clones, the members of which are identical as opposed to the variable grexes or strains. Strong colors predominate—Cinnabar, upright-flowering, is maroon; Prosperity, outward-facing is lemon; Fireflame, recurved, is red. July.

Olympic Strain. White, flushed green or reddish on outside of trumpets. Pastels such as Pink Perfection strain also offered. 6 feet; July.

L. regale. A favorite Lily of a generation ago, now being superseded by the more colorful, disease-resistant strains mentioned above. 4 feet or more. Fragrant, white flowers flushed pink on outside. The mutation Royal Gold is highly desirable.

L. rubellum. A lovely Lily too seldom planted. Rose pink flowers on 2 foot stems in May.

Lilium

L. speciosum. A Lily for late summer and early fall. Var. *rubrum*, with pink and red markings is admired, best in the form Red Champion. 3-4 feet. Var. *album* is white. Prone to mosaic attacks, so should not be included in gardens with *L. tigrinum*, which endures the disease and infects other Lilies.

L. tigrinum. 4-6 feet tall, hardy, bright orange, spotted, reflexed. Familiar in old gardens during late summer, but not desirable for reason noted above.

This list is quite incomplete. Serious lily fanciers are referred to The International Lily Register, a thorough work which offers full descriptions, provides parentages if they are known and distinguishes between grex and clonal lilies. It is a priceless guide through this enormous genus.

LILY-OF-THE-VALLEY—See *Convallaria-majalis*.

LIMONIUM—Sea-Lavender.
This genus of the Plumbago Family (Plumbaginaceae), formerly included under Statice, recalls the cloud-like Babys-Breath.

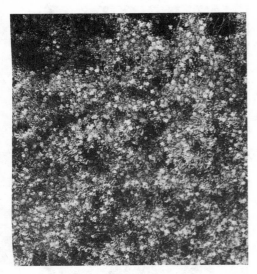

Limonium latifolium

Linum perenne

Rosy-purple flowers good in fresh and dried arrangements. Deep tap roots can be transplanted only in early spring. Young plants move best. Full sun, light soil. Easy from seed. Stems may snap off at the base in windy gardens unless staked. Flowers remain most of the late sumer and early fall. Pest- and disease-free. There are several interesting dwarf species, but 2-3 feet tall *L. latifolium* is most common.

LINUM—Flax.
A few species of this genus of the Flax Family (Linaceae) are useful garden plants because of their graceful form and long display of bloom.

L. perenne. Well known for its dime-sized blue flowers early to midsummer. Feathery foliage. 2 feet. Full sun, light soil. Best wintered in a frame in North. Self-sows freely. Especially fine where it enjoys the morning sun and opens early. Blooming extended if cut back.
L. flavum. Yellow, 1 foot, not reliably hardy.
There are several less well-known species, similar to the above, but varying somewhat in height, flower size or hardiness.

LIRIOPE—Lily Turf.
This genus of the Lily Family (Liliaceae) is best known in *L. Muscari*, with grass-like leaves and purple fall flowers. Not hardy in the North. Foliage makes a useful accent in southern gardens.

LOBELIA.
This genus of the Lobelia Family (Lobeliaceae) contains many species, only 2 of which are of importance in the perennial garden. These are at their best with their roots close to water, but they will make satisfactory, though shorter, plants in humusy, moist garden soil. Self-sowing common in favorable situations. Division possible in fall, or in areas where the plants suffer during winter, clumps may be stored inside and split in spring.

L. cardinalis—Cardinal-Flower. 4 feet tall at the water's edge. Scarlet flowers, late summer-early fall. Hardier in the wild where it

V. Above *Delphinium, hardy phlox, the shasta daisy, anthemis and petunias are combined in a colorful border. Hybrid anthemis, one of the sturdiest summer flowering perennials, provides an abundance of long-lasting cut flowers as well as bright yellow color in the border.*

VI. Above *Aquilegia, a McKana giant hybrid easy to raise from seed, is effective in the garden or as a cut flower.*

VII. Opposite *For dramatic contrast among other flowering plants, the pure white delphiniums are unsurpassed. In addition to white and familiar blue, the hybrids are available in lavender, orchid, purple and pink shades, with attractive combinations of these hues.*

is protected by twigs and grasses over the crown. May survive longest in the most unkempt part of the garden.

L. siphilitica. Less well known than the above, but hardier. About 3 feet. Blue flowers; late summer. Self-sowing common. A white form is seldom offered, but very likely to appear from a large sowing.

LOOSESTRIFE—See *Lythrum*.

LUNARIA—Moonwort, Satin Flower.
This long-cultivated genus of the Mustard Family (Cruciferae) is best known in the species *L. annua*. Although a biennial, this purplish-flowered plant so freely self-sows that it becomes a permanent garden feature. A white form is handsome combined with the deeper shades. Moist soil, partial shade. When cleaned of outer husks, the central white portions of the seed pods can be used in dried arrangements. If they are to be saved, the branches must be cut as soon as the green fades from the seed heads, or else the weather will quickly disfigure them. 3 feet, if well grown.

Liriope

Lunaria rediviva

Lobelia cardinalis

LUPINUS—Lupine.
This familiar genus of the Pea Family (Leguminosae) is seldom satisfactory except in cool, moist sections, particularly if growing such hybrids as the Russell Strain is attempted. Species such as *L. polyphyllus* and its forms are useful for naturalizing, but hardly effective garden plants. It is better to try the hybrids and hope that the following June will not be hot and windy. A satisfactory mixture may be had by sowing seed in the open in midsummer. Keep seeds well watered. Seedlings are easily transplanted before the second set of true leaves appear, as long as the root is inserted straight down. Favorite colors must be increased by division or, better, by cuttings in early spring. Lift the clump when new growth starts. Trim shoots free, leaving a piece of the yellow crown attached to the cutting base. Insert in moist sand or vermiculite, place in a plastic bag and leave on the north side of a building for a month. Cuttings should then be rooted enough to set out.

Aphids are a major problem. Begin spraying early with nicotine sulphate or malathion. Never allow more than 6 or 8 stems to flower. Stake these early and tie them often. Lupines may last many years in light, lime-free soil. The Russell Lupines are not uniformly hardy, however, perhaps because of the presence of annual species in their background. It is best to keep a new lot coming along. They can be used as a cut flower if hollow stems are filled with water before inserted in a vase. When through flowering, cut back stalks to encourage another crop. They do not need transplanting.

LYCHNIS
This genus of the Pink Family (Caryophyllaceae) contains some of the most vividly colored plants in cultivation. Most are easily grown in any light soil in full sun. Though seldom long lived, they often self-sow freely. Division easy for the double forms.

L. chalcedonica—Maltese Cross. Bright red flowers with attractive clefted petals. June-July; 3 feet. Snaps at base in windy gardens unless staked.

L. Coronaria—Mullein Pink, Rose Campion. Maroon flowers and gray foliage always attract comment, even though the plant has been cultivated for centuries. 2 feet; blooms through much of summer.

Lychnis chalcedonica

Lupinus hybrid

L. Flos-cuculi—Ragged Robin, Cuckoo Flower. Rose-pink flowers on foot high stems. Best in wet places. Double form increased by division.

L. Viscaria—German Catch Fly. Rose-red, 18 inches; June.

LYSIMACHIA—Loosestrife.
Strong-growing plants for the wild garden, hardly superior border plants. Grows well in any soil, but are most lush in moist areas. One of the most robust of all genera of the Primrose Family (Primulaceae).

L. clethroides. Curving white spikes in midsummer; 2-3 feet tall. A curious, old-fashioned perennial, but terribly invasive. Useful cut.

L. Nummularia—Creeping Jenny. Even more of a spreader than the above. Yellow flowers, midsummer. Sometimes suggested as a ground cover for shady areas, but better plants offer less trouble.

L. punctata. Brilliant yellow, July; 3 feet tall. Appropriate in old-fashioned or wild gardens.

Lythrum Salicaria

Lysimachia

Macleaya cordata, Iberis, Phlox, and Sanguinaria

L. vulgaris. Another yellow loosestrife, somewhat earlier and shorter than *L. punctata,* with greater need for shade and moisture.

LYTHRUM
This genus of the Loosestrife Family (Lythraceae) has become naturalized in many American meadows. Tall, purple flowers are useful accents in late summer. Extensive roots of old plants are shrub-like, so no delicate plants should be nearby. Tall stems sometimes need staking. Moves well only when young. Pest- and disease-free.

L. Salicaria—Spiked or Purple Loosestrife; 3 feet or more. The species is easy from seed. Named varieties raised from cuttings taken when growth has become firm. Varieties Robert, Morden Rose and Morden Pink, varying somewhat in their shade of rose, are worthwhile because of their more compact habit.

Macleaya cordata

MACLEAYA
Often recommended in spite of its defects is this genus of the Poppy Family (Papaveraceae). Though a showy plant, with numerous creamy flowers borne on 6 foot stems in late summer, it would be difficult to place even if it did not spread rapidly. Curiously shaped large leaves often attract attention. Only spring moving is recommended. Easily increased by seed or division. *M. cordata*—Plume Poppy, the species common in gardens is often still listed as Bocconia. Staking usually required. Both flowers and seed heads useful in arrangements. Hardy and pest free.

MALVA—Mallow.
This genus of the Mallow Family (Malvaceae) is usually represented by *M. moschata,* Musk Mallow, which bears light pink flowers on 2 foot stems through much of the summer. The common name comes from the musky odor given off by the bruised leaves. A white form is available. Incised foliage is especially attractive. Easy in any soil, and readily increased from seed.

Malva moschata

MEADOW-RUE. See *Thalictrum aquilegifolium.*

MECONOPSIS
This genus of the Poppy Family (Papaveraceae) has never been grown widely in the United States. Moist, humusy soil and partial shade are preferred. Fresh seed necessary for good germination.

M. cambrica—Welsh Poppy. One of the easier species. Yellow to orange flowers on foot tall stems through much of summer. Self-sows. Double form is admired, but less hardy.

M. betonicifolia. A variable species, the deep blues being especially handsome. Can exceed 4 feet. Often accused of being monocarpic—that is, flowering once in June and then dying. This may not occur if young plants are disbudded their first year. Partial shade improves the flower color; perfect drainage helps in over-wintering. One of the handsomest plants in cultivation, and well worth trying no matter how short-lived it may be. Several other species are worth growing, especially *M. grandis,* similar to *M. betonicifolia* but usually with more of a perennial nature; the shorter and also usually perennial *M. simplicifolia;* and Reginald Farrer's favorite *M. quintuplinervia,* more easily remembered as the Hairbell Poppy, with many-shaded bluish-purple flowers on foot-high stems.

Meconopsis cambrica

MENTHA—Mint.
This well-known genus of the Mint Family (Labiatae) has little to commend it other than its fragrance. Coarse, small-flowered, fast-spreading, it is hard to place it even in the herb garden where it properly belongs. However, mint may serve a purpose in a moist, shady corner where it will not interfere with other plants. Easily divided in early spring or after flowering. *M. piperita,* Peppermint and *M. spicata,* Spearmint are both about 2 feet tall. *M. rotundifolia,* Apple Mint, and several other species are listed by specialists.

Mentha rotundifolia variegata

Mertensia virginica

Monarda didyma

MERTENSIA—Bluebells.
This genus of the Borage Family (Boraginaceae) is typical of a number of wildflowers
which are charming in spring, but which
disappear during summer, making it easy to
uproot them while working, unless the site
is labelled. Therefore, they are best as filler
plants and in moist thin woodland, where
they look their best and may be let alone.
Seed may be sown in spring, but division
during the summer and fall dormant period
is the usual form of increase.

M. *virginica*—Virginia Bluebells. Pink buds
and blue flowers late April-May; 18 inches.
May pass out of bloom quickly if its season
is warm and windy. Several other species
such as M. *paniculata* and M. *lanceolata* are
quite robust, but less common in gardens.

MICHAELMAS DAISY—See *Aster.*

MILFOIL—See *Achillea.*

MILKWEED—See *Asclepias.*

MIST-FLOWER—See *Eupatorium coelestinum.*

MONARDA—Bee-Balm, Horse Mint.
This is one of the most delightful genera of
the Mint Family (Labiatae). Fragrant-
leaved, blooming over a long period, easy to
grow in any soil which is not too dry, the
Bee-Balms are among the best of old-fashioned perennials, but can become rambunctious if not restrained in spring. A single
stem will in a year produce many young
plants, and can become invasive. Division
every 2 or 3 years after flowering is necessary. If given adequate space, the plant will
branch well. Useful when cut. A favorite of
bees and humingbirds. Pest- and disease-
free.

M. *didyma*. Variable in color, many forms
of which have been selected, or crossed with
M. *fistulosa*, Wild Bergamot. Cambridge
Scarlet and Croftway Pink are self-explanatory. A white form usually has disappointingly small flowers. Height of these all vary
greatly, from 2-5 feet, depending upon
amount of light, moisture and space given
them.

MONKSHOOD—See *Aconitum.*

MOUNTAIN BLUET—See *Centaurea montana.*

MULLEIN—See *Verbascum.*

MYOSOTIS—Forget-Me-Not.
This genus of the Borage Family (Boraginaceae) is represented by two perennial species less attractive than the biennial *M.
sylvatica.* All do best in moist, shaded situations. Propagation is by seed or division
after flowering.

M. scorpioides, True Forget-Me-Not. Blue
flowers in spring. Stems average a foot,
rarely erect. Not a showy garden plant, but
attractive viewed at close range. *M. alpestris*
is compact, but suffers in dry weather.

NEPETA
This genus of the Mint Family (Labiatae)
contains over a hundred species, only a few
of which are useful garden plants. Gray
foliage is attractive. Division after the lavender flowers fade is the easiest form of propagation. Cuttings may be made of new growth
made after spent flowers are cut back.

N. Faassenii—The most common Nepeta
in gardens. Bluish-purple flowers on foot-
long stems during early summer. May bloom
even longer if cut back after the first flowering. Useful as a large edging plant.

NIEREMBERGIA—Cup-Flower.
At best a half-hardy perennial, this genus
of the Nightshade Family (Solanaceae) is
useful in southern gardens, where it flowers
from late spring to early fall.

N. hippomanica Var. *violacea,* often listed
as *N. caerulea,* has violet-blue flowers. It
prefers a sunny location. *N. repens,* white
with pink or blue tints, does better in shade.
Both are low growers, the latter creeping.

OENOTHERA—Evening-Primrose.
A large genus of the Evening Primrose Family (Onagraceae). Oenotheras usually have
yellow flowers, rarely white or rose. Only a
few of many species are commonly planted.
A sunny, perfectly drained site is best. Division in early spring or after flowering, or
seed-sowing are both satisfactory methods
of propagation.

Oe. fruticosa—Sundrops. Yellow flowers
early to midsummer; 18 inches. One of the
showiest lemon-yellow perennials.

Oe. missouriensis—Large yellow flowers
borne, not always plentifully, through much
of the summer. Trailing. Winged seed pods,
tan often streaked crimson, are excellent in

Myosotis   Royal Blue

Nepeta Mussini

Nierembergia rivularis

Oenothera biennis

decorations. Does not transplant well when mature, because of long, stringy root.

Oe. speciosa. White fading to rose-pink fragrant flowers over a long period; 18 inches. Sometimes invasive.

Oe. tetragona. Yellow flowers on 2 foot stems most of summer. Branching form increases quantity of bloom. Attractive long leaves.

ONOPORDUM.
This thistle-like genus of the Composite Family (Compositae) contains a score of species, one of which *O. Acanthium* is sometimes found in gardens. Purple flowers in July; average height 4 feet. Easy from seed, not particular about soil.

OPUNTIA—Prickly-Pear.
This genus of the Cactus Family (Cactaceae) is hardly common in northern gardens, but one species, *O. compressa*, is quite dependable in cold climates as long as there is sharp drainage. Although large yellow flowers are striking in early to midsummer, the plant is not attractive at other seasons. It is likely to become clogged with weeds, which are difficult to remove because of the spines. Easily

Onopordum Acanthium

increased by placing a joint flat on the ground, and weighting with a stone. Roots will develop on the underside. Move to permanent position before these become too rangy. Best considered a curiosity.

ORIENTAL POPPY—See *Papaver orientale*.

ORIGANUM—Marjoram.
This especially aromatic genus of the Mint Family (Labiatae) is more familiar in the herb garden than the perennial border, but it is always pleasant to keep some fragrant-leaved plants in the latter. *O. vulgare*—Wild Marjoram bears variable pink to purple flowers on 2 foot stems in midsummer. Unless supported, majoram will sprawl, especially if grown in good soil. Like so many of the herbs, it prefers a sweet, well-drained soil in full sun. Easy from seed.

PACHYSANDRA
No introduction is needed for the genus of the Box Family (Buxaceae). *P. terminalis* must surely be the most widely planted ground cover in this country. Only Myrtle and Ivy offer much competition. Although there are dozens of other ground covers which might be used to lend additional gar-

Origanum vulgare

Opuntia compressa

Pachysandra terminalis

Paeonia hybrid

den interest, Japanese Spurge need not be looked down upon. Hardy, pest- and disease-free, evergreen, easily increased from cuttings or runners, reliable in a variety of soils and exposures, this 6-8 inch favorite will continue to be used in great quantities. The rate of increase will be greater in humusy, fertile soil. In less favorable situations, Japanese Spurge may be disappointingly slow to get started. The American species *P. procumbens* is less of a spreader and seldom evergreen.

PAEONIA—Peony.
One of the great garden plants, this genus has traditionally been included in the Crowfoot Family (Ranunculaceae)) but recent scientific work indicates it belongs to its own family (Paeoniaceae). Incredibly long-lived and free-blooming, if reasonable care is given in selecting and preparing a position, this perennial will ordinarily survive the gardener who planted it. It is one of the few perennials which do not require periodic division to maintain vigor. In fact, it resents being disturbed. Annual top dressing with bonemeal or complete fertilizer will do much to insure satisfactory flowering. As is the

case with all fleshy-rooted perennials, Peonies require properly drained soil. Dig deep holes for large roots. Full sun is preferred, but light shade away from tree roots is not detrimental. Because the plant will remain in place many years, the soil should be enriched with bonemeal and compost. Each plant needs 2 or 3 square feet. The importance of shallow planting has been well publicized, but there should be about 2 feet of well-prepared soil beneath the root to support the plant over the years. The bright red shoots or "eyes" should be no deeper than 2 inches after the soil's final settling. Fall is the best planting or dividing time. Peonies are not trouble-free. (Botrytis sometimes a problem.) Good sanitation measures and regular applications of a modern fungicide such as Captan are recommended. Spray with Sevin to control rose chafers. Early staking is necessary to keep the heavy short-lasting blooms from toppling. They are excellent as cut flowers, with fine fragrance. When cutting, leave 2 sets of leaves on the base of stalk and ⅓ of blooms. Division, the usual form of increase, is not an easy job, calling for plenty of energy to lift the plant, and more to slice the tough root.

Several recent and very thorough publications which have discussed Peonies should be consulted in addition to the brief list below. Peonies have been hybridized as widely as other favorite perennials, but old names endure longer than those of Iris or Day-Lilies. Specialist catalogs offer useful descriptions of modern introductions as well as old favorites.

Peony species are not now widely planted, but a few of interest are:

P. anomala. Single crimson, May; 2½ feet. Cut leaves.

P. lactiflora. White, fragrant, widely used in hybridizing. 3 feet; June.

P. officinalis. Crimson, also important as a parent of many modern Peonies. 2½ feet; late May-early June.

P. tenuifolia. Excellent finely cut foliage. Under 2 feet. Red to purplish. May. One of the more valuable species for garden use.

When selecting Peony hybrids, it is well to keep in mind the flower form, height and blooming time as well as color. Doubles remain most popular, with many old favorites such as white, flecked red Festiva Maxima, pink Sarah Bernhardt and red Karl Rosenfeld still sold by the tens of thousands. In this category, new more or less yellow introductions are particularly interesting, but few are widely distributed. Single Peonies meet with little favor in this country, which is unfortunate, for they not only offer pleasing form, but also extend the blooming season. Many catalogs group single Peonies with Japanese types. In both classifications, a central cluster of yellow stamens provides a striking contrast for the red petals of such varieties as Mikado; the white, tinted pink of Rosy Dawn; and the deep pink of Helen.

PAPAVER—Poppy.

This genus of the Poppy Family (Papaveraceae) is represented in perennial gardens by the striking forms of *P. orientale,* Oriental Poppy. Although gay while they are in bloom, Poppies do not stay long in flower. Any large grouping of them leaves a considerable gap when foliage dies after flowering; the space traditionally being filled by the sprawling of nearby Gypsophila, Limonium, or similar plants. The species and the more robust named Poppies may prove invasive. However, loss of some varieties may be considerable during wet winters unless the long roots are planted in well-drained soil. Full sun is also preferred. Poppies may be safely transplanted only during the summer dormant period, but most garden centers offer potted plants which may be planted at any time. Dig deep holes for their large fleshy roots. Division of old roots is possible during late summer, and root cuttings of pencil thickness are also best taken at this time. See also Propagation from Seed. Poppies make a handsome cut flower if picked as the buds are about to burst. Cut ends should be flame-seared. Seed pods are good in dried arrangements.

Most Poppies bloom in June on 2-3 foot stems and may need staking. An exception is double Crimson Pom Pom, earlier and shorter. Much is made of white forms such as Field Marshall Von der Glotz and the old Barr's White, but these are not always robust. Various shades of pink should be seen in bloom so the most desirable color can be selected. Unspotted Helen Elizabeth, light pink Spring Morn and rose pink Salome are excellent. Blood red Warlord and self-descriptive Claret are nearly as brilliant as orange-scarlet Oriental and Curtis Giant Flame. An unusual color-range is provided by the "old rose" group, of which Henry Cayeux is senior member. Huge May Curtis is a newer introduction in this shade.

P. nudicaule—Iceland Poppy. A handsome, too seldom seen poppy in a wide range of colors, but little better than a biennial. Their long blooming period rivals that of the annual Shirley and California poppies.

PEACHLEAF BELLFLOWER—See *Campanula persicifolia.*

PEARL EVERLASTING—See *Anaphalis.*

PENSTEMON

Few of the 250 species of this genus of the Figwort Family (Scrophulariaceae) have been widely planted. Their intolerance of

Papaver orientale

Penstemon   Garnet

winter wet has always counted against them, but at least one species, *P. barbatus (Chelone barbata)* often survives in heavy soils and produces slim red flowers on 3 foot stems through much of summer. It is easily raised from seed or divided after flowering. The shiny green foliage is especially attractive.

P. heterophyllus is offered in several blue selections, most of which are only a fraction of the 5 foot height of the wild form, hence more useful in gardens. Not reliably hardy.

P. ovatus. Variable bluish-purple flowers average 3 feet; late summer. Attractive foliage. Usually treated as a biennial.

P. Newberryi—Mountain Pride. Rich flowers on 2 foot stems through much of summer.

Although many other species are often described in perennial books, those above are most commonly offered for sale. Whenever a good seed source is located, a number of other species should be tried to see how they behave in your locality. Hybrid Penstemon of mixed ancestry are often easier to find in catalogs. Pink Beauty blooms on 3 foot stems early to midsummer. Rose Elf is about half that height, while crimson Firebird averages 1½ feet tall.

PEONY—See *Paeonia.*

PERIWINKLE—See *Vinca minor.*

PHLOX

Few perennials have been so poorly treated as has this genus of the Phlox Family (Polemoniaceae). It has been a tradition in American gardening to buy the worst types and grow them as badly as possible. Thus we have the most ineffective shades of Ground Phlox studded with grass and sorrel, while equally frightful flowers of Summer Phlox are borne on gaunt stems clothed with diseased foliage, or without any leaves at all. These misfortunes are no doubt partly due to this perennial's ability to last almost forever under the worst conditions. They do best if divided every three or four years. Occasionally some will die out in very poorly drained soil, but this is exceptional. Although the *P. subulata* selections do well in light, well-drained soil, the cultivated varieties of *P. paniculata* appreciate compost both in the soil and as annual top dressing. Full sun or light shade is preferred. Nematodes are a common pest controlled best by removal of plants to new soil during the late summer division time or, better still, by starting new plants from root cuttings at the same season. A miticide is often necessary to control red spider. Deterioration of foliage as the plant comes into flower can be controlled by generous feeding, by spacing two feet or more apart to allow for air circulation and by beginning a weekly fungicide spray during May. Modern phlox stands up against weather much better than old forms, but staking is still good insurance in windy gardens. Phlox is sweetly fragrant, but is a mediocre cut flower because the florets drop.

P. amoena. Similar to Ground Phlox, but flowers intermittently through summer, after a major spring show. Rose-pink.

P. divaricata—Wild Sweet William or Blue Phlox. One of our most beautiful spring wildflowers. Lavender blue, a foot high. May spread into other plants. Easily increased after flowering by division, which also promotes health. Many varieties, of which *Laphamii* is most commonly offered.

P. paniculata—Summer Perennial Phlox. It is still common to see cultivated varieties of Summer Phlox that were worthy varieties twenty years ago, but which have been since replaced in better gardens by such strains as that of B. H. B. Symons-Jeune. Modern phlox are distinctly different. They are generally more compact, better branched, with round, sturdy florets of remarkably lively colors. Most are highly fragrant. They deserve the best care, not the neglect that was endured by older types. Deep, humusy, well-drained soil enriched with super-phosphate, bonemeal or complete fertilizer, is essential. Light shade will help the color of pastel kinds, but heavy shade or competition of tree roots should be avoided. Removal of dead heads will prevent self-sowing and the appearance of poorly-colored seedlings.

A few older varieties are worth growing. Miss Lingard, properly placed under *P. carolina*, is still useful for its early white flowers and glossy foliage, but it is not always vigorous, and likely to snap at the base unless staked. Sir John Falstaff, with its great, floppy, salmon florets, still attracts attention, but it is hardly a superior Phlox. Mary Louise and World Peace are very tall whites, but they can be somewhat controlled by pinching back a month or six weeks before flowering. Dresden China, one of the taller Symons-Jeune Phloxes is a handsome light pink; Fairy's Petticoat is another light pink with deeper eyes; Gaiety is one of the best bright reds. There is a great color range among other modern Phloxes. Because they are so freely raised from root cuttings, they are sure to be widely available in the coming years. Many are generally distributed now.

P. stolonifera—Creeping Phlox. Both the common and botanical names indicate the plant's shortcoming—it is a great spreader, good as a ground cover, poor near choice plants. Lavender-blue, early spring.

P. subulata—Ground Phlox, Ground-Pink, Moss-Pink. This must surely be the most commonly used of all "rock garden" plants.

Phlox   Fairy King

Phlox

One still must do some searching for the large-flowered, clear-colored forms, but it is worth the effort. Blue Hills is an excellent lavender-blue, starting to flower in late April in New England, before most other cultivated varieties. Scarlet Flame is a better red than many old rosy forms which have been inaccurately described as red. The J. H. Alexander series among the best available. Division after flowering is more successful if only smaller, non-woody stems are replanted.

Several other species are of interest, but those above are generally easier to grow, and adequate for most garden purposes.

PHYSALIS—Husk Tomato, Ground Cherry. This showy weed, a genus of the Nightshade Family, is best known in the species *P. Alkekengi*—Chinese Lantern Plant. Flowers are inconspicuous, but orange-colored husks are prominent in the fall. A fast spreader, best placed in a remote corner. Not particular about soil. Easily grown from seed or divisions set out in spring. If cut before autumn rains disfigure it, the Lantern Plant provides useful material for dried arrangements.

Physalis Alkekengi

PHYSOSTEGIA—False Dragonhead. Although this genus of the Mint Family (Labiatae) is best known for such rose-pink species as *P. virginiana* and cultivated varieties such as Vivid and Bouquet Rose, the white var. *alba* is more easily combined with other plants. Such association cannot be too close, however, for the Physostegias are fast spreaders. They flower in late summer for a month or more. Most garden forms average about 3 feet, a few others, nearly twice that height, are distinguished by such names as *gigantea* and *grandiflora*. None are particular about soil, and will do as well in partial shade as full sun. Sow seed or divide in early spring. Dig up every couple of years so they do not get out of hand. Staking of taller forms is necessary in exposed gardens. Botrytis is a problem in some areas. A strong-stemmed long-lasting cut flower.

PINK—See *Dianthus*.

PLATYCODON
This genus of the Bellflower Family (Cam-

Physostegia virginiana

panulaceae) is one of the best perennials. Beautifully formed Campanula-like flowers are produced generously in late summer. Only one species, *P. grandiflorum* is grown. Its common name, Balloon-Flower, comes from the bud shape. Bluish-purple type is most common, but an excellent white and pale pink are also available. There are also double forms. All may exceed 2 feet. Require staking, which is hard to do attractively, hence Var. *Mariesii,* somewhat over a foot tall, is preferred. Pest- and disease-free. Full sun or partial shade. Well-drained soil needed for the long, fleshy roots. Plants are very late to start in spring, and should not be moved after growth is much advanced. Clumps are seldom easily divided. Best means of increase is from seed. Plants may stay in one location many years, not requiring division to maintain vigor.

Platycodon grandiflorum

PLUMBAGO—See *Ceratostigma Plumbaginoides.*

PODOPHYLLUM
This genus of the Barberry Family is best known for the species *P. peltatum,* May-Apple, 1-2 feet tall; white flowers in May, followed by greenish-yellow fruit. Lobed, shiny foliage is attractive. Requires a shady position and humusy soil. Both this species and more showy *P. emodi* are easily raised from fresh seed. Divide in early spring.

POKER-PLANT—See *Kniphofia* (Tritoma).

POLEMONIUM
A genus of the Phlox Family (Polemoniaceae) best known for *P. caeruleum,* Jacobs-Ladder. The common name comes from the form of the attractive foliage which, unlike that of many spring-blooming perennials, remains in good condition through summer. Lavender-blue flowers carried on 2 foot stems. A white form is also available. Easily divided after flowering or raised from seed. Not particular about soil or position, but light shade and moisture are needed for best appearance. *P. carneum* is useful for its dwarf habit, but suffers during dry periods. Of all compact forms, *P. Richardsonii* is

Podophyllum peltatum

most dependable. *P. reptans* is also worth having, but may tumble over choicer plants nearby. All species are useful for cutting.

POLYGONATUM—Solomons-Seal.
This grand genus of the Lily Family (Liliaceae) includes one of our most delightful and easily grown wildflowers. It should find a place in every lightly shaded, moist garden. Delicate white flowers are suspended in June from curved stems. *P. commutatum* may exceed 3 feet in an ideal situation, while *P. multiflorum*, a Eurasian species, is under 2 feet tall. Foliage remains attractive until late summer. Division after flowering is an easier method of increase than seed sowing.

POLYGONUM—Knotweed.
This coarse genus of the Buckwheat Family (Polygonaceae) should be used only in difficult positions where a robust ground cover is needed. Most species are too invasive for garden use. Some are useful as vines.

P. affine, nearly evergreen, bears pinkish flowers on foot high stems through late summer. Darker colored Darjeeling Red is preferred.

P. Aubertii—China Fleece-Vine, Silver Lace-Vine. Hardy perennial vine. A fast grower covered with greenish-white, fragrant flowers in late summer. Will do well under difficult conditions.

P. Reynoutria, one of the most commonly offered species, also pink flowered in late summer, is a fast spreader.

POTENTILLA—Cinquefoil.
Although the yellow-flowered, shrubby *P. fruticosa* is a well-known representative of this genus of the Rose Family (Rosaceae), few gardeners plant the herbaceous species. Attractive, divided leaves make an unusual ground cover. The best for this purpose is *P. tridentata,* not strictly herbaceous, but worth mentioning here. Foliage of the readily available *P. nepalensis* is coarser, but appealing, at least before the long wand-like stems appear. Reddish blossoms in midsummer. Var. *Willmottiae* is somewhat better colored. Often self-sows. Divide after flowering.

PRIMULA—Primrose.
This favorite genus of the Primrose Family

Polemonium   Blue Pearl

Polygonatum

Polygonum Aubertii

Potentilla

(Primulaceae) contains over 400 species, many of no horticultural significance; some of interest only to expert rock gardeners; a few have more general garden value. For average border use, *P. polyantha* hybrids are most satisfactory. These are easily grown in any rich, moist soil and bear numerous large flowers in many colors during May. Unless fresh seed is sown immediately after ripening, germination will usually be very erratic. Division after flowering not only provides additional plants, but also maintains vigor. Unless shade and moisture is provided, the foliage will deteriorate and may become infested with red spider, always difficult to control even with superior miticides. Very likely to be heaved out of the ground during winter, these Primulas survive if given a light, airy mulch.

Primulas are grouped in various sections. Those of the Auricula Section, containing *P. Auricula* and its cultivated varieties are difficult except in milder sections of the United States. Fleshy leaves are frequently evergreen.

Those of Candelabra Section are among the most showy of Primulas, with colorful flowers in June and July held high on stems from 1-3 feet high. It is unwise to attempt them unless a partly shaded location with even moisture can be provided. *P. japonica* is the easiest of this section but the flowers, in various rose shades, are not outstanding. The cultivated varieties of *P. pulverulenta* are better colored, and often as readily grown.

The Sikkimensis Section includes *P. Florindae*, a tall, yellow Primula not difficult if abundant moisture is present. It blooms with the Candelabra Section in early summer. Most other members of this section, such as variable *P. alpicola*, are under 2 feet tall, but *P. sikkimensis*, yellow, is often taller.

Diminutive plants of the Farinosae Section are seldom easily grown, though rose-colored *P. frondosa* may not prove difficult in a shady, moist garden. It displays the yellow eye typical of this section.

The Vernales Section includes the familiar *P. vulgaris*, yellow or shades of blue, as well as rose to purple *P. Juliae*, much used in hybridizing. *P. veris*, the English Cowslip, is included here also.

There are several other sections of interest to specialists.

PRUNELLA
One of the minor genera of the Mint Family

Prunella grandiflora

Primula japonica

(Labiatae) Prunella is a vigorous, self-sowing perennial suitable for a moist, out-of-the-way corner. *P. vulgaris*—Heal-All is best known. Purple flowers are carried on 2 foot stems through summer. Pinkish and white varieties are also offered. Easily divided.

PULMONARIA—Lungwort.

Containing one of the finest blue-flowered perennials in the April garden, this genus of the Borage Family (Boraginaceae) often flowers well into May. Though its species multiply moderately, they are never invasive. Divide after flowering. Best results are obtained in moist, humusy soils in lightly shaded positions. Elsewhere, spring blooming will be satisfactory, but appearance of summer foliage will suffer.

P. angustifolia. Blue flowers carried on stems a foot tall or less. Dark green foliage.

P. saccharata—Bethlehem Sage. A larger plant, usually more admired than the above. Pink flowers blue with age. Foliage spotted white.

PYRETHRUM—See *Chrysanthemum Coccineum*.

RANUNCULUS—Buttercup, Crowfoot.

Although easily grown in any moist garden, this genus of the Crowfoot Family (Ranunculaceae) is not widely planted. Divide after flowering.

R. acris, in its double form, is desirable for its yellow flowers on 2 foot stems intermittently from June to August.

R. gramineus. Yellow flowers held a foot above grayish leaves. Earlier flowering than the above.

RHEUM—*R. Rhaponticum*.

Garden Rhubarb is the most familiar species in this genus of the Buckwheat Family (Polygonaceae), but there are a few others which may provide strong accents in a large garden. They grow in any soil or situation, but are most lush in rich, moist areas. Division of old clumps in early spring can be an exhausting task, for the roots are massive. Young leaves are effective in modernistic flower arrangements. Tall, white flower heads always attract comment.

R. palmatum, with 5 foot flower stems and unusual lobed foliage, is the best choice for ornamental purposes.

ROCK-CRESS—See *Aubrieta;* also *Arabis.*

ROSMARINUS—Rosemary.
This aromatic, anciently cultivated genus of the Mint Family (Labiatae) should be in every southern garden. In the North it is best treated as a pot plant and wintered inside. It is a shrub rather than an herbaceous plant. When kept outdoors, it should be placed in full sun. Limy, well-drained soil is preferred. *R. officinalis* is available in an awesome number of forms: white-, blue- and pinkish-flowered kinds are offered as well as the bluish-purple type. There are also prostrate, erect and arching forms. These all must be increased from summer cuttings, but the species can be raised, somewhat slowly, from seed.

RUDBECKIA—Coneflower.
This genus of the Composite Family (Compositae) contains many highly variable species, one of which, *R. purpurea*, is now housed under Echinacea. Seldom long-lived, but usually self-sowing, the Rudbeckias are best in the wild or cutting garden or, perhaps, at the rear of the border. The Gloriosa Daisy selections of *R. hirta*, with large single or double flowers, are preferred over most of the species. They bloom the first year from seed, and often are perennial, especially in well-drained soil. All are open field plants, so prefer full sun. They make excellent cut flowers.

R. lacinata var. *hortensia*—Golden-Glow. The familiar 6 foot double yellow form common in old-fashioned gardens. A fast spreader, difficult to place. A few hybrids such as Goldquelle retain the doubleness, but are only half as tall.

R. speciosa, a true perennial Black-Eyed Susan about 2 feet tall, preferred over the taller biennial *R. triloba*, which bears a similar dark-centered yellow daisy. The cultivated variety Goldstrum is highly recommended for its large flowers on 2-3 foot stems.

Pulmonaria angustifolia

Ranunculus acris

Rheum palmatum

RUTA—Rue.

This genus of the Rue Family (Rutaceae) should not be confused with Thalictrum, Meadow-Rue, a genus included under Ranunculaceae. Only one species, *R. graveolens* is cultivated. Inconspicuous flowers are less important than the aromatic much divided, bluish foliage. 3 feet tall. Propagated from seeds or divisions.

SAGINA—Pearlwort.

This mat-like genus, a member of the Pink Family (Caryophyllaceae) is most important for the species *S. subulata*, which bears diminutive white flowers in spring. A useful ground cover for a moist corner. Propagated from seeds or divisions. One of the most charming of moss-like plants.

SALVIA—Sage.

It is unfortunate that many gardeners still know this genus of the Mint Family (Labiatae) only in the species *S. splendens*, so famaliar with its mass of scarlet blooms. Inexperienced gardeners are still startled to hear there are blue Salvias; equally surprised to find some perennial. Most are easy from seed, an exception being the sterile hybrid *S. superba*, still often listed under its older name *S. virgata* var. *nemerosa*. Increased by division or summer cuttings, this handsome purple Salvia will flower through much of the summer, creating an especially good show if the old heads are periodically trimmed. Well-drained soil and full sun is preferred for most Salvias.

S. azurea var. *grandiflora*. One of the best light blue Salvias. Only half hardy. 3 foot stems must be staked. Rather too thin to make much of a show, but cutting back in early summer may improve its appearance. Late summer.

S. farinacea. Usually grown as an annual in the North, but occasionally it will overwinter. Often self-sows. Highly variable from seed, many shades of blue. Infrequently a white appears. To 3 feet tall. Finer-leaved than many Salvias.

S. haematodes. Seldom perennial, but easily kept going from seed, often self-sowing. 2-3 foot stems rise above a basal rosette of large, coarse leaves. Bluish-lavender flow-

Rosmarinus officinalis

ers on much-branched stalks during June and July.

S. *Jurisicii*. A foot-high plant easier to place than taller Salvias. Usually hardy. Purple flowers through much of summer.

S. *nutans*. Deep blue, pendant flowers on 3 foot stems in July.

S. *officinalis*. This culinary Sage belongs in the herb garden, and is of little value in the perennial garden. Properly it is a small shrub. Familiar coarse leaves and purple flowers.

S. *patens*. One of the clearest blues in the genus, but little more than a biennial in the North. Rather open, rangy branching habit. 2 feet.

S. *pratensis*. Generally hardy. Self-sows freely. Variable in color, purple most common. 2-3 feet.

S. *Sclarea*—Clary. An immense Sage, its large leaves and bracts making it seem even more massive. 3 feet even when casually grown. The Vatican variety is nearly white, with pink and purple tints. A freely-sowing biennial. Strongly aromatic foliage.

Ruta   Blue Mound

S. *superba*—A fine perennial with broad, bushy habit and long flowering period. Deep purple. 2 feet or sometimes taller. Not only the best of Salvias, but one of the most outstanding of all perennials.

SANGUINARIA

This fragile wildflower, which displays its beauty for a brief period in late April, is a genus of the Poppy Family (Papaveraceae). Only one species—S. *canadensis*, Bloodroot. White flowers on 6-8 inch stems. One of the easier wildflowers, usually spreading, though seldom invasively. Dies back after flowering. Light shade, humusy, moist soil. Single form not difficult from seed or division after flowering. A double variety is much admired.

SANGUISORBA

This long-blooming, hardy genus of the Rose Family (Roseceae) bears flowers shaped like a bottle brush. Occasionally it is still listed under its older name, Poterium. Reliable in any soil in partial to fairly heavy shade. Easily divided after flowering or raised from seed.

S. *canadensis*. 6 inch white flower heads

Rudbeckia   White King

on 5 foot stems. Best in damp soil. Heavily cut foliage. Flowers through much of summer.

S. *obtusa*. Pinkish-rose, rather lax flowers over a similar long period; 3 feet.

SANTOLINA

This genus of the Composite Family (Compositae) includes S. *Chamaecyparissus*—Lavender Cotton. A small shrub with aromatic, gray foliage, and one of the best edging plants for a well-drained, sunny position. It will grow about a foot tall and spread at least twice that unless thinned out each year. Small yellow flowers borne in midsummer are unimportant. Short tip cuttings root easily any time after new growth has become firm. The green foliage of S. *virens* makes a pleasant contrast, but this species is not as readily available. Both species are natives of the Mediterranean, so winter protection is desirable in the North. However, they are generally no more difficult to over-winter than Lavender.

SAPONARIA—Soapwort.

Best known for the old-fashioned S. *officinalis*, Bouncing Bet, this genus of the Pink

Sagina subulata

Salvia officinalis

Sanguinaria canadensis

Family (Caryophyllaceae) also includes the beautiful rock-plant S. *ocymoides.* The latter bears small pink flowers in June, and is easily grown from seeds sown where the plant is permanently desired. It does not transplant well. Also pink, Bouncing Bet is a great spreader, but certainly not out of place in a corner of an old garden. It is 2-3 feet tall, usually tumbling over when it comes into bloom.

SATUREJA—Savory.
This genus of the Mint Family (Labiatae) is not useful for display, but it is a delightful aromatic plant which need not be restricted to the herb garden. S. *montana,* Winter Savory, about a foot tall, produces light lavender flowers in late summer. Divide or increase from seed.

SAXIFRAGA—Saxifrage.
This huge genus of the Saxifrage Family (Saxifragaceae) contains some of the best of all rock garden plants, many of which are challenging even for experts. Like many mountain plants, most Saxifrages prefer an even moisture supply, but sharp drainage. Only those which are easily cultivated are

Santolina Chamaecyparissus

Sanguisorba obtusa

Saponaria officinalis

Satureja alpina

Saxifraga umbrosa

included here. Properly sited, they are long lived.

S. *Aizoon*. The best known of the encrusted section, with evergreen leaves, white at the edges. A number of varieties, with white, rose-pink or yellow flowers averaging 6 or 8 inches high. Late May-June.

S. *Cotyledon*. White, tinted pink, variable in height, 1-2 feet; June.

S. *lingulata*. Rosettes of this encrusted species are particularly attractive, white flowers, usually over a foot high; June.

S. *rosacea*. One of the easier moss types. Typically white, but rose-pink forms are also available. 6 inches; late May-early June.

S. *umbrosa*. London Pride. White, tinged pink. 18 inches; May. One of the showiest, useful wherever there is some shade and plentiful moisture.

S. *virginiensis*. A North American species. White. Averages a foot high; May.

Those interested in other Saxifrages are directed to the rock garden books of Reginald Farrer, which treat both well-known and rare species in a lively manner.

SAXIFRAGE PINK—See *Tunica Saxifraga*.

SCABIOSA—Scabious, Pincushion Flower. This genus of the Teasel Family (Dipsaceae) does not contain many species useful as garden plants, but S. *caucasica* is one of the best perennials. Long-flowering in the garden, long-lasting as a cut flower, this Scabiosa should be planted generously. The species are easily raised from seed, but cultivated varieties should be divided in early spring. Retain outer portions of the clump and discard the central thick-rooted part. Good drainage plus spring planting is important for successful over-wintering, as is adequate moisture for proper summer bloom. Full sun and well-limed soil are desirable.

S. *caucasica*. Large flowers in various purple to blue shades on 2 foot stems through much of summer. Named varieties are difficult to obtain, but a seed mixture of House Hybrids will produce many excellent colors. White forms provide welcome contrasts.

S. *graminifolia.* Grass-like foliage, as indicated by the botanical name, typical of a number of foot-high species useful for the rock garden. Rose-purple flowers in July.

SEA-LAVENDER—See *Limonium.*

SEDUM—Stonecrop.

This enormous genus of the Orpine Family (Crassulaceae) contains about 350 species, several good in the rock garden; a few in the border. Most are very long-lived in sunny, well-drained positions. They are easily divided after flowering. Several are weeds.

S. *acre.* One of the fast spreaders, but a useful ground cover where it can be contained. Yellow flowers; early summer.

S. *kamtschaticum*—Yellow flowers on 6 inch stems through late summer. Var. *variegatum* is as easily grown.

S. *maximum* var. *atropurpureum* is preferred over the type. Reddish purple leaves and rose-pink flowers during late summer; 1½ feet.

S. *Sieboldii*—A favorite Sedum, the most desirable variety having pink-edged grayish leaves. Rose-pink flowers on 8 inch stems in late summer and fall.

S. *spectabile.* One of the largest Sedums, averaging 2 feet tall. Large rose-colored flowers through late summer attract swarms of pollinators. Several deeper forms offered, of which Brilliant is best known. Indestructible but not invasive.

S. *spurium*—Dark red Dragon's Blood is the preferred form. Maroon leaves. Trailing stems 6-9 inches long; blooms July-Aug. A fast spreader.

SEMPERVIVUM — Houseleek.   Hen-and-Chickens.

This genus of the Orpine Family (Crassulaceae) contains many good rock garden species. Many are very similar except to an expert's eye, but those listed are all distinct

Scabiosa   Blue Nymph

Sedum spectabile   Autumn Joy

Sempervivum tectorum

Senecio Cineraria

in some way. Everlasting in well-drained soil and full sun. Each offset or "chicken" will produce a new plant, so division is the easiest means of propagation. Flowering is often erratic, and white, rose or yellow flowers are little more than curious.

S. *arachnoideum* – Cobweb Houseleek. Small rosettes covered with cobweb-like threads. One of the most admired species. Reddish flowers.

S. *tectorum*—Common Houseleek. Several varieties, many with "Hens" as large as a fist. Rose-purple 8 inch flowers.

Other useful Sempervivums are small S. *arenarium*, red-tipped S. *dolomiticum* and the sometimes similarly marked S. *montanum*.

SENECIO—Groundsel.
An immense genus of the Composite Family (Compositae), with over 1000 species, Senecio contains many weeds as well as a few useful plants. Many of the species are now included under Ligularia. Even the desirable plants noted below should be divided every other year to be kept within bounds. Those with large leaves look shabby by midsummer unless planted in a moist location.

S. *adonidifolius*. Less than a foot tall. A useful rock plant with orange-yellow flowers in early summer.

S. *macrophyllus* – Long leaves, yellow flowers on 3 foot stems in late summer.

S. *tanguticus*. A spreader 6 feet tall in damp gardens. Yellow flowers in early fall.

SHASTA DAISY – See *Chrysanthemum maximum*.

SHORTIA
Only three species are included in this genus of the Diapensia Family (Diapensiaceae). Best known is S. *galacifolia*, Oconee Bells, with handsome foliage attractive throughout the year. Large white flowers appear on 2-3 inch stems in early spring. S. *uniflora* is the more familiar of two Japanese species. Moist, humusy soil and a partly shaded loca-

tion are preferred. Increased by division after flowering.

SIDALCEA
This genus of the Mallow Family (Malvaceae) is not widely included in gardens. Although *S. malvaeflora* is easily raised from seed, its rose-pink blooms carried on 3 foot stems are inferior to those of cultivated varieties. These newer forms display many fine pink and red colors, but plants are not generally available in the United States. The genus is similar to Althaea with the advantages of being shorter and rust-free. Moist soil, full sun or light shade.

SILENE—Catchfly, Campion.
This large genus of the Pink Family (Caryophyllaceae) contains several good species for the rock garden. Most are readily increased from seed, but some, such as *S. acaulis*, are reluctant to bloom. When conditions suit it, rose-pink flowers cover this low green cushion in May. Good drainage and summer moisture are essential. *S. maritima* var. *rosea* is another pink Silene which blooms about the same time. *S. Saxifraga*, growing 6 inches or more, produces white flowers with green or red outer markings. Flower intermittently through much of summer. *S. Schafta*, Moss Campion, is a fall bloomer, bearing purplish-rose flowers on trailing stems. Some summer shade is desirable for choicer species, especially when grown in warmer areas.

SMILACINA—False Solomons-Seal.
Bearing some resemblance to the growth habit of Polygonatum, though none to its flower form, this genus of the Lily Family (Liliaceae) actually appears, at least in its foliage, to be nearer Lily-of-the-Valley. Easily grown in any moist soil, but it is a fast spreader and should not be planted near choicer material. A common woodland ground cover in moderately shaded areas. Divide after flowering.

S. racemosa. 1-3 feet tall, depending largely on moisture available. Airy white panicles in May.

Sidalcea malvaeflora

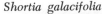

Shortia galacifolia

S. stellata. Similar to the above, except about half as tall.

SNEEZEWEED—See *Helenium.*

SNEEZEWORT—See *Achillea.*

SNOW-IN-SUMMER — See *Cerastium tomentosum.*

SOLDANELLA
A genus of small rock garden plants of the Primrose Family (Primulaceae). Not the most easily grown alpines, Soldanellas require shaded, moist locations. They can be raised from fresh seed or careful division after flowering.

S. alpina. Attractive leaves not unlike those of a small garden Nasturtium. Violet-blue flowers. 4 inches high in early spring.

S. montana. With larger leaves and light lavender flowers an inch taller than the above species.

SOLOMONS-SEAL—See *Polygonatum.*

Silene acaulis

Smilacina racemosa

Soldanella alpina

SPEEDWELL—See *Veronica*.

STACHYS—Betony.
One of the most decorative of all gray-leaved perennials, this genus of the Mint Family (Labiatae) should find a place in every sunny, well-drained garden. In wet winters they may be damaged, but spring division of the surviving portions revives the planting.

S. *corsica*. A useful carpet form with light pink flowers through much of summer.

S. *grandiflora*. Purplish flowers on foot-high stems in late June-early July. A moderate spreader. Satisfactory for cutting.

S. *officinalis*. A tall species, with rose-purple flowers on 2-3 foot stems in midsummer.

S. *olympica*—Lambs-Ears. The common name perfectly describes the felt-like leaves, always fascinating to children. Rose-purple foot-high flowers through much of summer are hardly attractive, and might be removed if the plant is used as edging.

STATICE—See *Armeria Maritima* and *Limonium*.

Stokesia laevis

Stachys grandiflora

Symphytum officinale

Tanacetum vulgare

Teucrium Chamaedrys

ST. JOHNSWORT—See *Hypericum*.

STOKESIA—Stokes Aster.
This perennial is one of the handsomest of all Composites. Large flowers, white or in many lavender shades, are carried through most of the late summer. Seldom over a foot tall, but somewhat sprawling. *S. laevis* is the sole species, but many cultivated varieties are offered. Large flowered Blue Moon, displaying many lavender shades, is one of the best. Like other selected forms, it should be increased by spring division. The species is readily increased from seed. All prefer a well-drained position in full sun. An excellent cut flower.

SUNFLOWER—See *Helianthus*.

SWEET ROCKET—See *Hesperis matronalis*.

SWEET VIOLET—See *Viola odorata*.

SYMPHYTUM—Comfrey.
This genus of the Borage Family (Boraginaceae) has been long cultivated, but it has little value in modern gardens. The largest species are sometimes used as compost ingredients, and might be grown for this purpose, if space permits. Increased from seed or spring division.

S. *asperum*—Prickly Comfrey. An immense plant, often man-high in damp ground. Rose-pink flowers fading to bluish-purple, through much of summer if kept trimmed back.

S. *officinale*—Common Comfrey. Variable white to rose-pink or purplish flowers on 3 foot stems through much of summer. S. *peregrinum* is similar, but a foot or so taller.

TANACETUM—Tansy.
It is difficult to imagine this familiar Composite weed as a garden plant, except in out-of-the-way corners around old dwellings. A cut-leaved form is sometimes included in the herb garden, but it is as terribly invasive as the type *T. vulgare*. Foliage is strongly aromatic, and button-like yellow flowers appear on 3 foot stems in late summer. Increased by division or seed sowing at any time.

TEUCRIUM—Germander.
This genus of the Mint Family (Labiatae) is best known for the beautiful evergreen *T. Chamaedrys*. This shiny, small-leaved perennial slightly exceeds one foot in height when bearing its thin lavender flower spikes, but these are unattractive, and often sheared back. Easily divided in early spring or increased from summer cuttings. Full sun and light soil. Seldom dependably hardy in open winters, so it is best to protect well with boughs or overwinter 2 or 3 plants in the frame. The plant is traditional used as edging for Rose beds.

THALICTRUM—Meadow-Rue.
This genus of tall perennials belonging to the Crowfoot Family (Ranunculaceae) creates the same airy effect at tall heights that the Gypsophilas do at middle levels. They are best staked. Spring division is the easiest means of increase. Light shade and moist, humusy soil are preferred.

Thalictrum dipterocarpum

T. aquilegifolium. One of the most familiar species, with attractive Columbine-like foliage. 3-4 feet tall. Light purple flowers in early summer.

T. diffusiflorum. Perhaps the best thalictrum, but not yet widely distributed. Lavender flowers on 3 foot stems in midsummer.

T. dipterocarpum. Both the typical purple and the less well-known white are attractive in late summer. 4 feet tall even when casually grown. *T. rocquebrunianum* is more robust and larger flowered.

T. minus. A highly variable species, most notable for its fern-like foliage. Yellow flowers, borne in early summer on average 18 inch stems, are not striking.

T. rugosum. Often still listed under the older name *T. glaucum*, which describes the grayish bloom on the foliage. Yellow flowers on 4 foot stems in July.

THERMOPSIS
Containing a score of species, this genus of the Pea Family (Leguminosae) is best known for *T. caroliniana*, which carries yellow blossoms rather briefly on 4 foot stems in mid-

Thermopsis

summer. Plants are usually raised from seed, young specimens being set in their final places at an early stage. Mature plants have shrub-like roots. Though not too particular about soil or position, Thermopsis is best in light soil and full sun. Staking is required, but otherwise the plant requires little care.

T. montana. A compact 2-3 foot species more desirable in small gardens. Similar yellow pea-like blossoms in late June-early July.

THRIFT—See *Armeria.*

THYMUS—Thyme.
This common inhabitant of the rockery and herb garden is a genus of the Mint Family (Labiatae). Thymes are small shrubs rather than herbaceous perennials. Manner of propagation depends upon the particular species. Prostrate growers are easily increased from division, as long as care is taken to plant a section with roots and not merely a section of trailing stems. Woody species 6 inches to a foot high often divide poorly, as is frequently the case with subshrubs. However, these are easily increased from summer cuttings. All prefer full sun and light soil. The value of prostrate Thymes as filler between flagstones is somewhat questionable, for they

quickly cover the paving, and when in bloom attract swarms of pollinators which make use of the paved area all but impossible. This group which may become clogged with Sorrel and other weeds, which seldom can be completely removed.

T. Herba—barona. A seldom seen low grower, worth having for its caraway scent.

T. lanuginosus. This so-called woolly species, much admired for its prostrate gray foliage, often is injured in open winters.

T. nitidus. Another gray-leaved species. About 10 inches tall, with purplish flowers in late spring.

T. Serpyllum—Mother of Thyme. A number of varieties with flowers, white and various shades of rose-pink. A carpet species, blooming intermittently through summer. Var. *vulgaris,* lemon-scented, often appears in catalogs as *T. citriodorus.*

T. vulgaris—Common Thyme. A robust, invasive species with 6 inch purple flowers. Useful in the herb garden if it can be contained.

TORCH-LILY—See *Kniphofia* (Tritoma).

TRADESCANTIA—Spiderwort.
Although a number of species of this genus

Thymus Serphyllum splendens

Tradescantia virginiana

VIII. Opposite *This charming one-color effect was created with lupines and pyrethrum, with contrast of height and form to avoid monotony.*

Tritonia (Montbretia) crocosmaeflora

Trollius europaeus superbus

of the Spiderwort Family (Commelinaceae) are familiar house plants, only one, 2 foot tall *T. virginiana*, is important in the perennial garden. This lavender-blue species and its white, rose-pink and light blue varieties will grow in any soil in full sun or light to moderate shade. They flower through much of the summer. Division is easily accomplished either in early spring or after flowering. Though not a neat growing perennial, it is useful in difficult situations where few other plants succeed. It often is difficult to eradicate once established.

TRITONIA
A genus of South African bulbous plants of the Iris Family that produce slender spikes of showy bright red, orange or yellow flowers in summer not unlike gladiolus. Commonly listed in catalogs as Montbretia. Grows 3-4 feet. Plant bulbs in May 3-4 inches deep and 4-5 inches apart in rich but sandy, well-drained loam in full sun. North of Washington, D. C. requires a winter mulch. North of N. Y. City lift bulbs in autumn. *T. crocosmaeflora* and vars. most commonly grown.

TROLLIUS
This Buttercup-like genus of the Crowfoot Family (Ranunculaceae) is particularly useful in heavy, damp soil where many other perennials might prove short-lived. They do best with some shade, though will do well in sun if soil is moist. Propagation is accomplished by sowing fresh seed or dividing after flowering. However, division is not necessary to maintain vigor. Though slow to establish, plants may be left in one location for 4 or 5 years. In dry locations Trollius may not be long lived. Useful as a cut flower, especially if buds are cut when first opened. Many varieties will repeat bloom if faded flowers are promptly removed.

T. europaeus—Globe-Flower. Many cultivated varieties, many of mixed parentage, of which Lemon Queen is one of the best known. Most attain 2 feet, but a few exceed this height. They all flower in May and June, and it is possible to get almost any shade of yellow or orange one desires.

T. Ledebouri is similar, but a month or so later flowering. The type is deep orange. Larger-flowered Golden Queen has yellow anthers and gold-colored blooms. Both *T. pumilus* and *T. yunnanensis* are useful lower growing species.

X. Opposite *A large perennial garden is bright with color. Purple globe-thistle, red bee-balm, pink phlox and coreopsis are in full bloom, with annual calliopsis. The large clump of rudbeckia (left front) will produce abundant yellow flowers until frost.*

Tunica Saxifraga

Valeriana officinalis

TUFTED PANSY—See *Viola cornuta*.

TUNICA

Although there are about 30 species of this genus of the Pink Family (Caryophyllaceae), only *T. Saxifraga* and its varieties are cultivated. The single pink form is easily raised from seed, but the double white as well as the double deep pink kinds are increased by division in summer. June sees the greatest blooming of these 6 inch rock plants, but flowers are produced intermittently until fall. However, the thin foliage is seldom in good condition after midsummer. Full sun and any well-drained soil.

VALERIANA—Valerian.

In old gardens, this genus of the Valerian Family (Valerianaceae) is represented by *V. officinalis*, Common Valerian, Garden Heliotrope. It will grow in any soil, and does not mind a little shade. Heavily fragrant, light lavender flowers are borne on 4-5 foot stems in midsummer. Finely cut foliage. Occasionally attacked by black mites and affected by crown rot. Cats are especially fond of the shallow roots. In spite of these troubles, the plant is everlasting. Staking is needed in windy gardens. Divide after flowering. Self-sowing is also common.

VERBASCUM—Mullein.

The most familiar species of this genus of the Figwort Family (Scrophulariaceae) is the immense yellow weed, *V. Thapsus*. Although the plant is of small value in bloom, the felty, basal foliage rosette provides an effective accent all summer. Several other species have equally limited garden value, but in a well-drained soil and given full sun, such hybrids as Pink Domino, 4 feet tall, are attractive in late June and July. Miss Willmott is a fine 5-6 foot tall white, while the Cotswold group displays shades of yellow to copper on stems under 4 feet tall. All cultivated varieties are increased by root cuttings made in spring.

VERBENA

Most species of this genus of the Vervain Family (Verbenaceae) are grown as annuals in the North. However, *V. bonariensis* may survive in moderate winters. Even if it does not, self-sown seedlings will carry on. Showy purple flowers are carried on the 3 foot plants all summer.

V. corymbosa, also 3 feet tall, bears bluish-purple flowers over a similar long period. It does very well with plentiful moisture, and is often surprisingly hardy. Increased from seed and cuttings, as is *V. hastata*. Varies from 3-5 feet. Violet spikes through late summer.

VERONICA—Speedwell.
This genus of the Figwort Family (Scrophulariaceae) contains several weeds as well as some excellent garden plants. The species may be divided. Raised from seed, they can be expected to show considerable difference among their progeny. Named varieties are increased by division after flowering. All are easy in full sun or light shade and average, well-drained garden soil, but many low growers suffer unless adequate summer moisture is available. Taller forms, which are best staked, provide good cut flowers. This tall group's foliage often looks poorly as the summer advances. Nomenclature of Veronicas is rather confusing, many species having two or more synonyms.

V. incana. One of the most attractive of low growers with deep blue spikes carried a foot above gray foliage in early summer.

V. latifolia. Better known as *V. Teucrium.* Highly variable, both in height and color. It is better to select cultivated varieties such as Royal Blue or Crater Lake Blue, whatever their true parentage may be rather than plant the uncertain species.

V. longifolia. Two foot tall var. *subsessilis*, July flowering, is deeper blue than the type, but cultivated varieties are more desirable. Sunny Border Blue, Blue Champion, Blue Peter and Blue Spire are all good, while rose-pink Barcarolle and light pink Minuet are also outstanding. Icicle remains the favorite white. Most modern Veronicas bloom through much of summer.

V. prostrata. Long known as *V. rupestris*, this species bears light blue 6-8 inch spikes over a long midsummer period.

Verbascum

Verbena hybrid

Veronica subsessilis

Vinca minor

V. repens. One of the bluest of prostrate Veronicas. Other color forms less desirable. May blooming.

V. spicata. Like *V. longifolia,* this is now overshadowed by the large family of hybrids noted above, so its white and rose-pink forms are seldom seen, although the blue form is still found in old gardens.

Veronicastrum virginicum, Culver's Root, often appears in catalogs as *Veronica virginica.* In any case it is a cool, white perennial for the late summer garden. However, its 4-5 feet height makes it hard to place.

VERVAIN—See *Verbena.*

VINCA—Periwinkle.
This genus of the Dogbane Family (Apocynaceae) needs no introduction. Except for Pachysandra, no ground cover is more familiar than evergreen *V. minor,* which displays bright lavender-blue flowers in spring and intermittently through the growing season. Vinca grows in any soil or exposure, but looks best when planted in rich, humusy soil and given partial shade. It has no shortcoming other than a tendency to discolor in severe, open winters. Easily divided at any time. A host of varieties, including a beautiful white and the large-flowered Bowles Variety.

VIOLA—Violet.
Although this genus of the Violet Family (Violaceae) contains many weedy species and some others that are only half-hardy, it continues to be one of the best loved of all genera. An enormous genus with hundreds of species, Viola is perhaps most effectively represented in the perennial border by the many cultivated varieties of *V. cornuta.* These are easily raised from seed, but they are intolerant of hot summers or open, wet winters. Humus, moisture, shade and shearing after the first rush of May and June blooms will help them greatly. Cut back severely, fertilize and water to produce more and better flowers. Chantryland is a handsome apricot, while Arkwright Ruby and White Perfection are other members of a long list of useful varieties.

V. odorata is available in many colors—white as well as several shades of pink and purple. Like *V. cornuta*, these are useful low edging plants, but they are best increased by division.

VIRGINIA BLUE BELLS—See *Mertensia virginica*.

WILD BLEEDING-HEART—See *Dicentra eximea*.

WOODRUFF—See *Asperula*.

YARROW—See *Achillea*.

YUCCA
This genus of the Agave Family (Agavaceae) contains several warm-climate species, but only one, *Y. Smalliana*, usually appears in northern gardens. It is better known as *Y. filamentosa*. Numerous bell-like white flowers appear briefly in late summer on stems averaging 6 feet tall. Yucca can be raised slowly from seed, or small plants may be separated from the parents' base. Swordlike evergreen leaves make a strong garden accent. Easily raised in full sun and light soil.

ZAUSCHNERIA
The chief species of this genus of the Evening Primrose Family (Onagraceae) is *Z. californica*, with bright red flowers borne in late summer on foot high stems. Useful only for warm areas in light soil. Increased by cuttings made before or after flowering.

Yucca Smalliana

Zauschneria californica

Viola   Hearts-Ease

Part II

Garden Housekeeping, Planning and Planting

1

Basic Garden Procedures

A place to live, good food, fresh air, some covering against the exigencies of climate, and a few basic health practices—these are as important to the flora of the world as to the fauna. In many respects, therefore, this chapter on soil, food, mulches, staking and pruning is the most important one in the book.

TEST AND IMPROVE SOIL

It will be well worth the effort involved to have your soil tested. Use an inexpensive home-testing kit or mail a representative pint of dry soil in a cardboard container to your State Experiment Station or local Extension Service (both listed under United States Department of Agriculture). Most soils need more organic matter or humus which lighten heavy clay soil, give better drainage, and increase water-retention capacity of sandy soil. Well-rotted manure, peat moss, leafmold (rotted leaves), and compost are the materials most commonly used. Soil well supplied with organic matter is of a good texture, friable, and easily worked. Plants quickly respond by richer growth and larger flowers. Since most nutrients enter a plant through the roots, the better the root system, the more nutrients can be absorbed.

If soil tends to bake hard When dry, use 50 lbs. ground limestone to 1,000 sq. ft. or a large shovelful to an area 10 x 10 feet. Work or spade this into the soil to a substantial depth.

Most plants grow best in a soil with a pH between 6.5 and 7.0, about neutral. The pH designates the degree of soil acidity or alkalinity, a pH of 7.0 indicates a neutral condition. Above this figure, it becomes increasingly alkaline; pH 8.5 is very alkaline. Below 7.0 it becomes increasingly acid; pH 3.5 is extremely acid.

To make soil more alkaline, add lime. Unleached wood ashes, a form of lime not a fertilizer, also sweeten sour soils. To bring a slightly acid soil to neutral, use 10 lbs. ground limestone per sq. ft.; to make it strongly alkaline, use 20 lbs.

To make soil more acid, add aluminum sulphate or powdered sulphate. Use 2¾ lbs. aluminum sulphate per 100 sq. ft. to bring a slightly alkaline soil to neutral. Flowers of sulphur can be used to make the soil more acid. It is cheap and easily available, but takes longer to be effective. Apply at ½ the rate given for aluminum sulphate.

If drainage is very poor, break up the hardpan at the bottom of the bed or border and use a bottom layer of 3 to 4 inches of stone or coarse gravel before refilling the bed with the enriched soil.

If the soil is very poor, and you must keep costs and labor to a minimum, a few important plants may be strategically placed on "made" soil at some focal areas with effective results.

PREPARING THE SOIL

At least a week or more before planting any perennials, preferably in the fall, prepare the soil properly; this will be well worth your time and effort in end results. Many perennials are deep rooted and will suffer much less from midsummer drought if their roots are in cool, moisture-laden soil. Also, advance planting gives soil time to settle.

1. Place a large piece of canvas or an old sheet next to the flower bed. Dig out soil onto the canvas a few shovelfuls at a time. Mix in humus and fertilizer to improve the soil. One-fourth humus by volume is a good proportion to use with topsoil. Then enrich with some good chemical fertilizer. For

amount of fertilizer to use, follow directions on the package. Then mix soil, humus and fertilizer thoroughly.

2. Continue digging to a depth of 18 to 24 inches. Return improved soil to bed and dig out another block until you have taken care of the whole border.

3. If there is a large area to spade, rent a rotary cultivator in the fall when they aren't in such great demand as in the spring. This will be far easier than hand-spading.

WHEN TO PLANT AND TRANSPLANT

Most gardeners plant perennials in the spring, when the urge, enthusiasm and excitement of gardening take hold. The late-flowering and less hardy sorts, as well as those with evergreen foliage are usually best moved in the spring. Other perennials not usually transplanted in the fall in northern states, include *Anemone japonica,* aster, ceratostigma, late-flowering chrysanthemums, shasta daisy, helenium, and monarda.

However, except for plants like the above, midsummer and early fall planting is often advisable. There is not as much work to be done in the garden in the autumn, and the soil works more easily. The summer warmth still retained in the soil induces root action. If plants are transferred early enough, they should be well established by spring and start into growth earlier and with better root systems. Thus they are better able to withstand dry spells the following summer.

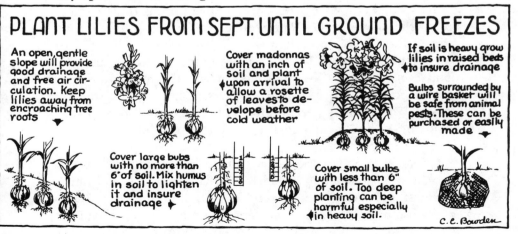

PLANT LILIES FROM SEPT. UNTIL GROUND FREEZES

An open, gentle slope will provide good drainage and free air circulation. Keep lilies away from encroaching tree roots

Cover madonnas with an inch of soil and plant upon arrival to allow a rosette of leaves to develope before cold weather

If soil is heavy grow lilies in raised beds to insure drainage

Bulbs surrounded by a wire basket will be safe from animal pests. These can be purchased or easily made

Cover large bulbs with no more than 6" of soil. Mix humus in soil to lighten it and insure drainage

Cover small bulbs with less than 6" of soil. Too deep planting can be harmful especially in heavy soil.

C. C. Bowden

Fall planting or transplanting should be done at least four or six weeks before freezing weather; two months would be even better, so that plants become established before freezing weather sets in. Resting plants do not take hold of the soil and when not established will heave unless mulched. If set out late, give protection the first winter. In dry sections where there are severe drying winds, new beds should be thoroughly soaked soon after planting and then mulched to retain as much moisture as possible.

If it is necessary to move plants during the summer, cut them back some. Do not transplant in moist soil which may cake around them, but add plenty of water after transplanting until roots have taken hold.

FEEDING

After growing a crop of perennials on a piece of ground for one season, for vigorous plant growth the following season replenish the soil with some organic matter and a commercial fertilizer. Well-rotted cow manure has long been a favorite but it is now expensive and hard to get. Present-day gardeners find a compost of decayed vegetable and plant material complemented with a commercial fertilizer equally good. Sulphate of ammonia is used as a substitute for the old-fashioned liquid manure, one ounce in 2 gallons of water. It is powerful and quick-acting and ½ lb. to 100 sq. ft. is ample.

Many good all-purpose fertilizers under various trade names are on the market today. These chemical fertilizers have a numerical formula of three figures as 5-10-5 which indicate the percentages in alphabetical order of nitrogen, phosphorus and potassium, the three essential elements in the mixture. Some are compounded for fast action, others release their elements gradually over a long period. Most are made so that part of the fertilizing value is available at once, the remainder at a slower rate.

Bonemeal is one of the safest general fertilizers for flowers; because it is slow acting there is little danger that it will burn plants. It is especially recommended for bulbs. Superphosphate is also useful for all sorts of flowers. Too much nitrogen causes plants to make tall, spindly soft growth, an abundance of foliage, and poor flowers. Always work or rake the fertilizer into the soil and then add water to dissolve it.

Some people apply a fertilizer only in early spring using a shallow application of humus and one of the slowly available fertilizers. Fertilizers must be soluble in water to be available to the plants, so always water them well into the soil. Read directions on bag or package for method of application and quantity to use. Some people apply a fertilizer in three installments.

In general, use 2 to 3 lbs. for every 100 sq. ft., 1/3 at time of planting, 1/3 when first growth comes, and 1/3 just as plants commence to bloom. Do not overuse as there can be injury from over-application. "A pint is a pound the world around." You may find it easier to measure than to weigh.

Dirt gardeners who have had practice prefer to broadcast the fertilizer evenly by hand, feeling this is the easiest method of application. Apply carefully around specimen plants and distribute along the sides of rows using smaller applications, two weeks apart to avoid the burning of young foliage. Do not have fertilizer on foliage as it may kill or injure the leaves. Rake in and water immediately after application.

Fertilizer can be applied by means of cartridges attached to the garden hose but care must be taken to apply evenly. Foliar fertilizer applications (fertilizers in solution sprayed on the foliage), require special equipment, and are not a timesaver to the average gardener. This method requires more applications for equal results.

In porous soil or in very rainy seasons, additional fertilizing may be needed. Sprinkle light applications around each clump, hoe in gently and water.

WATERING

Water is essential for the intake of nutrients from the soil. If the soil has been properly prepared, watered and mulched, watering should be necessary only during dry spells; however, perennials can not survive without moisture in the soil and wilting generally means dryness. Many plants may be encouraged to bloom a second time with a little water and fertilizer for encouragement.

Frequent light watering does more harm than good. A soil

soaker applies moisture with little evaporation or runoff. The water seeps slowly into the ground where it is needed. To water the perennial border properly, give each plant a slow soak, a good long drink. Deep watering encourages deep rooting. Roots near the soil surface are susceptible to the hot sun and these surface-feeding roots may parch. Shallow-rooted plants like monarda will need more frequent watering than deep-rooted plants such as baptisia.

Since disease spores germinate readily on wet foliage, water at a time when the leaves will quickly dry, well before sunset if possible. However, evening watering is better than none at all. Water, air, warm temperature and light are necessary to plant growth.

CULTIVATING

About a week or so after planting lightly cultivate, that is, dig into the top inch of soil with a hoe or scratcher to uproot any young weeds. Occasional cultivation throughout the season is usually necessary to remove weeds. Hoe gently, as deep cultivation may damage shallow-rooted perennials. Mulches keep down weeds and eliminate the need of cultivating.

SUMMER MULCHING

Since chemical weed killers or herbicides can harm perennials, more and more gardeners use summer mulches to keep the weeds down, spreading an inch or two of mulch loosely over the border between plants. These mulches tend to discourage weeds and conserve the moisture in the soil. Apply only after the soil has first been well soaked. If a few weeds do come up, pull them out by hand.

There are no set rules for the depth of a mulch. It depends on the type of mulch and soil. A sandy, gravelly soil needs a thicker mulch than heavy, clay soil. Experiment. You will want a mulch deep enough to kill weeds and prevent the soil from drying out, yet not too deep to prevent air and water from reaching the surface soil. Apply a summer mulch well before the summer droughts and before the weeds start active growth. A mulch should last for several years.

WINTER MULCHING

Extreme cold is not entirely responsible for winter killing of perennials. Plants are protected not to keep them from freezing but to keep the soil cold. There are several factors that are responsible for winter killing of perennials. The alternate freezing and thawing of the soil creates much damage if the roots are not deeply anchored, since this causes plants to be lifted from the soil, exposing the roots to extreme cold and drying. A covering of snow which remains on the ground until spring serves as an ideal mulch or protection, keeping the soil cold.

Drying winds are injurious to perennials which keep their foliage through the winter. Water standing on the crown will kill most perennials. Low temperatures may kill the less hardy. Warm spells will encourage permanent growth too early and extended rains may induce rot.

The purpose of a winter mulch is to maintain a solidly frozen border all during the winter. For less hardy perennials, winter covering will be necessary. Protection is best applied after the ground freezes hard. The plants will then remain frozen. A mulch applied too early will cause perennials to make a soft growth during the warm days of fall and may also invite mice into the beds. More tender perennials are best removed to the coldframes for the winter. Care must be taken not to smother plants with a mulch that will mat and exclude air. After the first year, delphiniums, irises, peonies, Oriental poppies and many other perennials do not need protection; day-lilies never need a covering.

In late fall when stalks wither, cut them back to 3 to 4 inches; the stubs catch and hold any winter cover used. Any old foliage or material that might be infected should be burned to prevent carrying over insects or diseases.

A 3- to 4-inch mulch with evergreen boughs or tree branches as weights to prevent wind loss of lighter mulches is advised. Mounds of sand or ashes placed over crowns of delphiniums will prevent rotting. The thickness of the winter mulch is not too important with perennials which die to the ground, but for evergreen perennials like iberis only a light mulch is recommended. Care must be taken not to exclude light or the plants could be severely injured.

More perennials are injured by cold in the spring than in the winter. Loosen but do not remove the winter mulch on the first warm days of spring. Uncover the perennial border gradually. Take off the mulch when the last killing frost is passed.

In the south, winter protection is needed in many cases to keep plants from starting into growth during premature hot spells.

SUITABLE MULCHES

The type of mulch to use will be influenced by your location, the weather in your area, what results you are after and cost, usually determined by availability. Experiment to find which of the following work best for you.

1. *Buckwheat Hulls*—A 1" summer mulch is good and may be retained through the winter, but do not use buckwheat hulls around small succulents that grow flat on the ground. Since the hulls are black they absorb the heat on a hot summer day and leaves coming in contact with them might burn. Crushed gray stones around succulents is good.

Mrs. Edward G. Howe, New Vernon, New Jersey, endorses this material: "There is very little work to do once the planning and planting is done for the season. I am a firm believer in mulch and use buckwheat hulls generously. They have more than paid for themselves in the droughts we have had. The garden survives very well indeed while the lawn has turned to brown nothing. And as I am the gardener, I appreciate not having to weed constantly."

2. *Cocoa Shells*—If you live near a chocolate factory the shells from the cocoa bean which are light, dry and easily handled should be inexpensive. If their potash content will not be injurious to the plants you are growing, they will make a good mulch. A mulch of 2" to 3" will retain soil moisture and control weeds.

3. *Coffee Grounds*—They are so fine that they will cake, so never make an application of more than 1" deep.

4. *Cranberry Vines*—On Cape Cod where cranberry vines are plentiful they are used as a winter mulch held in place by evergreen boughs. Wiry and light, they never pack.

5. *Evergreen Boughs*—Where plentiful, evergreen boughs are

are excellent for a winter mulch. They do not mat down and thereby provide adequate aeration.

6. *Grass Clippings*—If used too green and too deep, grass clippings will heat up and form a dense mat. They are better on the compost heap.

7. *Ground Corncobs*—In corn-growing and rural areas ground corncobs are easily obtainable and very cheap. Apply to a depth of 2″ to 3″.

8. *Leaves*—Leaves are nature's own mulch and practical because they are always plentiful. Dried leaves are combustible and also may blow away, sometimes the larger kinds are unsightly. Results in many cases are better if the leaves are broken up or ground. Do not use too deep mulches of soft leaves such as poplar, willow, and maple as they tend to pack tightly and are also likely to rot. A few inches of oak leaves are ideal for mulching because they do not pack so tightly. Elm and maple leaves may have a slightly alkaline reaction.

9. *Paper Mulch*—Made up in rolls of various widths, paper mulch is efficient for large-scale planting in rows and was originally used on Hawaiian pineapple fields. It is also sold in squares provided with a slit in the center for slipping over individual plants.

10. *Peanut Shells*—Peanut shells are used in southeastern United States. They are lightweight and easily handled.

11. *Peat Moss*—Although peat moss is widely used as a mulch, when dry it becomes impermeable and water runs off to other areas. If it is moist it absorbs much of the water itself with only some reaching the soil below. Roots will form in the moist mulch of peat. This shallow rooting process is detrimental to some plants since they are more easily damaged in winter and dry out in summer. Once roots form in a mulch it becomes a part of the soil medium and no longer serves as a mulch. Peat is used for acid-soil plants.

12. *Pine Needles*—In pine-growing areas, pine needles are plentiful, easily lifted and applied with rake and fork. Use a depth of 3″ or 4″. Excellent for acid-loving perennials, white pine has soft flexible needles which make a very fine mulch. Red pine needles are coarser and may not deteriorate for 3 or 4 years. No weeds will grow in them, yet rain and air will filter through to the soil.

13. *Polyethylene Film and Aluminum Foil*—These may be used between straight beds of plants or around single plants to prevent water from evaporating. Black polyethylene film has all the properties of the clear plastic except that it excludes light so prevents all weeds from growing. Since it does not let water into the soil after it is in place on the ground, punch holes at 6" intervals with an ice pick or make a few knife cuts in depressions to allow rain water to drain into the soil. For mulching, use a thickness of .015 inch. Watch out so field mice do not get underneath. In the fall, plastic film can be lifted and stored for use again. If handled carefully it will last 4 years or so.

14. *Salt Hay*—Salt hay as a winter covering provides a light, yet dense mulch and is largely used by commercial growers of pansies. It must be raked off in the spring and stored for future use or burned.

15. *Sawdust*—If you live near a lumber mill and sawdust is cheap, use it as a 2" to 3" mulch. It will break down and become humus. However, apply a generous application of a complete fertilizer to the soil before applying the sawdust. Otherwise its use may result in a nitrogen deficiency in the soil, causing yellow foliage and stunted growth. After several years when sawdust deteriorates, apply more fertilizer and sawdust.

16. *Wood Chips and Wood Shavings*—Use them 2"-3" deep. They will last 2 years or longer. As with sawdust, fertilize first. Chips are preferable to shavings since they are coarser, less flammable, less subject to blow away in high winds and less apt to pack.

Lumber companies grind up the bark of redwood, pine, yellow birch and other trees; an inexpensive mulch if you live near a lumber company.

17. *Spent Hops*—If you are near a brewery you can obtain spent hops for the hauling. Never apply wet on a real hot day of 90° or above as the material heats noticeably. Keep it about 12" away from the basal stems. A mulch 4"-6" thick will last a couple of years before disintegrating appreciably.

18. *Sugar Cane*—If you are near a sugar mill, ground cane can be used as a mulch. It decomposes into almost pure humus. Use 2" thick.

19. *A Mulch of Perennials*—Mrs. Paul A. Younge, Wellesley Hills, Mass., points out in answer to our questionnaire that per-

ennial plants make a good mulch for shrubs. She says: "Our garden is shaded, has mostly acid soil and is for the larger part planted in flowering shrubs with underplantings of such perennials as wild bleeding-heart, lily-of-the-valley, shortais, false Solomons-seal *(Smilacina)* and violet which form a living, green mulch for shallow rooted shrubs."

ADVANTAGES OF MULCHES

1. After the first application, should cut down on labor by lessening the need for weeding and watering.
2. Reduce weed growth.
3. Reduce water loss from the soil.
4. Keep soil cool in the summer.
5. Keep soil cold in winter and prevent alternate thawing and freezing.

POSSIBLE DISADVANTAGES OF MULCHES

1. Might it keep rain from entering the ground? Water must seep through to the soil underneath.
2. Will mulch dry out and blow away?
3. Is it a fire hazard?
4. Is it too expensive?
5. Will it look well?
6. Crowns of herbaceous plants may become imbedded too deeply?
7. Excellent place for disease spores to winter and multiply but if garden is kept clean there is little danger of this. If it does become infected remove mulch and burn.
8. It can harbor insects and rodents.
9. May it encourage late fall growth, delaying hardening and maturing processes of the plant? May it also slow up early growth in spring?
10. A mulch that packs down or cakes and excludes air could do more harm than good. Feeding roots need air which must seep through mulch to soil underneath.

STAKING

The taller, more slender perennials may need staking. On the market today are many good supports that will encircle the whole plant loosely. Make the support inconspicuous, never obvious. Bamboo canes make good stakes. Paint or buy them green and place in the center of clumps or use in other ingenious ways to keep everything looking natural and unsupported. Raffia tied first to the stake and then loosely around the stems will give a natural effect. Tall, slender plants tending to bend in strong winds will require staking both for appearance and safety. Some of the heavy double peonies will need a support. Low-growing perennials which are inclined to sprawl are best supported by digging inconspicuous twiggy branches of shrubs and trees into soil among the plants. Supports should be placed in position before the stems begin to lean.

REMOVE FADED FLOWERS AND SEED PODS

To continue and stretch the season of bloom, and to economize the strength of the plant, prevent seeding, for it is hard work to produce seed. Removal of the old, faded flowers also keeps the garden looking tidy and neat. Snip off only the flower or flower cluster as the foliage below will continue to manufacture food. It is wise to burn the old flowers in case they harbor any insects or disease.

CUT BACK FOR SECOND BLOOM

When through flowering, cut back stalks of perennials to encourage a second crop. If this is done promptly and after a 2-

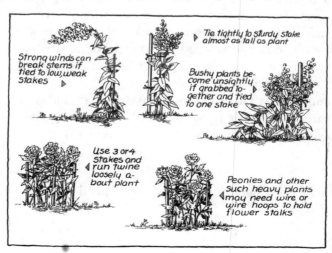

Strong winds can break stems if tied to low, weak stakes

Tie tightly to sturdy stake almost as tall as plant

Bushy plants become unsightly if grabbed together and tied to one stake

Use 3 or 4 stakes and run twine loosely about plant

Peonies and other such heavy plants may need wire or wire hoops to hold flower stalks

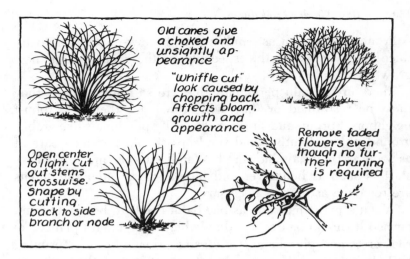

Old canes give a choked and unsightly appearance

"Whiffle cut" look caused by chopping back. Affects bloom, growth and appearance

Remove faded flowers even though no further pruning is required

Open center to light. Cut out stems crosswise. Shape by cutting back to side branch or node

weeks rest a complete fertilizer is worked in around the plants a second bloom will appear on many. *Anchusa Azurea* sheared back at least 6″ from the tops of the plants, after their first blooming period, will encourage them to bloom again.

THINNING, PINCHING, DISBUDDING, PRUNING

With multiple-flowered plants, notably the hardy delphinium, aster, helenium and phlox, superior flowers and plants are developed if stems are thinned to about four in each clump, soon after they appear above the ground, eliminating the weak shoots which wouldn't do well anyway. This sends more strength into the remaining stems.

Pinching out or removing the tip or terminal shoots with thumbnail and finger is practiced with flowers as the aster and chrysanthemum to promote bushiness and reduce the ultimate height.

If you are interested in larger flowers, the side buds of some plants which never amount to much anyway, as the peony, should be removed as soon as they are large enough to handle. This concentrates the strength in the terminal buds. This procedure of disbudding is used with the carnation (not the cluster-flower type), large-flowered chrysanthemums and dahlias. Disbudding is practiced if you want large flowers for exhibition purposes. Pinch off the lateral or side buds as soon as they form, leaving only the terminal or top buds.

Prune plants such as candytuft and snow-in-summer to induce thick new growth, especially in the rock garden; new growth is rapid.

There are certain perennials that are so rambunctious they must be restrained or they will crowd out their less robust neighbors. Spring- and summer-flowering perennials like arabis, ground phlox, dianthus and sundrops should be taken care of as soon as they have flowered. Watch late-bloomers and late-starters such as bellflower and plumbago so offending shoots are removed as soon as necessary.

When a perennial such as bee-balm needs to be pruned and curbed it should be dug up, divided and reset. With plants like rock-cress and plumbago (*Ceratostigma*) simply use a pruning knife to cut out the encroaching shoots at or near the base. Try to maintain the natural habit and appearance of the plant and not have it look shorn.

Some plants can be restrained by chopping around them with a sharp spade. Plants like gypsophila, the day-lily and others set out near Oriental poppies to hide the dying foliage of the latter, should be watched in the fall and cut back, as the new leaves of the poppies appear, to give the poppy leaves space and light.

Prune spring-flowering vines just after they flower in the spring to encourage new and better growth. For late summer- or fall-blooming varieties, prune while dormant in the winter or in early spring, just before the leaf buds open and just as growth is starting. This will encourage better and stronger shoots.

BREAK UP LARGE CLUMPS

Even though there are many perennials which would persist indefinitely, in many cases they produce much better results if dug up, divided and reset as the need arises. When a clump gets too big, crowded and weak, when it seems to be dying in the middle, or when display of bloom is less lavish, dig it up and pull it apart. Replant the good sections separately or give them to a friend. This need not be a lot of work if you take one genus at a time. Always be sure to have well-developed roots on the clumps you save. This rehabilitation process is beneficial for many rampant growers such as chrysanthemums, some asters, helenium and physostegia if done annually. When the

Above   Cut off two inches of root before replanting shoots.

Above.   When clumps are six inches high, lift with garden fork and shake free of soil.

Below.   As laterals form, snip off half-inch of each for compact plants that flower heavily.

Below.   Replant 12″ apart.

soil has thawed in the spring dig up old plants of hardy 'mums and divide. Replant 12″ apart.

The performance of each clump will determine when division is necessary. While not a hard and fast rule, in general divide spring-blooming perennials in late August or early September and late-blooming plants in early spring as soon as the frost is out of the ground.

Bearded iris and primrose, both early-blooming, may be successfully divided a few weeks after flowering. Whenever done, water carefully until new roots have developed and the clump is well established.

PUT GARDEN TO BED

Some gardeners like to let 3″ or 4″ of top growth (stalks) remain in the border to catch the snow which is an ideal cover, or to hold the winter mulch in place since tops prevent wind from blowing it away.

If there are no diseases, insect pests or seeds of weeds, the material pulled up or cut from the border can be laid flat on the ground to serve as a mulch. Many people, however, prefer to use such material on a compost heap where it will disintegrate more quickly.

The tendency today, when tidying the border for winter, is to cut all top growth level with the ground with a scythe when frost comes, then to use a winter mulch if necessary. Beds look neat and tidy this way and are quickly and easily done. Be careful not to smother plants with a too heavy cover or one that mats and excludes air.

2

Insect and Disease Pests

To keep perennials healthy learn to recognize and control the common pests and diseases. This is not too difficult. No one material will cure everything, but there are some "all-purpose" or combination sprays and dusts on the market which provide good control. These all-purpose compounds accomplish in one operation what would otherwise require separate applications. Use these in either a liquid or powder form, whichever you choose.

DUSTING

For the amateur, dusting is usually preferable to spraying. Dusts are handier in small quantities for quick jobs. Dusters are lighter and easier to carry, and easily assembled, operated and cleaned. Dusts are usually pre-mixed and it is unnecessary to wash out equipment after use. Unused dusts may be left in the duster until the next application is needed.

Only light applications are necessary and should be applied when the air is still. Good all-purpose compounds may be purchased. They may contain DDT, rotenone, sulphur, Aramite, and ferbam. Another mixture is DDT, Captan, Karathane, and Malathion.

A good plunger-type duster equipped with a deflector plate to direct the flow of dust at the angle desired is advisable. A two-quart dust gun or a bellows or crank type are good. Some dusts, packed in inexpensive cardboard cylinders fitted with dispensers, eliminate the need to transfer the dust to a regular garden duster. They work well, but are not economical unless only a small quantity is needed.

SPRAYING

Most commercial operators with large areas to control use sprays. Spray materials are sold either as powders to be mixed with water or as liquid concentrates to be diluted with water. The liquid concentrates are easier to prepare than the powders, and leave less noticeable residue on plants. However, they must be applied exactly as directed or they may burn the foliage.

Professional gardeners prefer sprays over dusts because weather conditions at the time of spraying are less important, sprays are more economical from the standpoint of coverage, they provide longer protection since the dried residue is more resistant to changing weather and if one makes up his own all-purpose spray the ingredients are easier to combine than dusts in a duster.

Buy a well-made sprayer adequate for your particular job. Then operate, clean and store as recommended by the manufacturer for long-time service. Spray tanks must be cleaned after each treatment.

Spray bombs now on the market are handy for treating a few plants or spot infections, but are not economical if a large area is to be covered.

GOOD DISEASE PREVENTIVES

Diseases are more easily prevented than cured so take the necessary preventive steps to avoid unnecessary trouble and disappointments.

1. Properly grown, healthy plants. Sickly, overcrowded plants are susceptible to disease and the most seriously affected.
2. Sunlight.
3. Proper air circulation.
4. Destroy, by burning, any diseased parts of a plant.

5. Spray or dust to prevent the spread of disease to other plants.

FUNGICIDES AND INSECTICIDES

Fungicides are designed to combat diseases caused by fungi, while insecticides are used to combat insects. Neither can fulfill the purpose of the other, so they are combined in many of the products on the market today. DDT, hailed as a cure-all during the last war, was found not to be, but is still used as a general insecticide for beetles, worms and caterpillar-type pests. It is not recommended for fruits and vegetables. Methoxychlor serves the same purpose as DDT and is safer. Residual poison is not as long-lasting as DDT. Certain insects with continued exposure to DDT become less easily killed, building up an immunity to it.

Plants become diseased when they are prey to fungi and harmful bacteria. Viruses will cause them to be stunted, marked with a mosaic-like pattern or golden-yellowing of branches. These viruses are carried by infected insects which puncture the plants to their destruction. Plants so infested cannot have the affected part removed as a control, because the virus is all through the plant. Such plants must be pulled up and destroyed. Aphids or plant lice and leafhoppers are the main carriers, so get rid of them. Materials to control insect pests are all poisonous. None should be used carelessly. Read all information on the container carefully and follow the manufacturer's directions.

Ants—If ants become annoying, treat the soil around the plants with a dust or solution of nicotine sulphate, chlordane or lindane. Ants may spread fungus spores so should be eliminated.

Aphids—These plant lice live on plants, suck their juices and are one of the main carriers of virus diseases, so get rid of them. They like lupines, golden-glow, etc. Use an insecticide as malathion (one of the better insecticides), Black Leaf 40 (highly poisonous), rotenone or pyrethrum, (both have low toxicity to humans). The latter two should not be kept over from season to season as they lose their value after long storage, as does malathion.

Beetle, Blister—This black beetle, ⅝" long, sometimes found on asters, dahlias and calendulas, may be controlled by dusting with DDT, methoxychlor, rotenone and lindane (poisonous so handle with care).

Beetle, Japanese—Hand pick, knock the insects into a can containing water and kerosene, and spray with combined DDT and malathion, or methoxychlor or Sevin. Also treat the soil. Chlordane may be applied to the soil as a dust or granules as well as a spray to control beetle grubs. This will also discourage moles that live on grubs.

Borer, Iris—This is really a large cutworm. Over-winters in the egg stage, larvae hatch in spring, feed on leaves and gradually bore down to the rhizome. Cut and burn leaves if seen in the early stage, kill the borers if found in the stem, or if found in rhizomes when plants are being divided.

Cutworms—These insects chew off the plant near the surface of the ground. Dust plant with DDT or methoxychlor and soil with chlordane or lindane (poisonous).

Leafhopper—Leaping insects which suck the juice of plants. Main carriers of viruses so kill them by using DDT or methoxychlor, malathion (relatively safe to handle) or lindane.

Leaf Miner—Troublesome with columbine and other perennials. Use malathion, DDT, methoxychlor or lindane (poisonous so handle with care).

Mites—Thiodan or endrin are good miticides.

Cyclamen Mite—Destructive to delphiniums. Use Thiodan which is quite safe to handle or malathion. Cyclamen mite is an entirely different kind of mite than red spider.

Red Spider Mites—A minute pest, barely visible to the eye, occurring on the foliage of many plants during hot dry weather; particularly injurious to phlox. If foliage has mottled yellow appearance, look at undersides of a leaf with a hand lens. If mites are seen, dust or spray with Aramite (quite safe to handle), Kelthane or malathion.

Nematodes—These tiny eelworms tunnel through the feeding roots, causing irregular swellings or nodules. Infested plants are stunted, weak in growth and pale green. If infested, discard the entire plant and do not plant in the same area. Consult your County Extension Agent about nematicides used to fumigate soil.

Root Lice—White or bluish-green lice on the roots, their presence indicated by weakened growth and yellowish foliage. Form a cup by scraping away a small amount of soil at the base. Pour in ½ cup to 1 cup of dilute Black Leaf 40 spray solution.

Rose Chafer—A beetle which enjoys feeding on the flowers of peonies. Use DDT, methoxychlor, chlordane or Sevin.

Scale—Use malathion in summer; when dormant, use dormant oil spray.

Slugs—These are shell-less snails abundant around seedbeds, rock gardens and shaded spots. Dust metaldehyde on the soil.

Stalk Borers—Striped caterpillars that burrow in the stems of many garden flowers. Get rid of all weeds, old stems and rubbish to control and prevent their occurrence.

Thrips—Minute insects which cause flowers to be malformed and blotched with brown. Spray developing growth of plants subject to thrips at weekly intervals, as soon as they attain 6 inches in height, with DDT, methoxychlor or malathion.

FUNGUS DISEASES AND CONTROLS

The control of fungus diseases depends generally upon the use of fungicides.

Botrytis—Peonies, madonna lilies and some of the other perennials are subject to this fungus disease. One of the copper fungicides should be used to spray the soil and young shoots when they start to grow.

Damping-Off—Avoid getting seeds and seedlings too wet to prevent damping-off disease. Captan is useful for this fungus growth.

Leaf Spot—Use ferbam (Fermate) for leaf spot control. Cleanse skin after using. Maneb (Manzate) and zineb (Parzate) are excellent fungicides.

Mildew—A thin, dirty-white felted mass or growth is produced on the leaves by this fungus. Control with Karathane (also called Mildex) or sulphur. Sulphur, both a fungicide and insecticide, has been largely replaced by ferbam (Fermate), phaltan and Karathane. Karathane will not burn foliage at high temperatures and is much safer in hot weather than sulphur. Karathane is compatible with Aramite, captan, and malathion for a combination dust or spray. Any of the fixed copper compounds (COCS) are good fungicides for mildew.

Mosaic Disease—A virus disease characterized by mottling of the foliage which sometimes affects lilies. Segregate susceptible kinds. Use an insecticide to destroy insects which are capable of transmitting the virus from infected to healthy plants.

Rust—This causes spots or discoloration on leaves and stems. Controlled with captan, maneb (Manzate), zineb (Parzate).

Wilt—Fungus and bacterial diseases characterized by wilting and withering of leaves. Make tip cuttings of strongest shoots in fall or spring and burn the old clumps.

OTHER PESTS AND CONTROLS

Chipmunks—These little animals can be pests in some areas. They dig and eat or carry away the smaller bulbs. Trap and drown, or dust peanut butter with zinc phosphide and drop into holes or put in woodpile or under a piece of wood so birds and pets cannot get it.

Earwigs—Spray surface of soil around plants to keep them in check.

Grasshoppers—If they are causing trouble dust or spray with chlordane.

Mice—Mice often use the mole runs and eat the bulbs. A good commercial bait of zinc phosphide on steamed oats is often recommended.

Moles—Moles cause destruction and much annoyance by burrowing among the flowers. Get rid of their food, grubs and earthworms, by spraying soil with chlordane.

Rabbits—May be kept away by freely using tobacco dust or dried blood along the garden border lines.

Woodchucks—Eliminate by dropping gas cartridge into burrow. Obtain from County Agricultural Agent.

RULES TO OBSERVE

1. Read all the information on the container carefully and use only as directed. All dusts and sprays are poisonous to a greater or lesser degree and cannot be used carelessly. All

sprays and dusts are required by law to be labeled as to contents, degree of toxicity to humans with suggested antidotes, the amounts required and methods of preparation. Read this information carefully and use as directed by the manufacturer.

2. Dusts and sprays should be stored in a dry, cool place out of reach of children. All packages or bottles should be kept tightly sealed, out of direct sunlight and adequately labeled.
3. Do not dust or spray plants when wilted.
4. Do not dust or spray plants when temperature is above 85° F.
5. Dust or spray only to control some pest that is present or one you are certain will appear.
6. Thorough coverage is important. Reach the underside of the leaves so no uncovered areas are left open to attack.
7. Be aware of the dangers that lie in the careless or ignorant handling of dusts and sprays.

Mrs. Don F. Smith, president of the Federated Garden Clubs of Maryland sums up: "I have found that most plants in the perennial border are disease-resistant if the ground is well prepared first with humus, peat moss, cotton seed meal, rock phosphate and bonemeal. If it is well drained and good care is taken in housekeeping (old flower heads removed and destroyed, yellow leaves and stems removed, etc.) the perennial bed is a real pleasure. I use no sprays or dust except on the chrysanthemums."

3

Propagating Perennials

For some people, half the fun in gardening is growing the plants from seed or cuttings. Propagating perennials is relatively easy, and a real economy but it does take time and a little know-how. It is always nice to have a few extras of favorite plants, to fill in bare spots, give to flower loving friends and neighbors, or to donate for sale at charity benefits. To increase your supply of perennials you may propagate from seed or cuttings or by division, depending upon the particular flowers you want to grow. For best methods of propagation specific genera, see Part I.

COLDFRAME

A coldframe is not essential but it can be a big asset. In early spring before outdoor sowing is possible, and again in August and November, biennial and perennial seeds may be sown in flats in the coldframe. It is handy for rooting cuttings in early summer. In winter it will serve to carry over plants, not reliably hardy outdoors, to provide cuttings or divisions in the spring.

The site must be well drained, in a sheltered corner; if possible the frame should slope toward the south. A height of 18″

160

Make the Most of a Coldframe

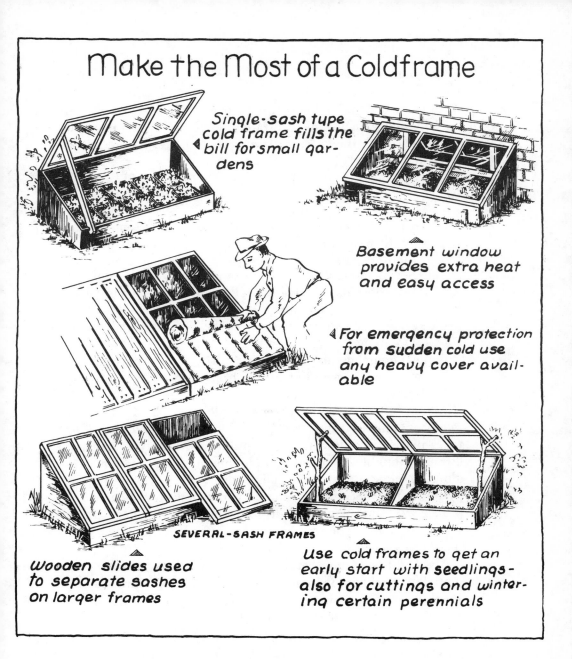

Single-sash type cold frame fills the bill for small gardens

Basement window provides extra heat and easy access

For emergency protection from sudden cold use any heavy cover available

SEVERAL-SASH FRAMES

Wooden slides used to separate sashes on larger frames

Use cold frames to get an early start with seedlings - also for cuttings and wintering certain perennials

at the rear and 12″ in the front will afford a good slope to shed rain and catch the sun's rays. To insure good drainage plan to have the soil 2″-3″ higher than the soil level on the outside of the frame. Use 6″ of a good soil mixture inside the coldframe

161

or for small quantities sow seeds in tin cans or flats filled with soil and set them on a base of sand or cinders for good drainage until the seedlings are ready for transplanting.

A hotbed is a heated coldframe, but most amateurs prefer to manage with the latter, starting a month later and requiring only sun heat.

FROM SEED

Many perennials may be easily grown from seed. Some germinate rapidly within two to three weeks and the plants may bloom the next season. Germination of others as dictamnus or trollius, even though sown at the same time, will be delayed until the warmer days arrive the following spring. Some take a long time to flower. Seedlings of dictamnus, some lilies and peonies may not flower for three to five years, requiring considerable patience.

Other perennials like hemerocallis, iris, peony and phlox do not come true to variety if grown from seed because of their hybrid nature.

A few self-sow. While perennials do not self-sow as commonly as annuals, if the top-soil is well cultivated before seeding takes place the following may reproduce themselves: balloon-flower, columbine, coreopsis, delphinium, forget-me-not, foxglove, gaillardia, heliopsis, hollyhock, lychnis, phlox, poppy, pyrethrum, sweet william, tunica and veronica. When of the proper size, transplant these little seedlings to the place where you want them in your garden. To keep plants from propagating themselves, keep seed from forming.

The right soil temperatures and adequate moisture are essential for seed germination. Some need direct exposure to light, as achillea, centranthus, thyme, valeriana and some of the violas, so will not tolerate deep planting.

For perennials easily grown from seed and those seldom grown from seed see page 166. Decide which perennials you want to grow from seed and order early from a reliable source. Seeds should be stored in a dry, cool place in an air-tight container properly labeled. Envelopes in which seeds are purchased usually state when to sow, list time required for germination, and other pertinent facts, so read printing on envelope carefully.

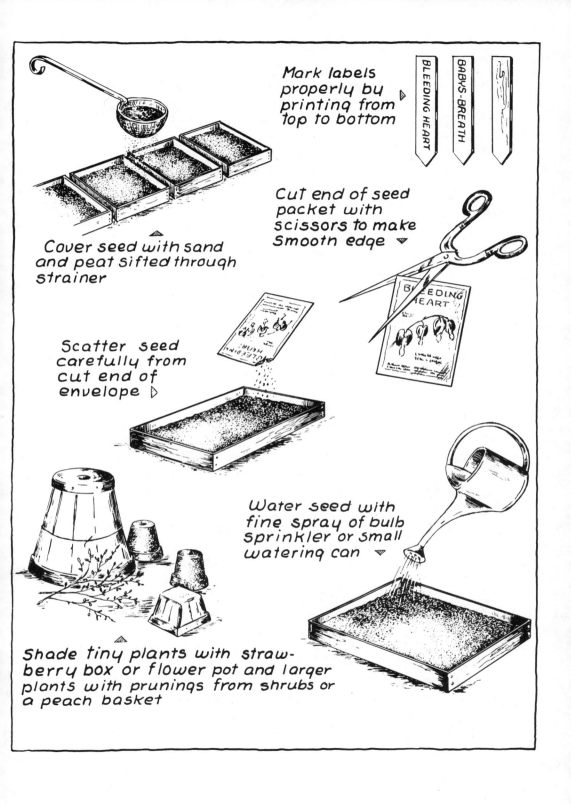

Mark labels properly by printing from top to bottom ▷

BLEEDING HEART

BABY'S-BREATH

Cover seed with sand and peat sifted through strainer

Cut end of seed packet with scissors to make smooth edge ▼

BLEEDING HEART

Scatter seed carefully from cut end of envelope ▷

Water seed with fine spray of bulb sprinkler or small watering can ▼

Shade tiny plants with strawberry box or flower pot and larger plants with prunings from shrubs or a peach basket

Mrs. C. C. Buckbee, past president of the Colorado Federation of Garden Clubs, Inc. says: "I enjoy starting perennials from seed. I have grown *Alyssum saxatile, Coreopsis lanceolata,* heliopsis, iberis and shasta daisy with success."

The Seed Bed

The seed bed or flat is prepared the same for either spring or fall sowings. Prepare a porous soil, mixing one-third peat moss, one-third sharp sand and one-third top soil or loam and add one cup of superphosphate to every bushel of mixture. Use one-half to one inch sifted sphagnum moss over the soil, sow the seed in this and then cover lightly (not over ⅛ inch) with sifted sphagnum moss. Several other weed- and disease-free, sterile materials with good drainage may be used for seed germination such as a clean, sharp sand, or equal parts of clean, sharp sand and sifted peat moss, or a garden grade vermiculite. Sow seeds and keep the soil thoroughly moist until germination. Always place the flat or seed bed in a well-drained location where there is no danger of an accumulation of water.

How and Where to Sow

Do not sow more seed than you need. Sow far enough apart not to crowd, as seedlings need plenty of light. If seeds in seed flats indoors are planted sparsely much tedious thinning later on will be avoided. Properly label all rows of seed. Record date of planting and transplanting on label. If fluorescent light is used it should not be over 6″ above the soil surface. Seed beds placed in a coldframe make an excellent arrangement.

Seeds may be sown in rows or broadcast over the surface using tin cans, flats, coldframes or in the open ground. Sowing in rows is preferable. Slowly germinating varieties are often best sown separately in pots. Make rows about 2 inches apart with seeds barely touching in the row. A 6″ to 12″ row should be ample for most home use. Sow in a shallow furrow $1/16$ to ⅛ inch deep, gently shaking seed from cut end of an envelope. Sift a thin layer of the germinating material over seeds. Cover seeds to a depth equal to three times the diameter of the seed. Very small ones are merely scattered and gently pressed in with a board. Firm lightly with block of wood, water slowly and carefully. If seed is sown in a coldframe in March use glass or plastic sash until danger of frost passes.

Never let seedlings dry out or become too wet. When second or third pair of leaves develop, and they are large enough to handle, transplant them where they will have more space to grow. When well enough along, place in their permanent location in the garden, in the spring after danger of frost is over, allowing adequate distances for proper growth. If transplanted in the fall a light covering of evergreen boughs put on after the ground freezes late in the fall will keep the young plants from heaving.

When To Sow

Our good friend, Dr. R. Milton Carleton, nationally known gardening authority writes—

"I hope that in your book you will inveigh against the silly custom of aping the British by sowing seeds of perennials and biennials in June. In their maritime climate, that is good practice because they have cool nights and not too hot days. But in our continental climate, many perennials simply will not germinate due to too high temperatures, causing failures for which the seedsman is blamed. I always recommend seeding as soon as the soil can be worked and allowing them to grow when proper soil temperatures occur."

EARLY SPRING

Most perennial seeds do well in the relatively cool ground (52°-59°) of early spring. Prepare the soil for the seeds in the fall just before the weather stops outdoor work. Coldframes are not necessary but do provide a protected space easily weeded and cultivated. Adonis, asperula, delphinium, linum and papaver like a cool temperature to germinate. Today specially stored and treated delphinium seeds boast a higher percentage of germination and do well planted in early spring.

The perennials listed below like a steady soil temperature of 68° for seed germination but may be sown at the same time as the above group. They will simply lie in the soil a few weeks longer and germinate when a steady soil temperature of 68° occurs.

Althaea rosea	Gypsophila
Alyssum saxatile	Lathyrus latifolius
Anemone	Lunaria biennis
Anthemis	Lupinus
Armeria	Lychnis
Aster alpinus	Malva
Bellis	Myosotis
Cerastium	Nepeta
Chrysanthemum	Primula
Coreopsis	Ranunculus
Dianthus	Senecio
Doronicum	Silene
Gaillardia	Statice
Gerbera	Thalictrum

Several of these plants germinate erratically. If the seed is fresh, alyssum may do better at 86° days and 68° nights. Anemone is quite unpredictable and may take 80° days to germinate fully. Some seeds of Aster alpinus, doronicum, ranunculus and statice look sound but have no embryo. Don't expect more than a 25% stand on these, although under ideal conditions 50% may germinate.

Seedlings from spring germination may not flower during the first year. The Chinese larkspur, gaillardia, hibiscus, Iceland poppy, lychnis, platycodon and shasta daisy will bloom the first year if the seed is sown as early as the soil is workable; most others however will not. Seeds which ripen late in the season as those of the chrysanthemum are usually held over for spring sowing.

June—Seeds that need fluctuating soil temperatures, fairly warm during the day (86°) and cooler at night (68°) will germinate in June when this soil range is reached in the northern part of the United States. Included in this group are: anchusa, aquilegia, asclepias, Campanula carpatica and pyramidalis, digitalis, echinops, geum, helianthus, heuchera, kniphofia, liatris, penstemon, pyrethrum, rudbeckia and salvia. The biennials digitalis and Campanula Medium may be sown with this group or earlier.

August—Seeds that need 90° days and 55° nights to germinate are best planted in August. This soil temperature range usually occurs in the north in August as the result of the more rapid cooling of the soil as the sun begins its southward swing. These seeds are best placed in coldframes since if frost comes early the coldframe protection allows them to mature to a point where they can stand exposure later to winter temperatures. Several of these do best if the seed is sown on the soil surface exposed to direct light. Moisture can be controlled better if seeds are sown in flats or pots. Achillea, Campanula lactiflora and persicifolia, centranthus, lavandula, thyme, valeriana and viola belong in this August group.

Seeds of a number of plants like the biennials (canterbury bell, English daisy, forget-me-not, hollyhock, pansies and sweet william), lychnis and Oriental poppy that mature by midsummer can be profitably sown as soon as the seeds are ripe in August for bloom next season.

While pansies and violas are best sown in August, if you failed to start them then, you can sow them later. Your seed will not produce spring plants as large as those from early sowings but if you have a shady place to grow them you can have flowers all summer. Transplant seedlings in October.

Fall And Late November—Many perennials sown in the fall, any time before the freeze-up, will bloom late the next summer. Seeds will lie dormant until spring and germinate long before you would be able to start spring operation.

Some seeds will not germinate unless first subjected to a low temperature. Fall planting is recommended for this group. Placing the seed for several weeks in a temperature above freezing but below 42° will work equally well. Seeds which germinate best after cold treatment include aconitum, dicentra, dictamnus, some iris, various lilies, peony, and *Phlox paniculata* and *divaricata*. Excellent results may be had sowing such seeds as spring crocus and jack-in-the-pulpit in 4-inch pots and plunging them in a sheltered spot over winter; excellent germination the following spring.

The hard-coated seeds of the primulas and rock garden plants from alpine regions give best results sown in the fall. They are often treated by alternate freezing and thawing in an ice cube compartment for several days before sowing to duplicate the natural winter conditions.

The safest way to sow perennials in the fall (late November is all right for spring germination), is in a seed bed or flat. A coldframe is not needed to protect the box over winter, although it is preferable and a good thing to have. With no coldframe, set the seed box outdoors in a protected corner of the house or garage, covered with leaves until spring. In a flat, seeds escape many winter hazards which seeds sown in the open garden encounter such as drowning in surface water, washing away in heavy rains or being uprooted by alternate thawing and freezing. Next to a flat, a raised bed surrounded by a wooden curb is a good place. Fill it with soil and sow the seeds in rows, properly labeled so you can easily identify the plants.

FROM CUTTINGS

Remember that cuttings will produce plants exactly the same as the plant from which the cutting was taken, all new plants will be like the parent plant. Cuttings are best rooted in a sterile, well-drained medium as sharp sand or coarse vermiculite (the grade sold for house insulation). Unless grown under mist, shading and wind protection is necessary, and the bed must be kept moist at all times.

Stem Cuttings Many perennials as chrysanthemums, delphiniums, rock plants and sedums, are grown from stem cuttings. These are made from the tip growth taken during June and July. Make cuttings with a sharp knife, 1 to 2 inches in length, depending upon the variety and size of stem. Remove the lower leaves and insert ½ to 1 inch in a slit in the cutting bed, a flat filled with 3 to 4 inches of clean, sharp sand or equal parts of sand and peat moss or vermiculite. The bases of the cuttings may be treated with root-inducing substances but follow directions carefully. It is better to use none than too much. Hormodin #1, #2, #3, and Rootone are the materials most commonly used.

Glass or plastic should be kept over the flat until the cuttings are stored, and the medium used must be kept moist. Place cutting bed in the shade of a tree or on the north side of a building to protect it during the heat of day. Rooting will require 10 days to 3 weeks when the cuttings should be transplanted into a growing bed same as the seedlings. Keep shaded after transplanting until roots are established.

Root Cuttings   Anchusa, gaillardia, Oriental poppy and *Phlox paniculata* are some of the perennials propagated by root cuttings. Cut the root into 1-2 inch lengths in October or November. Bury them ½-inch deep in sand in a coldframe until spring. Cover with leaves to a depth of 4 inches for the winter. Plant in nursery bed the next spring.

BY DIVISION

Most perennials are easily propagated by division of the established clumps. This is usually done when the clumps normally require division. The need for division is usually indicated by the size and appearance of the clump, and the lack of vigor and smaller size of the flowers. Fall and late summer bloomers are best divided in the spring. Those flowering in the spring may be divided just after they have bloomed or in August. Iris are usually divided in July. When dividing clumps cut or break the parent clump into as many parts as desired but do not make the divisions so small as to destroy the garden value of the clump. Remove any dead, damaged, weak or diseased parts and to compensate for loss of roots which might have been broken, injured or cut off, cut stems back about a third. Replant and you will soon have a vigorous plant.

Lots of perennials can be multiplied without bothering to dig up and divide the parent plant by gently loosening or yanking away a little shoot on the side with roots and putting it back in the border. Mr. Fred J. Statt, Flower Department Manager, Joseph Harris Seed Company, Inc., Rochester, N. Y., recommends: "Varieties grown from divisions should be propagated when plants are dormant. This is usually in early spring about the time new growth is commencing. Varieties which make extra early growth such as peonies and Oriental poppies should be divided in August and September."

4

Favorite Perennials and Places to Plant Them

In our questionnaire to 300 horticulturists and amateur gardeners, we asked for lists of the 10 to 20 favorite perennials. Phlox, hardy chrysanthemums, peonies, iris, delphiniums, daylilies, coral bells and aquilegia topped the list. The reasons included easy to grow, hardy, dependable, most beautiful and most showy.

MOST FREQUENTLY MENTIONED

The following thirty-five perennials are those most frequently mentioned on the answers:

Achillea	Dicentra	Lythrum
Alyssum	Dictamnus	Monarda
Anemone	Digitalis	Paeonia
Aquilegia	Echinops	Papaver
Artemisia	Gypsophila	Penstemon
Aster	Hemerocallis	Phlox
Astilbe	Heuchera	Platycodon
Baptisia	Hosta	Primula
Campanula	Iberis	Shasta Daisy
Chrysanthemum	Iris	Trollius
Delphinium	Lilium	Veronica
Dianthus	Lupinus	

FOR SUCCESSION OF BLOOM AND EASY MAINTENANCE

Prof. E. C. Volz, Professor of Horticulture, Iowa State University, comments: "I consider the first nine in my list as basic perennials in that they are all outstanding and time tested and if used in any border or garden will supply "succession" bloom from April to October." His first nine were: tulip, iris, peony, shasta daisy, delphinium, hemerocallis, perennial phlox, hardy chrysanthemum and hardy aster. The other eleven plants in his list were also selected to provide color from spring until frost. They include dwarf *Dicentra eximia,* aquilegia, *Thalictrum aquilegifolium,* veronica, salvia, *Platycodon grandiflorum,* lythrum, dictamnus, hosta, *Eupatorium coelestinum* and *Sedum spectabile.*

From New Vernon, New Jersey, comes this report from Mrs. Edward G. Howe: "We have two peaks of bloom. One in May when the tulips, blue phlox and candytuft are full. The next big splash is late September or early October, when the fall garden is at its best. I do some planning and planting in the spring and fall, the rest of the time I just enjoy my garden. After all that's what a garden is for, isn't it?"

"After experimenting for many years with a perennial garden," writes Mrs. George F. Hoysradt, Horticultural and Greenhouse Chairman, Belmont Garden Club, Belmont, Mass. "we have come up with these perennials that are a joy, disease- and pest-free, requiring no staking and with leaves on some plants that can be used for arrangements. With a spring and fall fertilizing, separating every 2 or 3 years, they require a minimum of care." Mrs. Hoysradt lists: ajuga, astilbe, dicentra, *Doronicum caucasicum,* gypsophila (single lavender), *Hosta plantaginea,* iberis, mertensia, *Phlox stolenifera* "Blue Ridge", *Phlox subulata, Plumbago Larpentae, Pulmonaria,* sedums (all kinds), and Trollius.

THE PLACE

All home grounds, no matter how small, have space for some perennials. The plantings need not be elaborate, just enough to add color and interest to the shrubbery and supply a succession of bloom, giving a change of scenery to the landscape and adding pleasure and enjoyment to summer days. The location of the flowers is frequently predetermined or controlled by conditions the home owner is unable to change. Even then, however, it is amazing what beauty can be created by careful consideration. The truism "The way to make a thing possible is to believe that you can do it" is the right thinking under such circumstances.

Try to develop an intimate relationship between garden and house, placing the flower border so that pleasing vistas may be enjoyed from indoor windows or from outdoor living areas as a breezeway, terrace or porch. Flowers near the outdoor living area are handy to view and enjoy, pick and tend, and can easily be made a delightful center of interest.

Opposite. EASY MAINTENANCE   A shade-dappled path lined with lush hosta foliage is attractive all season and requires minimum care.

Below. CONTINUOUS BLOOM IN A SMALL BORDER   Spires of blue delphinium, light and dark gaillardia, and fillers of yellow marguerites bloom first, with tall hollyhock, yellow yarrow and white phlox soon after. Large clumps of early yellow lilies and white astilbe bloom at both ends, followed by pink asters in the fall. Gray-leaved, blue veronicas interspersed with pink dianthus make a lovely edging.

Most landscape architects suggest that lawns at the front and rear of the house be kept open, but we have seen many charming central plantings. In many ways, these islands in the middle of the garden offer ideal conditions. Usually there is no competition from roots of shrubs and trees, there is plenty of air circulation around the plants, and there is some sun. Nevertheless, it is true that an unbroken central lawn is easier to mow and also increases the apparent size of your garden, since an open expanse appears larger than the same space broken up.

Obviously, the garden should harmonize with its surroundings, at least in spirit. Plantings at the seashore must be made with salt-resistant plants, and in a shady glen it would be ridiculous to expect sun-loving perennials to do well. It is possible to correct soil, to water dry areas and perhaps to open up some heavily shaded places if you are willing to go to a lot of trouble and if you want to experiment, go ahead and do so. On the whole, choose only plants that will survive under your conditions. The lists at the back of the book will help you select the plants appropriate to their situation.

Better plan on a garden smaller than you think you can manage. In summer, the optimism of the spring garden enthusiast is easily squelched. Someone has estmated that for every hour of the week you can work in your garden, you can plant 36 sq. feet.

Narrow borders make maintenance easier, but a wide border makes continuous bloom easier to achieve. A four-feet-wide border is a fairly good compromise even for the smallest bed.

A Shrub-Perennial Border: Low, slow-growing shrubs make an effective background for flowers, provided you choose the ones that can take light, shade and root competition. Hardy ageratum, bee-balm, the various campanulas, day-lilies, sweet rocket, Siberian iris and meadow-rue *(Thalictrum aquilegifolium)* are a few of the many perennials that do well in such a combination.

Opposite. FLOWERING SHRUBS AND PERENNIALS White deutzia, fothergilla, tree peonies and bulbs underplanted with pansies and blue phlox, make a charming spring garden. White petunias and sweet alyssum, with tuberous begonias in shady spots, replace tulips and pansies.

Allow three feet between shrubs and perennials to avoid serious root competition. Sever any roots an inch or so thick along the border's edge nearest the trees or large shrubs with a sharp spade every couple of years in the fall. This will not hurt any well-established sizeable tree or shrub and will keep the roots in check.

Mixed Beds: In addition to all-perennial borders, fine mixed beds include bulbs, annuals and perennials, the latter supplying season-long beauty and color. Plant the bulbs in groups in well-defined positions, using the tall kinds like the lily toward the back where developing perennials will hide any unsightly foliage after blooming. Use those of medium height, as tulips and hyacinths, toward the center and place the small bulbs in the foreground, since their foliage ripens quickly.

Early spring-flowering bulbs will supply color even before and with the early perennials. Plant daffodils or tulips around peonies or between clumps of platycodon. These are permanent plants, unlike iris or phlox which must be lifted and divided every few years with the inevitable spearing of any bulbs in the vicinity. Use bulbs around such perennials as the Japanese anemone and dictamnus which are late in making early growth. Annuals can be set around or directly over the bulbs without any harm and will cover the spaces left when the bulb foliage dies. Annuals are valuable for filling in around early-blooming perennials, to give color later in the season, and to hide bedraggled foliage of Oriental poppies and other plants with poor mid-summer foliage.

In Deep Shade: A shady terrace is a delightful retreat on a hot summer day. If you do not want to go to the expense of paving, plant-tried and true perennial ground covers such as ajuga, pachysandra or hostas, are decorative throughout the season. Many perennials (see list) will thrive in light to moderate shade.

On Slopes And Steps: In 1625 Francis Bacon wrote "Nothing is more pleasant to the eye than green grass kept finely shorn" to which we heartily agree. This still holds true some 300 years later. There is no substitute for a well-kept, beautiful lawn. But in places where great expense and effort are required, it is better not to try to grow grass. It is foolish to become a slave to a lawn that never looks its best, no matter how long you labor.

ON A SHADY TERRACE   Pachysandra does well in partial shade where grass will not thrive. Other ground covers are listed on page 253.

ABOVE THE CITY Even here, space is made for a few perennials in a raised bed, with potted plants to add color.

Grass, being a cool-weather and moisture-loving plant, does poorly on steep, sunny slopes and is very difficult to mow. Why not let hemerocallis or Cypress spurge *(Euphorbia Cyparissias)*, a lusty perennial, or some suitable ground cover take over the slope? It will look well with little cost and much less labor.

In the Williamsburg gardens the old-time hardy periwinkle, *Vinca minor*, is used within flower beds. Bulbs such as narcissi are planted under it, and after they have bloomed in the spring the ground continues to be covered by the periwinkle and there is no problem of digging up or replanting. These ground covers are effective in winter, too, and they work well around other plants such as peonies and shrubs. If planted in the usual way, periwinkle plants will need to be weeded for the first two or three seasons, after which they usually take over the ground completely and need no further maintenance.

Use ground covers for bank and terraces where it is difficult to get grass to grow. To soften the lines of steps, suitable ground covers, alpines and dwarf perennials may be grown informally between, over, or in the steps. If the pockets in which the plants are tucked are well drained, the plants will last for years and reduce the tedious job of trimming.

City Garden: With space at a premium in a cramped area, with dense shadows and deep shade cast by towering neighbors, cold drafts, soot and fumes, the city gardener has many problems. The garden area is likely to be small, a private patio or terrace, with tall buildings on either side and a fence at the rear.

Smallness need not be a major problem since a well-planned tiny garden can surge with color from spring until fall. There are also various clever ways of forcing perspective and creating the illusion of distance and size.

White or light walls seem to increase the size of an area. Small spaces may be made to appear larger if they are given a light background, which also creates the impression of distance.

It sometimes takes a bit of doing to find plants that will long withstand the unfavorable growing conditions of the large city. Spring gardens with emphasis on bulbs, sturdy perennial ground covers and plants grown in tubs, to be easily replaced as necessary, are good. In the fall, chrysanthemums which have been grown elsewhere are not costly, can be transplanted to the garden, making it a vivid fairyland.

In limited space, a vine-covered trellis, a brick or stone wall, a picket or wooden fence with espaliered shrubs or small trees, raised beds, wall planters, and hanging pots and containers such as tubs and strawberry barrels, are widely used to gain more planting area. If you really want to garden, you'll find the space. The gardener restricted by area and environment improvises, invents, and creates new ideas to pursue his hobby.

Country Garden: The country garden should give the enthusiastic gardener a real thrill for here he can create a dream garden, unrestricted by space. In some locations a windbreak may be necessary, but otherwise there are no restrictions on planting the large garden. The tallest plant material may be

A TINY PINK-AND-GRAY GARDEN Materials: Rear—Russian olive
tree, two white clematis, rosemary plant in clay pot painted same "faded
pink" as the concrete blocks. Artemisia "Silver Dome" in black peat moss.
Dwarf Japanese juniper and snow-in-summer are in upper level. Pinks
of coleus, geraniums, and impatiens and *Nepeta Mussini*, show against
artemisia "Silver King." Rosy marble chips are in the foreground.

PATIO GARDEN Perennial iberis and *Phlox divaricata*, edging plants, bloom with white dogwood. Creamy white pansies flourish in Italian pottery containers flanking the steps. The stone wall holds iberis, hen-and-chickens and small ferns. Phlox and iberis are sheared after blooming and salmon pink geraniums and white petunias take over.

used in rear borders or in island flower beds in full sun, where a wonderful assortment of perennials will do well. Or a naturalistic, informal planting which requires minimum upkeep might be considered. The formal garden needs more care and must be well-kept to look attractive. However, many country gardens combine the two styles with charming results, using a formal planting directly around the house, with a naturalistic effect further away, blending into the nearby countryside.

Terrace Garden: During the summer, a paved area or patio against the wall of a house makes an ideal extension for the indoor living room, a delightful sitting area with screening to insure privacy and shade.

Some shade is necessary for comfortable sitting during the

181

day. The play of light and shadows from a well-chosen shade or flowering tree, as a native dogwood, is delightful to watch. A tree, tall shrubs or a vine-covered pergola all afford shade and seclusion.

Make this cosy, sitting area one of your choicest spots. The same considerations used in other plantings apply here as well. Experimentation on a sketch pad may prove rewarding. Choice specimen perennials, a combined shrub and perennial border, or a flower border at terrace level or in raised beds, may outline the paved area and supply abundant color. Plants seen at close range will be enjoyed for their lovely detail as well as landscape effects.

Cutting Garden: With the very small lot, the regular flower border planned as a part of the overall landscape usually also serves for cutting purposes. However, if you cut heavily you will soon leave gaping holes in an otherwise attractive border. For those who use many cut flowers for indoor arrangements, flower shows or as gifts to friends, a cut-flower garden is most useful. Then you can harvest without worrying about spoiling a garden picture.

A cutting garden in the service area or along the side of a garage, with flowers planted in straight rows for easy care, will provide ample flowers. Also, it will supply a reserve of perennials and annuals with which to fill empty spots which may occur in the regular flower border. Bare places will occur at times due to winter damage, disease and just plain old age. For a list of flowers valuable for cutting see page 248.

Raised Beds: Where space is limited or soil is poor, raised flower beds are practical. In many cases they are more economical than excavating poor soil and replacing it with good. If the soil is very poor cut down the size of the cultivated area to one you can manage. Mix enough artificial soil of the right consistency for a well-drained fertile bed to hold the plants you wish to grow. No need to excavate. Just pile this soil on top of the spot where you want the raised bed. For a higher bed use a rock base. If the bed is only a foot or so in height, it can be easily retained and concealed by planting a low clipped hedge such as yew or boxwood as a border, or by building a rock or brick wall or curbing around the edge. This raised-bed idea was frequently used in the old days, with bedding plants ar-

LIGHT AND SHADOW ARE DESIGN ELEMENTS   Dark and light, and smooth and rough textures, increase interest in this charming scene, with plants of hostas, day-lilies, rhododendrons and annuals (fillers in front).

DECORATIVE HERB GARDEN Broad-leaved English thyme, tarragon pots, (brought indoors in winter) and allium, artemesia, lavender, marjoram, mint, rosemary, sage, savory and thyme make a charming fragrant border.

ranged in geometrical patterns or "knots." We have all seen them in city parks and in pictures of early gardens.

The neatness and convenience of raised flower beds are assets in addition to the excellence of plant growth. Also with bench-high beds—like those constructed in homes for the blind, and in hospitals and homes for the crippled and elderly—gardeners can work outdoors without needing to bend.

Dooryard Garden: Dooryard flower gardens should have an old-fashioned, homey atmosphere and plenty of color. Such landscapes are well suited to informal cottage-type ranches, Cape Cods and Dutch Colonials. Flowers frequently supplement a hedge or fence which encloses the property.

Usually there is abundant sunlight for growing flowers and the garden is readily viewed and enjoyed from the living room as well as by passers-by. Old-time favorites as the hollyhock, peony, bleeding-heart, day-lily, iris, rose, foxglove, lily-of-the-

184

A GARDEN IN CAPE COD An old-fashioned dooryard garden in Massachusetts is filled with native flowers: hibiscus, hollyhock, bee-balm, peony, species of delphinium, pinks, foxglove, species hemerocallis, Madonna lilies, phlox and lavender.

valley, daffodil, candytuft and pansy, and often a collection of herbs grow in profusion, their varied colors concealing the fact that little thought has been given to design.

Rock Garden: Dwarf, spreading types of hardy perennials contribute most of the charming plants used in the rock garden, which should appear to be an honest part of the landscape, never obviously artificial. The area should show restraint, its colorful masses distributed for pleasing effects.

You may well ask, "Why or when should a home owner consider a rock garden?" If you love the beauty of alpine plants and have a bank or slope to contend with, a rock garden may be a practical solution. A natural outcropping of rocks or a ledge immediately suggests a rock garden. If you need to add rock to make pockets of soil and to increase the planting area, use the same kind of rock and follow the existing strata to make it look natural. The rock should seem to have belonged there. If care is used, lichens and mosses that enhance the naturalness of the scene can be preserved. The encrusted growths develop in beauty with each passing year and suggest age and permanence.

The use of a vertical rock garden allows a wider selection of plants and a more dramatic display. The low-growing plants are lifted up for closer inspection, brought out of their taller neighbor's shade and separated by rock barrier from their more aggressive neighbors.

Use plants that grow in association with rocks in their native habitat, such as the alpines or mountain flowers. In selecting plants, beginners choose the rapid growers, valued for their profuse flowering, to create a colorful spring display. Such perennials as creeping phlox, alyssum, aubrieta, hardy candytuft and violas produce lavish color. However, rare and unusual alpines offer a challenge to the serious gardener. Such little known plants are noted for their exceptional beauty, but sometimes present problems. The various gentians, some of the campanulas, the encrusted saxifrages, the choice auriculas and a host of other gems are all worth the effort they require. Actually, the most satisfying accomplishment is to combine the two groups in some measure. Something in flower from earliest spring to mid-November should be the aim. The first and the last bloom will come from early spring and fall bulbs. See list

WELL-PLANNED ROCKERY This garden was planned to take advantage of natural ledges. Thymes are between paving stones, pachysandra at left, *Dicentra eximia* behind it, *Phlox subulata* to the right, and stachys and primrose between two clumps of low white phlox. Lilies and creeping junipers complete the scene.

NATURALISTIC EFFECT   A man-made wall in front is related to the natural ledge in the rear. Coral bells, rock phlox, irises and daffodils fit the site.

of plants for rock gardens.

Woodland Or Naturalistic Garden: This type of garden requires little upkeep and can be lots of fun. The secret is in selecting the right plants for the location and getting them well established. Shade from large trees will limit the perennials you can grow but you can still have a lovely and interesting garden, quite different from the average. Some shaded areas are also dry because the roots of the large trees take up the moisture, but this can be overcome by watering. Also a stream or brook can be built to help the situation if you want to go to that expense. Although few flowers will grow in dense shade, many will do well in semi-shaded places. For perennials that will grow in shade or semi-shade see page 249.

Many native wildflowers that grow in wooded areas, if given semi-acid soil conditions, will thrive in shade. Some of these treasures include the wood anemone, hardy geranium, bleeding-heart, and hepatica.

A step-by-step transformation of an actual unspoiled site can point the way to what to cut down, how best to bring out the inherent beauty of what is left, and what to add in keeping with the original feeling of the plot. Just how to combine wild natural beauty, with one's desire for order and neatness is an interesting challenge. Natural ledges may be enlarged and tied together with other native rock to become both useful and decorative. They may form a natural slope to one side of the lawn and serve as the foreground for a colorful perennial flower border. Many kinds of plants, both indigenous and exotic, can fit into a naturalistic situation. Woodland, left to itself, quickly takes on the aspect of a primeval jungle, but a series of narrow paths opens up the whole area and makes it accessible as well as inviting. This is not a mammoth undertaking, and the old proverb properly reminds us that he who cuts his own wood warms himself twice.

The upkeep on this type of landscaping is comparatively simple. Plants grow easily under suitable conditions, and there is little need for manicured appearances since natural surroundings have intrinsic beauty.

Seaside Garden: Flower colors always seem brighter near the sea. Although many seaside gardens seem to depend mainly on annuals for gay color, many perennials will thrive in the

SEASIDE ROCK GARDEN In a difficult site, masses of plants are draped for good effect: Daphne in foreground, *Cotoneaster divaricata* in right foreground (down to railing), *Phlox subulata* starting to bloom atop wall, a clump of dwarf dianthus at left, and a mass of arabis at right.

Opposite. A WOODLAND PATH Silver-bell tree, birches and azaleas combine with primroses, phlox, forget-me-nots, trilliums, violets, spring vetchling, sweet woodruff and other wildlings in a gay spring picture.

sandy soil, salt spray and strong winds of the coast. Perennials have the advantage of being permanent and do not necessitate making an early trip to the shore to get the garden planted. Surely the following perennials should receive consideration for sunny, sandy, seashore locations where it is difficult to grow many plants.

Armeria maritima, thrift
Artemisia schmidtiana nana, "Silver Mound"
Artemisia Stelleriana, beach wormwood
Asclepias tuberosa, butterfly-weed
Aster hybrids, Michaelmas daisy
Baptisia australis, blue false indigo
Centaurea Cineraria, dusty miller
Erynigium maritimum, sea-holly
Euphorbia corollata, flowering spurge
Hemerocallis, day-lily
Hibiscus palustris, rose mallow
Lathyrus maritimus, beach pea
Limonium latifolium, sea-lavender
Oenothera biennis, evening-primrose
Oenothera missouriensis, Missouri primrose
Opuntia compressa, prickly-pear
Phlox subulata, ground- or moss-pink
Sedum spectabile
Thermopsis caroliniana, Aarons-rod
Thymus Serpyllum, mother-of-thyme
Thymus vulgaris, common thyme
Yucca Smalliana (filamentosa), Adams-needle

5

A Few Fundamentals of Design

Somewhere we read that it would be the height of gardening success to create "a garden more beautiful than you anticipated, with less care than you had expected and costing only a little more than you had planned." Certainly, beauty, ease of maintenance and cost are three main factors to be considered in any garden design. Too little knowledge at the outset usually produces disappointing and costly results. A good garden layout, adapted to the needs of the individual home-owner, and carefully selected plant material that will thrive under the given conditions, are essential for successful landscaping.

Successful design is basically a matter of common sense. It is obvious, for example, that the smaller the garden, the simpler it should be. Aim for an orderly arrangement of plant groups of sufficient size to create a non-cluttered, pleasing, over-all picture, yet with enough variation and interest to give zest. Broad simple effects are best, but they should never be monotonous, flat or dull.

In outlining the border, avoid odd and fancy shapes which are hard to keep trim and bewildering to the observer. Geometric lines are more pleasing than curves when space is limited; a straight line between two points makes more sense

COUNTRY BORDER When apple and crab trees bloom, there are daffodils, *Phlox divaricata*, day-lilies and true lilies. Irises, *Dictamnus fraxinella*, lupines, aquilegia, oriental poppies, peonies, lavender thalictrum, Johnny-jump-ups (a pleasant weed), dianthus, ajuga and violas provide a wide range of color later.

to the observer than a curved one. Therefore, if you want a curved path, create a reason for it by planting a small shrub or using a boulder or a garden seat at the point of detour.

CREATE BALANCE

To obtain formal balance, repeat the same plants on both sides of the center. For a feeling of informality, balance one or a few tall plants with a mass of lower ones on the opposite side of the axis.

Remember that solid forms have greater visual weight than delicate, open ones; that texture is more powerful than smooth surface and that vivid colors are more compelling than pastel ones. In a small garden, formal balance is satisfying because it is more obvious, and more restful, than asymmetrical balance.

TIE INTO SURROUNDING LANDSCAPE FOR UNITY

A border is far more effective if tied in with the landscape. Attractive garden pictures may be worked out by choosing flower colors to coincide with the bloom of nearby trees, shrubs and vines. White flowers of the hardy candytuft and white-flowering dwarf iris blend nicely into a background of white-flowering bridal wreath. Peonies and bearded iris chosen to harmonize or contrast with nearby climbing roses create pleasing effects.

REPEAT PLANT GROUPINGS AND COLORS

Repeat plant groupings and colors in a sequence at intervals;

PERENNIAL BORDER TWELVE FEET WIDE   To unify the old-time border, plant groups and colors are repeated. Note the varied shapes and heights.

this will create unity and make the border hang together. Compose the colors so that they occur throughout the border; avoid a solid block of color on one side and a green oasis on the other.

VARIETY

While diversity is to be desired, aim for consistency and pleasing transition and avoid busy, spotty or confused effects. Individual flowers offer a wide choice in size, form and type of inflorescence, from the tiny, delicate flat-topped flowers of the saxifrage pink to the huge, ball-like flowers of the double peony. The smaller, more delicate species and medium-sized plants are more in scale with the small border.

IN MIDSUMMER   Splashes of bold phlox bring color and consistency to a large planting.

SHADED RETREAT   A handsome wall enclosing a variety of textured plants creates a secluded garden.

Even the one-genus plantings of the specialist or hobbyist need not be dull. There is sufficient range of sizes, forms, textures and blooming season to bring variety.

Variety in foliage forms, texture and size can add immeasurably to the interest of a planting. The sword-like leaves of iris and yucca are nice contrasts rising from a smooth lawn. The coarser leaves of the hosta and hollyhock offer a pleasing contrast with the finer texture of the much-divided leaves of columbine and meadow-rue. Medium foliage size combines well with the fine, narrow leaves of blue flax. The beauty of the dark, scalloped leaves of coral bells is enhanced beside the pale, smooth, finely toothed leaves of peach bells.

197

Plan for contrasted plant forms, a judicious use of spiky subjects throughout the border. Alternate spiky plants with bushy growth and flat-topped flower head in the depth and length of the border. Bushy plants provide excellent masses of color, while spiky subjects add accent, grace and charm.

CONSIDER THE BACKGROUND

The word "garden" is derived from the old Anglo-Saxon word "gyrdon" which means an enclosed area. An adequate neutral background or partial enclosure enhances the beauty of a flower garden. It concentrates attention on the flower garden and shuts out any objectional view. A planting of trees and shrubs, a hedge, wall or fence will accomplish the purpose. Such an enclosure also adds enjoyment and pleasure by providing privacy and seclusion for the owner.

Hedges or shrubs that are allowed to grow naturally are less work than those that require clipping. Cedar, locust or redwood fencing need no painting and make a good background for flowers, offering no root competition. Use mowing strips which are narrow bands of hard paving, as bricks, laid so the brick length supplies the width of the strip. Level with and at the edge of the flower border, they provide a track for one wheel of the mower, simplify the chore of grass cutting and minimize hand trimming. They also keep the border shape intact and the lawn free from encroaching plants. Mowing strips provide a decorative, permanent border edging and strengthen the garden pattern where a crisp neat line is desired.

CONSIDER PLANT HEIGHTS AND SHAPES

The use of low spreading plants for edging, medium, well-rounded plants for filling, and tall spiky plants for backing will help you achieve a well-designed perennial bed.

Select a few dominant plants such as the lily, delphinium or gas-plant and repeat them at intervals throughout the border. A few accents in important places will relieve any monotony and give the planting distinction, and interest. Spires of hardy lilies, delphinium or thalictrum rising above lower, more rounded masses of phlox and other perennials, relieve any

DESIGNED FOR VARIETY Japanese irises, *Lilium regale,* and kni-
phopia (*tritoma*) bring varied shapes and heights to a planting stressing
simplicity and ease of maintenance.

GREEN-AND-WHITE GARDEN Showy Japanese irises and pyrethrum bloom lavishly in June and July, followed by fragrant white blossoms of *Hosta plantaginea* and white geraniums. Pachysandra, sheared during the season, will remain neat. (Shearings may be rooted and used elsewhere.) Note the excellent relationship in size of all plants.

monotony of undulating lines and make a pleasing and contrasted composition.

Mass flowers between the accents by grouping together
several plants of one kind. More pictorial effects are achieved
by planting with "drifts." Avoid groupings that are too regular
in shape and position; stagger them so one is not exactly in back
of the other for a natural, informal look. Pick two or more kinds
of perennials for each blooming season and use them in sufficient quantity to really be effective. The wider the border, the
larger the "drifts" may be.

Plant masses look best if they repeat in a general way the
shape of the whole border. With a curved border, plant groups
should in general follow the border curve. With a long narrow
border, tend toward long narrow groupings.

Low-growing plants used in the foreground should look well
all season, and have attractive foliage, as well as attractive
blossoms. Some like alyssum, arabis and candytuft, may spill
over the front edge to soften a hard, straight line.

Some herbaceous perennials are evergreen and are useful
because they retain their leaves the year round. They make excellent edging plants for borders and are also used in rock and
wall gardens as well as for ground covers. Among the most
popular are *Dianthus barbatus* and *plumarius, Heuchera sanguinea, Iberis sempervirens, Linum perenne,* sedum, *Teucrium
Chamaedrys, Thymus Serpyllum* and *Yucca Smalliana* (filamentosa).

KEEP MATERIAL IN SCALE

The size a plant will be after two or three years of growth
should govern the space allotted to it. Some of the rapidly
spreading kinds, which quickly engulf a neighbor, may need
annual division if grown in a limited area. On the other hand,
perennials like the globe-flower *(Trollius europaeus)* increase so
slowly that several may be set close together. A single globe
thistle *(Echinops ritro)* is picturesque, a large grouping would
be grotesque. The peony and gas-plant or burning-bush *(Dictamnus albus)* are also rewarding as specimens.

Sea-lavender and babys-breath taking up little space in April
swell into billowy masses by midsummer and space must be
allotted.

Foliage of the Oriental poppy, doronicum and bleeding-heart disappear during the summer so need to be hidden by other plants at this time. *Achillea filipendulina* which holds its form well and blooms late may be interplanted among these perennials.

Avoid large masses of any of the perennials that have a short blooming season such as bearded iris and many of the biennials to avoid stretches of dullness later. Choose perennials with foliage that looks well throughout the growing season, as do peonies.

Most gardeners tend to overplant and the border becomes too crowded after the first season when the perennials increase in size. Leave space for the natural growth of perennials, using a few annuals as fillers the first year. A well-filled border however does tend to restrict weeds. If the border is to be seen at a distance it will need masses of bold color and accent plants of adequate size and striking form. To be viewed at close range beside a garden path or outdoor living area dantier flowers, less striking in form and size, with interesting detail will serve the purpose nicely.

The width of the border determines the height of the plants you can use. A good rule of thumb is this: in a border 4 feet wide, the tallest plant should be no more than 2 to 2½ feet high; in a border 6 feet wide, the tallest plant should be no more than 3 or 3½ feet high. This is only a generalization—feathery plants such as gypsophila for example can be taller, since their effect is so light and airy.

CONSIDER COLOR

The color scheme is a personal matter. Some prefer vivid, striking combinations, such as scarlet Oriental poppy next to blue delphinium or yellow next to purple. Such contrasts bring vitality to the overall scene. Strong sun lightens vivid colors, so they can be used freely in such a situation.

Another possibility exists in blends of related colors, yellow and yellow-orange, for example, which fit into any color scheme. Or yellow may be the dominant color, used throughout the border, with yelow-orange introduced in lesser degree for contrast. In a restricted area, a one-color garden adds to the sense

TERRACE PLANTING IN TONES OF YELLOW Yellow, gold and orange perennials include achillea, alyssum, aquilegia, feverfew, digitalis, doronicum, trollius and viola. Later, come anthemis, coreopsis, gaillardia, helenium, heliopsis, hypericum, lilium, oenothera, rudbeckia, and pots of yellow button mums.

VERMONT VISTA   The countryside is the background for this terrace planting of spring bulbs, followed by blue and white *Campanula persicifolia* (under the window). Later anthemis, delphinium and Regal lilies take over. Dwarf-creeping nierembergia backed with blue pansies are the edging plants; heliotrope and petunias the fillers. White cosmos replaces peach bells (the cream and pink will come again if cut). Artemisia and lavender asters hide shabby spots in the fall. A cutting garden is maintained for replacements.

of space and well-ordered simplicity. Such a garden becomes a source of enjoyment to the owner, who will be constantly on the lookout for new and effective plants in the color of his choice.

Our first experience with a one-color garden was in Newport, Rhode Island, back in 1927. Mrs. Arthur Curtiss James had a famous blue garden at that time, rare because blue perennials are in the minority. At that time, we also saw an all-white "Moonlight Garden" in the evening and have never forgotten it. White flowers are luminous and lovely at night; during hot summer days they are cool and restful. Fragrance, always an asset, seems twice as strong in the night air.

With a one-color garden the possibilities are naturally limited so avoid monotony and create an exciting picture by planting many values of the same hue. If red is your choice, start with the palest pink tint graduating down to the deepest maroon shades for a delightful effect.

Accents and contrasts of sizes, form and textures are also necessary. Look for perennials listed according to fragrance on page 253.

Warm colors make objects appear nearer to the observer; cool colors make them appear farther away. The gardener may create the illusion of a larger space than he actually has by planting bluish flowers (cool colors) in the background and red and orange flowers (warm colors) in the immediate foreground.

In a wooded area, a vivid color scheme may be garish, for there is no sunlight to neutralize colors. Here is the site for pastel and white blossoms which look their best in shade.

Perennials in varying degrees of value and intensity are to be found in six standard colors, the three primaries; red, yellow and blue, and their three intermediates; orange, green and purple. There are many other hues, intermediates between the six standard colors. The blues and greens and related colors are cool colors, those in the red and orange range, warm. Green gets warmer as it grows yellowish, cooler as it grows bluish.

There is harmony among the warm colors because they are related, also among the related cool colors while the warm and cool colors do not harmonize but contrast with each other. Warm colors are conspicuous, aggressive and stimulating; cool colors, calm and restful. Something on the borderline between warmth and coolness may have the cheer of warm colors and the calmness of the cool. For restful, quiet, subtle effects combine some of the lovely blues and violets. Soft pinks and salmons are warm colors and can be given zest with a dash or accent of red and purple.

Unless you are planting a kaleidoscope of colors to be seen from a distance (where the atmosphere itself acts as a neutralizer) never plant blue reds next to scarlets. Red-purple petunias next to scarlet salvia or scarlet geraniums are unpleasant.

If flowers in many bright colors are to be used together introduce gray foliage plants as harmonizers. White and green are also useful blenders.

Do not disregard contrast in foliage color. Silvery-leaved artemisias and veronicas contrast with the very dark green foliage of aconitum. The gray-green, bearded iris foliage is well set off against the shiny dark leaves of dictamnus. The almost-white effect of the leaves of *Stachys olympica* or *Lychnis coronaria* increases interest by the contrast it makes with most other plants.

There is sufficient choice from among the perennials to satisfy all tastes. Personal preference will determine whether you want a blend of related colors or bold contrast.

6

The Actual Layout
and Planting

Most successful designs are carried out over a period of years. For this reason it is important that you start with a well-conceived plan on paper, showing the garden as it should be when completed. The location of trees, terrace, a projected fountain or swimming pool, any future additions should be marked and space allowed. Then and only then can you lay out your permanent perennial bed. Working with such a plan, you will save time and money and each year's work will see you a step closer to the final goal.

LAYING OUT THE BED

1. At least one or two weeks in advance of planting, mark off and outline the flower bed. Mark off a straight line with a stout string, rope or clothesline tightly fastened between two stakes. Use the garden hose for a curved edging. A rubber hose will stay where put. A plastic hose must be filled with water and capped at either end to stay in place. Caps are available in garden shops. Sprinkle the hose with lime so it will show on the grass. Then lift the hose and a white-lime outline of the curved edge will be there to follow. Using an edger, it is a simple matter to cut the sod along the curve.

Neat Edges Improve the Border

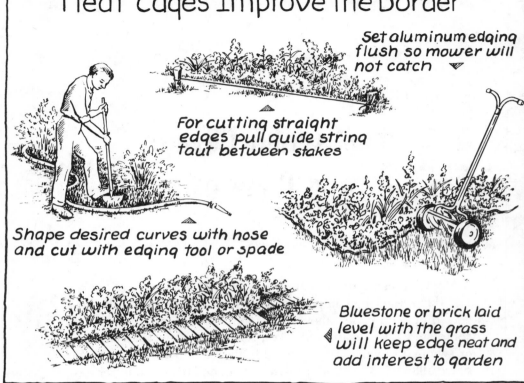

Set aluminum edging flush so mower will not catch ▽

For cutting straight edges pull guide string taut between stakes

Shape desired curves with hose and cut with edging tool or spade

Bluestone or brick laid level with the grass will keep edge neat and add interest to garden

2. Dig a trench two feet deep and prepare the soil thoroughly. See page 138. Let the soil settle a week or more before actually planting. Someone wisely said it is better to prepare a $5.00 hole for a 50-cent plant than to plant a $5.00 plant in a 50-cent hole.

PLANT ON PAPER FIRST

1. Using graph paper, make a scale drawing of your perennial border or bed. If yours is a small place, 1' may be drawn to equal ½". With tracing paper laid over the drawing, you can try many different experiments.
2. Select six or more basic perennials as the backbone of your bed. Long-lasting flowers, or foliage which is handsome for most of the growing season, and succession of bloom (for early, mid- and late-season displays) are important considerations. Our illustrations will help you decide. Work one section or unit of the border at a time.
3. Sketch in two or three groupings of tall perennials for the rear, two or three groupings of medium perennials for the middle, perhaps one or two to the front and side. Each grouping or drift (a good word to describe the natural casual effect you wish to achieve) should be similar in shape to the border, for best design. Allow groups of tall plants to come forward in places to avoid a stilted appearance.
4. Sketch in drifts of permanent edging plants for the foreground. The plants can be all one kind—preferably an evergreen to maintain winter form—or a combination of two or more edging plants of which at least one should be evergreen.
5. Back up the edging plants with filler flowers to bridge the gaps between the big displays. Mass the fillers in groups of three, five or seven plants of one kind. (Filler plants are those less dominant in character or those that bloom a short time or have foliage that disappears or fails to hold and turns shabby. Dainty, fluffy flowers like columbine are in the filler class. Bleeding-heart and Oriental poppies are fillers which die back soon after bloom. Perennials with foliage which disappears or turns shabby can be supplemented with plants nearby of later interest as babys-breath and annuals).
6. Repeat the drifts at intervals throughout the other sections

to give unity to the border and tie it all together. Allow a greater distance between the groups themselves than between the individual plants comprising the group. The more space you can leave between plant groups (up to the recommended maximum), the healthier the plants will be. If they look sparse at first, they will fill in quickly in most cases. Annuals can take care of bare places the first year.

7. Next to the sketch, list the plant varieties to be used. Record eventual height, spread, time of bloom, length of bloom, and color, numbered with a corresponding number on the sketch. This is the good way to double check your selections, being certain to allow sufficient space, have good height relationships, get the colors you want and achieve continuous bloom. Note when seed is to be sown.

Such a record is invaluable when placing your order. If labels get lost, it will show the location of spring bulbs, of plants whose tops disappear during the summer, etc.

HOW MANY PLANTS ARE NEEDED

In general at least three plants for each drift are needed to make a good showing. It is rather dangerous to generalize about spacing perennials since so many factors must be considered. The habits of the plants you are using will be the deciding factor.

Large Or Invasive Plants: A big plant of phlox needs about 4 square feet; a large peony about 6 square feet. The tendency today is to omit taller species which require staking, and select smaller ones that are easier to handle as dwarf fall asters, cushion 'mums, shorter summer phlox, and so on. Tall plants should be given as much space as possible—the more light and air they have, the stockier and shorter they will be. Also, many of the tall perennials have vast root systems, and need a lot of room so they do not compete. A square yard is a minimum for the large plants. Cerastium, plumbago or *Phlox subulata* and its forms spread like weeds. They too should have almost a yard of planting space.

Many perennials multiply quickly, and with economy in mind, you can limit your purchase the first year to just one or two of each. Mums, monarda and gas-plants are good examples.

Medium-sized Plants: Here too the element of branching is

PLANTED IN DRIFTS Annual ageratum, white sweet alyssum and verbena var. Sparkle in large drifts outline the border. In the background are hollyhock, hibiscus, and delphinium. Other perennials include achillea "Pearl", anthemis "Moonlight", artemisia "Silver King", campanula (still in bloom when delphinium start), shasta daisy, feverfew, sweet william, *Dictatmnus albus*, gypsophila, hemerocallis, irises, lupines, peonies, phlox, white salvia and veronica. Chrysanthemums are bought in the fall to fill in bare places.

important. Free-branching genera such as gypsophila need about a square yard, while more upright plants such as doronicum will do all right in a square foot. A well-planned border will use these plants in a clump, or perhaps three plants to a clump, or in long shallow drifts. The latter design is especially effective, for when a species passes out of bloom its absence is less noticed than if it were an isolated clump.

Edging Plants: Allow 1 to 2 square feet per plant. Iberis, dwarf lavender and santolina, as well as most other superior edging plants, may sprawl as they grow older, but seldom are rank spreaders. If a quick effect is desired with an edging plant, place fast spreaders so that a single plant occupies a square foot or less; twice that space would be better, to avoid crowding and postpone the need for dividing the clump.

BUYING PLANTS

1. Place your plant order in plenty of time so you will have a good choice of varieties for spring or fall planting. Remember, for every dollar you spend on a plant you will spend hours of work and waiting. Success will bring happiness and years of enjoyment, so start with something good.

2. If you need to economize, do not buy the newest varieties, which are collector's items, expensive because of the limited supply. Buy older varieties, perhaps equally good that have proven themselves, as the King Alfred daffodil, originated years ago but still one of the finest. This variety sells for far less than most new varieties. If new introductions prove to be superior to existing ones, they will be put on the market in large quantities and the price will drop.

Another way to cut costs is to buy small plants of good quality and grow them to a large size yourself, or propagate your own plants.

3. When roots, corms and bulbs are offered as bargains at the end of the planting season be sure you are getting a bargain and not leftover, poor quality material that may have deteriorated from poor storage. Do not be fooled by sensational advertising; resist a so-called bargain unless you know it is one. You will not get something for nothing so expect to pay for quality.

4. Shop early. If you have a good local nursery or garden center nearby, go talk with someone who knows his business, make

PERENNIAL AND DWARF SHRUB BORDER

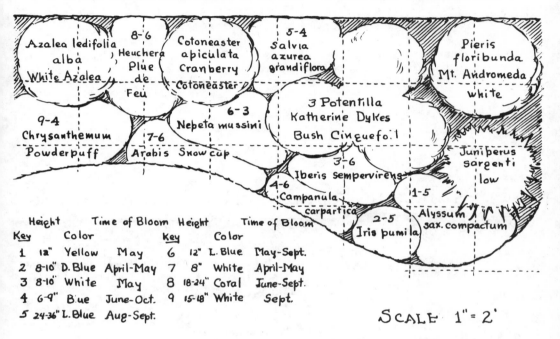

Azalea ledifolia alba
White Azalea

8-6
Heuchera
Plue
de
Feu

Cotoneaster
apiculata
Cranberry
Cotoneaster

5-4
Salvia
azurea
grandiflora

Pieris
floribunda
Mt. Andromeda
white

9-4
Chrysanthemum
Powderpuff

7-6
Arabis Snow cap

6-3
Nepeta mussini

3 Potentilla
Katherine Dykes
Bush Cinquefoil

Juniperus
sargenti
low

3-6
Iberis sempervirens

4-6
Campanula
carpartica

1-5
Alyssum
sax. compactum

2-5
Iris pumila

Key	Height Color	Time of Bloom	Key	Height Color	Time of Bloom
1	12" Yellow	May	6	12" L. Blue	May-Sept.
2	8-10" D. Blue	April-May	7	8" White	April-May
3	8-10" White	May	8	18-24" Coral	June-Sept.
4	6-9" Blue	June-Oct.	9	15-18" White	Sept.
5	24-36" L. Blue	Aug-Sept.			

SCALE 1" = 2'

Dwarf evergreens and shrubs are more in vogue these days, in keeping with the smaller homes and yards. Intersperse them with perennials for varity and added interest.

Foundation plantings need not be somber. Give them an air of gayety and welcome with colorful perennials.

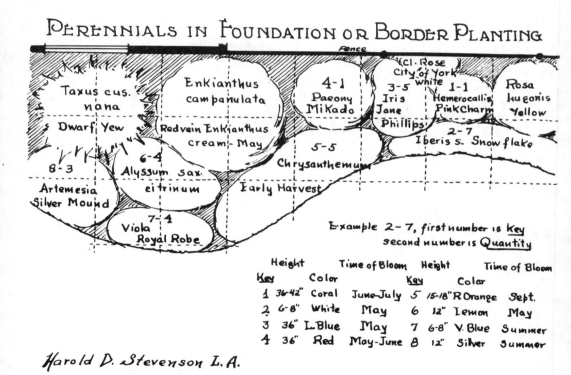

PERENNIALS IN FOUNDATION OR BORDER PLANTING

Fence

Taxus cus. nana
Dwarf Yew

Enkianthus campanulata
Redvein Enkianthus cream- May

4-1
Paeony MiKado

3-5
Iris Jane Phillips

(Cl. Rose City of York white
1-1
Hemerocallis PinkCharm

Rosa hugonis Yellow

2-7
Iberis s. Snowflake

8-3
Artemesia Silver Mound

6-4
Alyssum sax. citrinum

5-5
Chrysanthemum
Early Harvest

7-4
Viola Royal Robe

Example 2-7, first number is Key
second number is Quantity

Key	Color	Height	Time of Bloom	Key	Color	Height	Time of Bloom
1	Coral	36-42"	June-July	5	R.Orange	15-18"	Sept.
2	White	6-8"	May	6	Lemon	12"	May
3	L.Blue	36"	May	7	V.Blue	6-8"	Summer
4	Red	36"	May-June	8	Silver	12"	Summer

Harold D. Stevenson L.A.

your purchases and take the plants home in your car. This non-charge, self-delivery should save you some money.

5. If the local nursery doesn't have the stock you want, you will have to purchase by mail. Mail-order nurseries ship material at the proper planting time for your location. However, if you want your order properly filled, place it early to allow sufficient time and make substitutions unnecessary. As you become experienced you will learn who the plant specialists are and the best place to buy certain plants.

6. If you want named varieties and specific colors—and eventually most serious gardeners do—specify field-grown clumps or container-grown plants. Container culture is recommended for those varieties which transplant with difficulty, as for example babys-breath.

7. Need we say that you should write your name and address clearly on the order? Type, print or use a name sticker. When inquiring about an order, reordering or complaining, use the name exactly as indicated on the original order. When ordering, state alternate choices or state if no substitutions will be accepted. Specify planting date (or it will be shipped according to best date in your area) and keep a copy of the order.

8. Have the ground thoroughly and properly prepared for planting before the plants arrive (see page 138). Uncover the tops of perennials on their arrival but keep their roots in the packing material. Moisten roots if they seem dry. If for any reason there is to be a long wait, heel them in until planting can be done or put them in pots of soil. Water and place in a protected area in the shade until ready to be planted. Do not let the roots dry out, nor allow them to become waterlogged. Check materials against order list, and for quality. Don't blame the nurseryman or seedsman if you ruin the product through carelessness after arrival.

THE ACTUAL PLANTING

Do not hurry this particular job. Planning and planting should never be done under pressure or in a rush.

1. Spread a large piece of canvas on the lawn to lay plants on, this will save much clean up. A bushel basket or two for debris will prove handy and save steps.

PERENNIAL BORDER

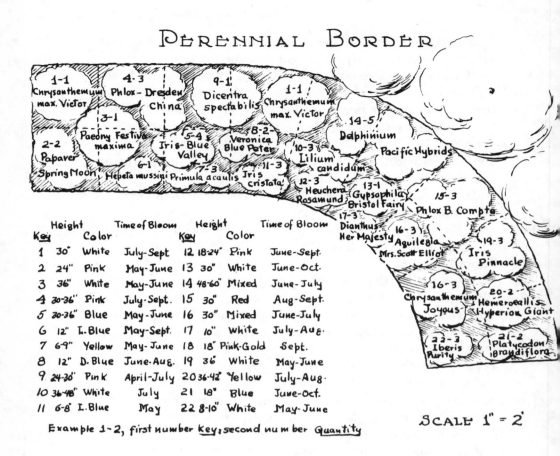

Key	Height	Color	Time of Bloom	Key	Height	Color	Time of Bloom
1	30"	White	July-Sept.	12	18-24"	Pink	June-Sept.
2	24"	Pink	May-June	13	30"	White	June-Oct.
3	36"	White	May-June	14	48-60"	Mixed	June-July
4	30-36"	Pink	July-Sept.	15	30"	Red	Aug-Sept.
5	30-36"	Blue	May-June	16	30"	Mixed	June-July
6	12"	L.Blue	May-Sept.	17	10"	White	July-Aug.
7	6-9"	Yellow	May-June	18	18"	Pink-Gold	Sept.
8	12"	D.Blue	June-Aug.	19	36"	White	May-June
9	24-36"	Pink	April-July	20	36-42"	Yellow	July-Aug.
10	36-48"	White	July	21	18"	Blue	June-Oct.
11	6-8"	L.Blue	May	22	8-10"	White	May-June

Example 1-2, first number key; second number Quantity

SCALE 1" = 2'

This curved perennial border will afford color from May to October with a continuous succession of bloom.

2. Make holes sufficiently large to allow roots to grow normally. See individual plant in A to Z of Perennials for guidance. If you plant ½″ to 1″ deeper than the plant was growing before (you can see the mark), to allow for soil settlement, you need not worry about proper depth. Firm the soil around the plant or bulbs so there will be no unfilled soil spaces or air pockets. Plant backbone perennials first.

3. Take care of individual soil needs. If lime is required for a plant, work in the proper amount where it is needed. For perennials liking more humus, mix the organic matter into the soil where the plants will be growing. Check off items as they are planted. Do not hesitate to make changes if they seem necessary when you start to actually lay out the plants. Note corrections on your sketch as well.

4. Insert stakes as you plant. Start with the backbone perennials, indicating exact locations by outline groupings with wooden labels or an old clothesline or rope. Plant in drifts, staggered to give an informal, natural effect.

5. Filler Groups—Trace shape of filler groups with planting trowel on soil surface. Then lay out or set plants on the ground, several groups at one time. Satisfy yourself the spacing is right. Then start planting fillers and edging plants.

6. Permanent plant labels, with pencil or stylus for writing them, should be at hand. Label each group with the full name of the plant—by genus, species and variety.

7. Water thoroughly following planting. A weak solution of soluble fertilizer may be used to stimulate root growth. Protect plants which have foliage that wilts badly when set out during mid-day from strong sunlight, by covering for a few days, with a basket; the roots can soon take up enough moisture so leaves will revive.

8. A week or so after planting, just lightly cultivate with hoe to loosen an inch of surface soil. This will uproot young weeds and make the soil more receptive to moisture.

TRANSPLANTING

When planting begins to crowd, about every fifth or sixth year, you may want to remake it or re-do a section or two each year. Early spring, September or early October are good times to do this.

To give added sparkle during the summer months these annuals, combined with the perennials, will supply the needed color.

PERENNIAL & ANNUAL BORDER

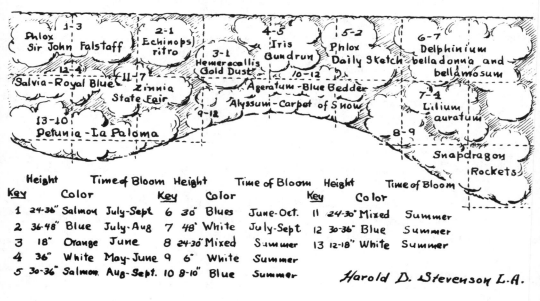

Phlox Sir John Falstaff (1-3)
Echinops ritro (2-1)
Hemerocallis Gold Dust (3-1)
Iris Gundrun (4-5)
Phlox Daily Sketch (5-2)
Delphinium belladonna and bellamosum (6-7)
Salvia-Royal Blue (12-4)
Zinnia State Fair (11-7)
Ageratum-Blue Bedder (10-12)
Alyssum-Carpet of Snow
Lilium auratum (7-4)
Petunia-La Paloma (13-10)
(9-12)
Snapdragon Rockets (8-9)

Key	Height Color	Time of Bloom	Key	Height Color	Time of Bloom	Key	Height Color	Time of Bloom
1	24-36" Salmon	July-Sept	6	30" Blues	June-Oct.	11	24-30" Mixed	Summer
2	36-48" Blue	July-Aug	7	48" White	July-Sept.	12	30-36" Blue	Summer
3	18" Orange	June	8	24-30" Mixed	Summer	13	12-18" White	Summer
4	36" White	May-June	9	6" White	Summer			
5	30-36" Salmon	Aug-Sept.	10	8-10" Blue	Summer			

Harold D. Stevenson L.A.

Retain in place the perennials which do not need (or resent) transplanting (see A to Z of Perennials).

Take up the other plants and split the clumps (see page 150). Discard the woody centers and replant only what is needed for the spaces to be filled. Enrich the soil deeply before replanting (see page 140). Save room for any new plants you may want to try.

7

The Low Maintenance Garden

A flower garden or backyard should be a pleasure. As soon as it becomes a burden its chief purpose is lost; in that case re-plan it to give the most value for the time, money and energy you can afford to expend. Gardening offers plenty of good exercise and therapeutic value for those who like it, in addition to the satisfaction and joy of creating something lovely for all to admire and enjoy, but it can be pure drudgery for the person who who rather be playing golf or fishing.

Almost everyone who answered our questionnaire stresssed that the scarcity of qualified garden workers and high cost of labor makes easy-to-manage perennial beds more desirable than ever.

THE NO MAINTENANCE GARDEN

Isabel Zucker, Michigan horticulturist and garden writer, gives encouragement to those interested in minimum maintenance. She writes:

"I grow hundreds of perennials and do not feel that any of them are hard to establish or have poor form or I wouldn't bother with them. I never stake any plant as I don't have the

AN EASY-TO-MANAGE UNDERPLANTING   Blue phlox (*Phlox divaricata*) is permanent, requires little care, and makes an excellent filler in drifts among ferns, wildflowers, perennials and spring shrubs.

time. We rarely if ever spray any plant, so if it gets pests it soon dies out. We never give any plant special care as that takes time, too. I am able to report there is at least one garden where plants grow on their own and thrive. I like particularly: *Anemones*, especially *pulsatilla* and *japonica*, Astilbes in variety, *Baptisia australis, Campanulas* in numerous species but particularly *latifolia* and *persicifolia* in both colors, the shrubby *Clematis*, particularly *Davidiana* and *mandshurica, Dictamnus* in both colors, true geraniums, hostas (I have all that are in commerce, have and am ordering seeds of some I saw in England), lily-of-the-valley, Penstemons, particularly Glenn Viehmeyer's hybrids, Peonies (the only care they get is fertilizing once a year with 10-6-4 with ureaform, which works wonderfully) and Veronicas. These perennials have been with me for years."

SELECT SLOW-GROWING, PERMANENT SPECIES

Use garden-worthy perennials, as self-sufficient as it is possible to find, those that once established are relatively easy to care for. Clumps of daffodils, day-lilies and peonies have frequently survived for years under conditions of neglect around foundations of old abandoned houses where little remains but the old cellar hole. In just the right location they seem to defy time and destruction. Slow-growing plants do not quickly outgrow their space. They require little pruning or attention.

AVOID PLANTS WITH NEGATIVE FEATURES

If minimum effort is your goal, avoid perennials described in Part I with such negative features as: hard to establish, need frequent division, invasive, need staking, flowers short-lived or susceptible to pests and disease. Any such negative qualities will require extra attention and effort.

PLANT PROPERLY AND AVOID TROUBLE

Mr. James Sutherland, Head Gardener, Christian Science Church, Boston, Mass., states: "I have had no trouble with the perennials I have listed and I do not use winter covering. If the

AROUND A SHADY POOL Requiring only occasional weeding, Jacobs-ladder, Virginia bluebells, and ferns in variety, with hawthorn and pines in the background, invite relaxation.

HERBS FOR A GOURMET   Santolina, lavender, sage and golden marguerites, easily picked and fragrant, are good choices for this patio garden
outside a good cook's kitchen.

soil is well-drained very little protection is needed with these
perennials and they do not need much care." He includes:
achillea, aconitum, anchusa, *Anemone japonica,* aquilegia, arabis, astilbe, *Campanula persicifolia,* chrysanthemum—Shasta
Daisy, *Convallaria majalis,* delphinium, dianthus (all vars.), dicentra, dictamnus, echinops, gaillardia, geum, gypsophila,
hemerocallis, heuchera, hosta, iris, mertensia, peony, phlox (all
vars.), pyrethrum, statice, trollius, and yucca.

SELECT RIGHT PLANTS FOR LOCATION

For easy maintenance choose only those plants that will thrive and keep healthy in the location where you want to grow them, that will take your climate, soil and exposure. See lists. Mrs. Edward W. Fenn, Concord, Mass., says: "My garden is mostly a shady one which dictates my choice of plants. I do not enjoy "temperamental" plants. If they do well in my garden, fine! If not I don't bother with them. I am more interested in landscaping with my plants than in growing prize-winning specimens."

A PATIO GARDEN   With a fence and wall to define the limits of the garden, and raised beds for convenience, this small planting requires minimum maintenance.

She grows astilbe, campanula (double bellflowers), *Chelone glabra* (pink turtlehead), *Dicentra spectabilis, Geranium sanguineum,* hemerocallis, mertensia, *Polemonium* (Jacobs-ladder) *Sanguinaria* (bloodroot), and *Valeriana officinalis.*

REDESIGN IF NECESSARY

If your garden is a headache to you, redesign it. You will save money in the long run. Think of these

• Two small or narrow beds are less of a chore than one large area—weeding and planting are easier.

• Plan the garden so a cultivator or sprayer can be used between the long rows if this is important.

REPLANNED TO CUT MAINTENANCE   Planned when garden help was plentiful, the borders were 8 feet wide and more than 10 feet in the corners. Decreasing width would change the proportions and ruin the over-all design. The happy solution was a 3-foot walk through the center, leaving 2½ feet of flowers on both sides—an improvement in design and function.

PLANNED FOR QUIET ENJOYMENT   Flowering trees and shrubs, a lot of ground cover, a few well-selected perennials and lots of brick add up to minimum maintenance and maximum pleasure.

• Replace lawns with paved areas and a few perennials. Lawns in the tropics and arid regions or in locations with extremely sandy soil are unnatural. Why waste time and money trying to grow grass? Paved areas using flagstone, stone, concrete or brick can cut down on upkeep. Add a few important perennials, strategically placed for striking effect. Use "made" soil for these plantings in order to get healthy plant growth.

227

Part III

Perennials
for Every Purpose

Calendar of Things to Do

JANUARY

1. Order seeds. Supply of choice material and novelties may be exhausted early.
2. Get tools and seed flats in shape, also sash for coldframe.
3. Inspect garden for low spots where water may collect and cause damage.
4. Study your perennial situation. If not satisfied rework your garden plans for more beauty and less maintenance.
5. Save wood ashes from fireplace. Add to compost or scatter light covering on the garden soil and hoe in.
6. In the South sow perennial seeds.
7. On warm days lift coldframe glass during middle of day for ventilation.
8. Lily-of-the-valley—If you have plenty, life a clump to enjoy indoors. Pot, give heat and sun gradually; should take about 3 weeks to bring into flower.
9. Christmas-rose—Cut flowers and enjoy indoors.
10. Bring single tulips, in storage to root, indoors. Do not force doubles until after February 15th.

FEBRUARY

1. Order new plant stakes (get old ones in condition), plant ties, fertilizers, mulching material or any supplies you may need.
2. If weather is mild, make garden rounds, pressing back into place plants which have heaved from the soil with the frost. Newly planted iris, peonies, rock plants and other perennials may have their crowns and roots exposed.
3. Seeds of some rock plants which like freezing can be sown.
4. In the South, plant perennials.
5. In the extreme South, flower seeds may be planted all winter; in the cotton belt from March on, but seeds may be started indoors in February.
6. Astilbe—Force into bloom indoors. Dig and pot up in heavy compost, soak well with water, place in cool spot until 2 or 3 inches of top growth is made. Water liberally. Then coax into bloom with warmth, water and sunshine.
7. Bulbs—Bring tulips indoors from storage where they have been rooted. After hardy hyacinths, daffodils and tulips are through flowering indoors and the tops have ripened let pots dry, store in garage or dry shed and plant in garden in fall.
8. Ventilate coldframe during mid-day for longer periods as weather permits.
9. Delphinium—Seedlings started indoors late this month will grow into strong plants capable of flowering about the time the heat of summer breaks and cool autumn weather is approaching.
10. Vinca minor—Sprays make lovely decorations. Underneath the snow the vine is still green. Cut long strips, wash in cold water and use indoors.

MARCH

1. Do not be too hasty to uncover protected perennial and bulb beds. Remove mulches from early, small bulbs so tiny shoots can come through. Keep tulips, daffodils and other bulbs lightly covered to keep sun from plants as long as they are frozen.

2. Compost Pile—Start one if you have none and have the room. On this heap put fallen leaves, lawn clippings and any other uncontaminated vegetable matter from the garden, wood ashes and the like. Turn and wet down occasionally.

3. In some sections of the country, garden work may be started now. Do not spade or plow until soil is dry enough to fall apart slowly when a little is squeezed in the hand. If it stays in a lump, it is not dry enough.

4. Garden perennials will benefit from an early feeding of a complete fertilizer.

5. Keep record book of perennials: record dates of sowing seed, planting and transplanting. Note time and length of bloom, where and when plants or seeds were purchased and results obtained.

6. Coldframe should be in operation. Get a head start. Seeds can be started in coldframe about 4 weeks ahead of outside planting dates.

7. Transplant seedlings started indoors to flats in coldframe. Thin out and separate, allowing ample room to develop. Support with toothpicks if needed. In transplanting young primulas, saxifrages, anemones and other rockery perennials give them some shade.

8. Spray the soil around hollyhocks, peonies and phlox with a copper fungicide and again later after the young shoots appear.

9. Cut back old growth on alyssum, hypericum and saponaria.

10. Clean up the garden.

11. Take up and divide chrysanthemums each spring, cushion varieties every other year. Make cuttings from old 'mum plants. When you discover green leaves under the mulch in the coldframe, remove mulch and shade but keep glass down except during warm part of day.

12. Ground Covers—Plant arabis, *Erysimum asperum, Phlox divaricata* and violas as ground covers for bulb beds.

13. Set out pansy plants as soon as ground is workable. Will flower continuously if blossoms are kept picked.

14. Divide such rampant growers as chrysanthemums, shasta daisy, Dianthus barbatus, gaillardia, kniphofia, lily-of-the-valley, phlox, *Rudbeckia lacinata* var. *hortensia* (Golden-Glow), and salvia.

15. Sift soil around rock garden plants that have heaved. Remove dead leaves from juicy leaved and woolly sorts.
16. Hardy violets can be forced into bloom indoors. Dig a chunk of frozen earth containing a plant or two, pot and place in a cool, sunny window.

APRIL

1. Order perennial plants now. You may not be able to get the varieties you want if you wait too long.
2. Remove any winter protection.
3. Apply lime in the correct amounts early before the ground is spaded over. Lime is not a plant food but makes heavy soils looser, sandy soils more compact, sweetens sour soils and increases the number of bacteria. An application every 3 or 4 years should be beneficial. Wood ashes contain lime.
4. When the ground can be worked spread fertilizer among the perennials in the border and work it in with a fork.
5. When cultivating be careful not to cut off the growing tips of lilies or disturb late bulbs. Be careful not to disturb the slow to appear anemone, hibiscus, platycodon and plumbago.
6. Coldframe should be left open throughout the day when the weather is warm for ventilation and to harden-off seedlings to be set out later.
7. Feeding any early-started plants with liquid fertilizer a few days before transferring from flats will prove beneficial. Liquid fertilizer in the furrows where seedlings are to be set will give them a quick start.
8. Protect perennials which have been started early by covering at night when there is danger of frost.
9. Keep some seedlings in flats to replace what the cutworms take.
10. Spray or dust delphinium, hollyhock, peony and phlox as soon as the plants start to grow. Dust or spray as required to deter pests or disease.
11. Be sure that none of last season's foliage is allowed to remain around delphinium, hollyhock, peony or phlox. Remove and burn it.

12. Sow seeds of biennials and perennials as soon as the soil is workable if they have not already been started in a cold-frame.
13. Many of the perennials can be divided now. The Japanese anemone, among finest of all autumn blooming perennials, gives best results if divided in spring.
14. Supports—Dry, twiggy growth from shrubby material may be set among low-branching perennials which will quickly hide the supports.
15. Alpines and Rock Plants—Scatter a mulch of stone chips around the crowns of those that need surface drainage as the saxifrages.
16. Bulbs—Small boxes with glass or plastic over the top are good for forcing early bulbs. After the weather gets warm, remove top and replace with wire mosquito netting if needed to exclude insect pests.
17. Prune and thin-out fall-flowering vines.
18. Clean iris plantings out by hand. Burn old leaves and all debris. Spray when leaves are about 6″ to control borer. Follow with second and third application 10 days apart.
19. The early *Iris cristata* can be dug from the garden in small mats and planted in pots so they may be enjoyed indoors. It is easily transplanted.
20. Tuck bits of sedum here and there for ground cover.
21. Easter lilies which finished blooming in the house may be set in the open ground. Even if they don't prove hardy they are likely to bloom again before the end of the summer.
22. Regal Lily—Tender when they first start to grow, to prevent late frost injury protect if a late frost threatens.
23. Lily-Of-The-Valley—Plant clumps now with the top of the pips just even with the ground.
24. Transplant pansies now.
25. Perennial Phlox—Pinch back some of the shoots while young for more and longer bloom.
26. Oriental Poppies—To discourage unwanted plants, dig out the roots and hoe off any shoots which appear later.

MAY

1. If frost threatens protect young plants.

2. Any perennials received by mail or express, if dry on arrival, should be plunged in water or buried in moist earth for a time.
3. Make a note of any changes you want to make in the fall.
4. Last chance to transplant rapid-growing perennials.
5. Middle of month apply second dose of balanced fertilizer to all established perennials. Use readily available food upon iris, peonies and other perennials coming into bloom.
6. On the first and fifteenth dust or spray as necessary; particularly watch delphinium, hollyhock, peonies and phlox. Watch lupine for lice, iris for borer.
7. Nearly all flower seeds can be sown in the garden during the next few weeks. Make sowings of spring-flowering perennials for next spring's bloom.
8. Cut off tops of *Alyssum saxatile*, forget-me-not and helianthemum for better growth.
9. When seedlings grown in a frame or house are set out choose a quiet, cloudy day. Plant long-stemmed seedlings with the roots an inch or so deep but avoid burying the crowns of plants that have their leaves borne in rosettes. Tall lanky growth should be pinched back to 2 or 3 sets of leaves.
10. Get rid of the weeds with a hoe.
11. Mulch late-planted perennials.
12. Encourage second crop—As arabis, anchusa and aubrieta go out of flower, cut tops to encourage new growth and second crop of flowers.
13. Stake delphinium before a storm breaks their lovely spires, also hardy asters, boltonia, and chrysanthemums if necessary.
14. Chrysanthemum—When newly divided plants have 6 leaves pinch out top to induce branching. Pinch back other branches as each of these develops 6 leaves. Pinch judiciously until the middle of July. Bushy plants look and bloom best.
15. Bulbs—Let the foliage of hardy spring bulbs ripen before removing.
16. Regal Lily—Seed may be sown now, using a coldframe or sow directly in open ground.
17. Violas and pansies—Set out now placing about 9" apart. Al-

ways keep the faded flowers well picked to encourage new blooms.

18. Peonies—For large exhibition flowers disbud peonies in early May when the buds are very small, about the size of a pea.
19. Phlox—For size, pinch out all but 5 stems of each mature clump.
20. Rockery—Plant now.
21. Shasta Daisy—Can be divided or planted now. Requires an abundance of room. Do not allow to flower too freely the first year.

JUNE

1. Take stem cuttings now or in July of edging plants such as arenaria, candytuft, snow-in-summer, pinks, dwarf phlox, rockcress, etc., when second growth starts.
2. Remove all faded flowers for long blooming season.
3. For a second crop of bloom cut back perennials which have flowered.
4. Pinch out all but 4 shoots in aster clumps and judiciously pinch back 'mums to make them branch until the middle of July. Stake if necessary.
5. Prune iberis and similar plants after flowering to induce thick new growth.
6. Sow perennial seeds, preferably in a coldframe, or in an open but protected seed bed, for early summer bloom next year.
7. Newly set-out plants and seedlings should be shaded for several days until they have become established if the weather is hot. See that they get ample water.
8. Mulch to keep down weeds and conserve moisture.
9. Stake if necessary before storms cause any damage.
10. Dust and spray as needed. Control iris borer.
11. If there are vacancies buy started perennials or annuals to fill empty spaces.
12. Cut flowers for indoors early in the mornings or late in the afternoon and plunge into water at once.
13. Turn over material in compost pile with fork and soak with a slow-running hose.

14. Hollyhock blooms may be improved by thinning the flower buds. Flowers do not last as long on crowded stalks and tip flowers are seldom good. Spray frequently for rust and mildew.

15. Grape Hyacinth—If permitted to seed they will self-sow over a wide area, which may be desirable.

JULY

1. If season is dry water as necessary. The usual garden requires one inch of rain a week to keep plants growing normally.

2. Dust and spray as necessary. If the weather is damp and muggy it could be a bad month for mildew and blight. Dust to deter. Hollyhocks—Keep dead and dying foliage cleared away from around the plants. Keep the under sides of the leaves well covered with a combination of sulphur and ferbam as a deterrent for red spider and to prevent the spreading of rust disease which appears as reddish-brown pustules. Iberis (Candytuft)—If humidity is high, dust for red spider. Forceful hose sprays directed from below break webs. Sulphur scattered on soil fumigates the spider away.

3. Turn over compost pile with fork and soak with a slow-running hose.

4. Stake tall perennials that need it before they break. Gusts which accompany thunder storms can play havoc.

5. Snip off blossoms as they fade to extend blooming season.

6. Cut back perennials as delphinium and lupines which have finished blooming to encourage a second crop. Prune some of the edging and rock garden plants to induce thick, new growth.

7. Bulbs—Order bulbs of fall crocuses and colchicums now. They should be planted as soon as they arrive and will bloom in the autumn. Crocuses may be used in the rock garden but the leaves of colchicum are too large for such a location. Decide now what bulbs you will need for later fall planting and order early.

8. Campanula pyramidalis (Chimney Bellflower)—Cut up roots and plant pieces 2 inches deep where they are to grow.

9. Chrysanthemums—Give a light feeding well watered-in for better fall display. Pinch back again for the last time the middle of the month.
10. Helleborus (Christmas-rose)—A few summer soakings through dry spells are beneficial.
11. Hemerocallis and iris are going through a rest period making this an ideal time to divide and reset them. Grow some of the many new lovely strains. Divide Madonna Lily as soon as it is through flowering. Make divisions of pyrethrum now or in September.
12. Iceland Poppies—Pick pods and sow seeds rather than depend on self-sowing.
13. Lilium testaceum (Nankeen Lily) and L. candidum (Madonna Lily)—Place order for bulbs now to plant in September. Plant about 3″ deep.
14. Linum (Flax)—To induce new growth remove at ground line some of the hardened older shoots which have flowered freely.
15. Nepeta Mussini (Border Catmint)—Make cuttings now. The new soft growth should be pinched off and placed in sand in a shaded coldframe.
16. Pansies—Order best seed obtainable for new beds to be made by first of August.

AUGUST

1. The last month to sow the general lot of perennial seeds.
2. Make root cuttings of anemone, babys-breath, bleeding-heart, Oriental poppy, phlox and statice.
3. Transplant seedlings of seeds sown in May or June. Space 6 wk. old plants 4″-10″ apart in a row or in coldframe. Water as needed.
4. Dust or spray, water or stake as needed. Use chlordane or spray with DDT for Japanese beetles.
5. Turn over and soak compost pile.
6. Order daffodils now. They need to be planted much earlier than many of the other bulbs.
7. If you do not wish perennials to self-sow keep seed from forming. Cut hollyhocks back to prevent seeds from scattering all over the garden. When they are through bloom-

ing cut to ground and burn all tops and leaves. Spray young seedlings with fungicide to prevent any infection.

8. Dicentra spectabilis (Bleeding-Heart)—Cut off foliage which has died and is unsightly and burn.

9. Doronicum caucasicum (Leopards-Bane)—Plant roots now when dormant. They will make good-sized plants by next spring and be sure to bloom.

10. Fall Colchicums and Crocuses—Plant now.

11. Forget-Me-Not—If tulips were not lifted sow seed directly in tulip bed for attractive carpet planting with tulips early next spring.

12. Gypsophila (Single variety or Bristol Fairy)—For dried sprays cut now when in full bloom. Cut on hot day and dry in shade. Store in cartons lined with paper. This applies to strawflowers and other everlastings although they should be hung, heads down, to dry. Cut and dry herbs to prepare for culinary uses. They are spiciest if cut just before the flowers open.

13. Helleborus (Christmas-rose)—Make planting now or in September. They do not like to be moved so place where they are to stay, in a location in partial shade.

14. Madonna Lily—Set out ahead of other bulbs, plant 2 to 3 inches deep. Old bulbs may be dug up and divided. Surround with sharp sand if soil is heavy.

15. Lupine—Wake up resting plants with a good watering and light application of fertilizer.

16. Peony—Order for September planting. Apply trowelful of fertilizer around each old clump carefully working it into the soil for good flowers next year.

17. Phlox—Take stem cuttings to increase supply. Cut back $^2/_3$, those that have bloomed heavily.

18. Rock Garden—Some of the rampant growers will need to be cut back.

19. Oriental Poppies—Dormant by late July. Do not disturb unless necessary. If division is essential, divide when plant is dormant and replant or cut roots into 2 inch pieces and plant in good soil. New growth should appear by end of a month.

SEPTEMBER

1. Herbaceous borders can be remade at this time. Most perennials, except the autumn flowering kinds, can be divided and transplanted now. Dig deeply and enrich the soil before resetting the plants.

2. Divide and reset any perennials which need it as a general housecleaning of the border.

3. Transplant seedlings from seed bed to coldframe or to rows in a protected reserve bed, 4" to 8" apart, depending on the variety. If you are planning a new border prepare the soil now and let it settle until next spring, before planting.

4. Newly set divisions and seedling plants will establish themselves more fully before winter if mulched after planting. It tends to maintain low soil temperatures for a longer period and thus makes for greater root development.

5. Watch for early frosts. In many cases garden plants protected through the first cold snap have a relatively long period of warm weather in which to continue growing and giving pleasure.

6. Now is the time to get rid of the perennials you consider weedy or no longer want.

7. Give final dusting or spraying as needed.

8. Place markers among perennials to indicate where lily bulbs are to go.

9. If you haven't one already, build a coldframe in which to sow seeds, root cuttings and to winter plants safely.

10. Bleeding-Heart—Divide now so they will become well established before hard frost.

11. Bulbs—Use a dibbler for planting but learn how to give it a swinging twist to make the bottom of the hole round and large enough so the bulb will not be planted with an air space under it.

12. Small Bulbs—Chionodoxas, crocuses, scillas, snowdrops and other small bulbs should be planted as early as obtainable, sometime during September.

13. Canterbury Bells and Foxgloves—Plunge spade in the soil near the plants. This breaks the root system and puts them to rest, resulting in greater hardiness.

14. Chrysanthemums—Fertilize when buds start to show.

Spray for aphids with nicotine. Transfer well-budded plants to the border, if you wish to, on a cloudy day, soak the day before and several days after moving; stake any that need it. The plants will bloom on without any interruption.

15. Eremurus (Desert Candle, Foxtail Lily)—Select light, well-drained, moderately rich soil for roots in a spot protected from high winds and morning sun. Somewhat tender so protect in the spring when growth starts. Set large baskets over them on cold nights.

16. Everlastings—Flowers like armeria (Thrift or Sea Pink) and *Catananche caerulea* (Blue Succory or Cupid's-Dart) should be picked when the buds begin to open; then tie loosely in bunches and allow to hang heads down for several weeks until they dry.

17. Hemerocallis (Day-Lily)—Divide at least every fifth year. The work may be done almost any time.

18. Heuchera (Coral Bells)—You can edge a border by dividing several large established clumps. Gently pull apart. Cut from the tap root only sections with some good roots of their own..

19. Hyacinth and Narcissi—Pot up those to be forced indoors and place in the cellar or a trench for root making. Darkness is required.

20. Iris—Bulbous iris may be planted now. Divide and reset crowded clumps. Cut tops half way back. Plant small divisions of bearded varieties 1 inch deep, and 15 inches apart. Face rhizomes in the same direction. Set 3 single pieces of Siberians 3 inches apart to form a clump. Water regularly after transplanting if weather is dry. Protect with mulch first winter.

21. Lilies—Order bulbs now although some may not be delivered until late September because they mature slowly. Madonna Lily should be planted as soon as possible.

22. Lily-Of-The-Valley—Separate every 3 or 4 years for best results. Select strongest crowns and plant 3 inches apart each way, just below the surface.

23. Narcissus Family—All members should go into the ground by late September if possible. Hyacinth bulbs may also be planted now or in October.

24. Phlox—Dig and discard any that are poor. Divide big

clumps into thirds every third or fourth year.

25. Iceland Poppy—Seeds planted now will come up before the end of the season but will endure the winter safely and bloom next spring long before spring-sown plants.

26. Tulips—Need not be planted for several weeks, may be planted in November, but place order now and have stock on hand.

27. Violas—Plant in coldframe now for good plants next spring.

28. Transplant any self-sown seedlings you want to save to the border or rockery.

29. Plant peonies.

OCTOBER

1. There is still time for making over the perennial bed. Do this now to conserve time so valuable during the busy spring. Re-do poorly designed sections or overcrowded spots.

2. Fill containers with leaf mold, good garden soil and sand and store in a frost-free place for use when planting seeds in flats and pots or rooting cuttings.

3. Put leaves from lawn on compost pile, adding lime or wood ashes and a commercial fertilizer. Burn any diseased or insect-ridden foliage left in the perennial bed.

4. To play safe mark with labels those perennials which start late in the spring such as the aconite, eupatorium, Japanese anemone, mallow and platycodon.

5. Give border a good cleaning. Lift out and divide plants needing it, discard poor varieties or those past their prime. Dig deeply, work compost and bonemeal into the soil and reset plants.

6. If month has been dry give perennials a good, deep, final soaking so they will go dormant in good condition and be less inclined to winter-kill.

7. Tie canes of clematis and other trained vines.

8. Label bulbs and roots dug up for winter storage and also mark places where spring bulbs and perennials are being planted.

9. Fill Coldframe—Plants of doubtful hardiness may be wintered here with late cuttings and small seedlings. A few

pansies and English daisies in the frame will bloom in late winter.

10. Arrangement Material—Collect seed heads before they are shattered by autumn's storms. Many late wildflowers such as limonium (statice), eupatorium and solidago hold their colors better if gathered earlier in the year when they are just opening but those collected now may still be useful.

11. Bulbs—Continue to plant hardy bulbs. Planting of such minor bulbs as crocus, scilla, snowdrop, chionodoxa and especially narcissus species should be completed at once. Large-flowering narcissus must also be planted immediately. Spring-flowering bulbs last longer if planted deeply —crocus set 5 inches and tulips 10 inches deep. Mulch lightly after the ground freezes the first winter.

12. Chrysanthemum—Clumps in flower may be dug and potted for house decoration or moved to other parts of the garden for fall color effects. As soon as through flowering, cut tops back and lift stock plants of doubtful hardiness. Place in an open coldframe and water once a week until a hard freeze occurs. Each clump will yield many divisions in the spring.

13. Eranthis hyemalis (Winter Aconite)—Plant tubers now for early spring bloom in the garden or rock garden. The yellow buttercup-like blossoms will open 2 weeks ahead of the crocuses. Plant tubers 2 inches deep and give light winter protection.

14. Iris—Remove leaves from plants the last thing in the fall. The eggs which produce iris borer are laid on the leaves. Burn them.

15. Kniphofia (Tritoma)—Not dependably hardy. If left outside protect the crowns.

16. Tulip plantings may be started as soon as the bulbs arrive although mid-October is early enough. If the bulbs are to be left for several years plant 10 to 12 inches deep, according to size. If they are to be dug up and stored in the spring plant them 6 to 8 inches underground.

17. Regal Lily—Effective planted between peonies and other large growing perennials or among rhododendrons and mountain laurel.

18. Lily-Of-The-Valley—Mulch lightly with old crumbly manure, peat moss or leafmold to increase vigor of the plants.

The same practice will benefit pachysandra. When mulching ground covers and creeping plants in the rock garden add sand to the humus used.

19. Peonies—Continue to plant peonies and hardy bulbs. Cut off and remove all peony foliage. Work in a trowelful of bonemeal per plant.

20. Hollyhock—Gather every leaf and stem and burn them if you are troubled with bud rot and rust.

21. Rock Garden—It is better not to set out rock garden plants after the middle of October. However, it is a good time to build a new rock garden or do any construction or repair work. The ground will then be ready and settled in preparation for spring planting.

22. Sunflowers—Remove seed heads before fully ripe and spread in a dry, airy place to cure for about 2 weeks before removing the seeds.

23. Tulips—In sections where field mice prey on tulip bulbs it may be necessary to put the bulbs in wire cages although the use of substances offensive to rodents is the modern plan.

24. English Violets—Place frame over beds out-of-doors in order to have early blossoms in spring.

NOVEMBER

1. After the ground is frozen give tenderer subjects some protection.

2. Spade vacant spaces in border and leave rough for winter.

3. Put a little covering on exposed perennial beds if ground freezes hard, but defer until early December.

4. Put coldframe to use by storing in it plants that need protection such as canterbury bells, English daisies, forget-me-nots, foxglove and pansies, and questionable chrysanthemums. Late bloom can be had on into the winter by setting a few roots of pansies and violets in a frame. Pansies started in August in a coldframe will bloom earlier than those left unprotected.

5. Sow seeds recommended for late sowing. (See page 167). Many gardeners sow delphinium seed now and carry flats through the winter in coldframe for an early start.

6. Stagnant surface water from melting snow during the winter months is dangerous to perennials. This condition can be averted in many cases by digging shallow ditches to carry off this surface water when the ground is frozen.

7. Mulching materials should be obtained now for use when the ground freezes hard, but not before. Mulch lightly all young plants just beyond the seedling stage.

8. Chrysanthemums—When through flowering cut back to within a few inches of the ground. After freezing weather mulch all except dePetris varieties. After mulching those in the frame, put down the glass and shade it. May not be necessary next month.

9. Helleborus (Christmas-rose)—Look to see if you have enough flowers for a bouquet. Do not cut the evergreen foliage. Add bonemeal lightly and a thin layer of compost.

10. Lilies—Continue planting as long as ground is open.

11. Lily-Of-The-Valley—If need division dig plants and reset them 1½ inches deep and 6 inches apart. Bonemeal and well-rotted manure worked into the soil will make a great improvement.

12. Peonies and Iris—Clean up tops and burn material if there is the least danger of disease.

13. In the North finish planting tulips.

DECEMBER

1. There is less to do in the perennial garden in December than in any other month.

2. Mulching is postponed until the ground freezes. It will not be long before mulches can be applied in most parts of the country to hold the soil temperatures even. See that protection does not become matted and smother plants. It should keep them cold and unstimulated by midwinter warmth. Only cover those plants that need protection.

3. Water should not be allowed to drip from the gutters into the perennial border.

4. Coldframe—Check the coldframe to make sure that plants being wintered-over have not dried out. Be certain there is no drainage problem which will cause standing water. If this trouble is present, make a runoff trench and a note to

correct the problem more adequately next year by laying gravel or cinders in the bottom of the frame. Ventilate coldframe in which campanulas, English daisies, pansies and other perennials are being wintered until the ground is thoroughly frozen. Then mulch lightly and replace the sash, covering it with straw mats for the rest of the winter.

5. Collected garden seeds keep well in stout paper envelopes. Mark and arrange alphabetically in boxes. Give garden friends choice perennial seeds as Christmas presents.
6. Read perennial books and send for seed catalogs.
7. Clean, oil and apply rust-preventing materials before putting garden tools away.
8. Bulbs—Examine potted bulbs in the cellar or darkened coldframe. If full of roots they are ready for forcing indoors. They force quickly.
9. Helleborus (Christmas-Rose)—Cut flowers now for indoor arrangements.

PERENNIALS PREFERRING SUN AND TOLERANT OF DRY, SANDY PLACES

The majority of perennials do best in the sun. Some shade is not objectionable over part of the border provided there is not too much competition from the tree and shrub roots.

Achillea Millefolium
Aethionema grandiflorum
Ajuga genevensis
Alyssum saxatile
Anaphalis margaritacea
Anemone Pulsatilla
Anthemis tinctoria and vars.
Arabis caucasica (albida)
Aremaria montana
Artemisia Stelleriana
Asclepias tuberosa
Aubretia deltoidea
Baptisia australis
Callirhoe involucrata
Campanula carpatica
   persicifolia
   portenschlagiana
Centaurea Cineraria
Ceratostigma plumbaginoides

Coreopsis grandiflora
Dianthus deltoides
Echinops Ritro
Euphorbia corollata
Galium mollugo
Gypsophila paniculata
Helianthemum nummularium
Hemerocallis
Heuchera
Hypericum calycinum (give shade)
Iris germanica vars.
Kniphofia
Lathyrus latifolius
Lavandula Spica
Linum perenne
Lupinnus hybrids
Lychnis chalcedonica
   Coronaria
Malva moschata

Monarda didyma
Nepeta Faassenii (Mussini)
Oenothera fruticosa
  missouriensis
Opuntia compressa
Papaver nudicaule
Penstemon barbatus
Phlox subulata
Platycodon grandiflorum
Potentilla pyrenaica
Prunella vulgaris (some shade)
Pyrethrum
Ranunculus repens

Rudbeckia laciniata
  speciosa
Santolina chamaecyparissus
Saxifraga Aizoon (some shade)
  decipiens (some shade)
Sedum album
  Sieboldii
  spectabile
Teucrium Chamaedrys
Thermopsis caroliniana
Verbascum olympicum
Yucca (filamentosa) Smalliana
Zauschneria

PERENNIALS FOR THE ROCK GARDEN

See list of "Perennials Preferring Sun and Tolerant of Dry, Sandy Places." Such plants are suited to the rock garden, where one of the main requirements is perfect drainage.

PERENNIALS GOOD AS CUT FLOWERS

(Those starred are "everlasting"—popular for drying)

Aconitum autumnale
Anaphalis margaritacea
Anemone
Anthemis tinctoria
Aquilegia
Armeria maritima
Artemisia
Asclepias tuberosa
Aster novae-angliae
  novi-belgii
Campanula persicifolia
Catananche caerulea*
Centaurea montana
Chelone glabra
Chrysanthemum vars.
Coreopsis
Delphinium hybrids
Dianthus barbatus
Digitalis purpurea
Doronicum caucasicum
Echinacea purpurea
Echinops
  Ritro*
  sphaerocephalus*

Eryngium
  alpinum
  amethystinum
  Oliverianum
  planum

Eupatorium
Gaillardia
Geum
Gypsophila
  paniculata vars.*
  repens Bodgeri*
Helenium vars.
Helianthus decapetalus
Heliopsis helianthoides vars.
  scabra vars.
Hemerocallis in var.
Heuchera
Hosta
Iris in var.
Kniphofia Uvaria
Liatris
Lilium in var.
Limonium latifolium*

Lupinus
Nepeta
Paeonia in var.
Papaver
Penstemon
Physostegia virginiana

Rudbeckia speciosa
Salvia superba
Scabiosa
Veronica longifolia vars.
Viola

PERENNIALS TOLERANT OF SHADE

Lack of sun is no excuse for not growing perennials. Many native wildflowers and hardy ferns prefer shade or partial shade. In a shady location, never use any plants that are listed as requiring full sun.

Aconitum in var.
Aegopodium Podograria
Ajuga in var.
Anemone japonica and vars.
   sylvestris
Aquilegia in var.
Aruncus sylvester
Asperula odorata
Astilbe in var.
Astrantia major
Brunnera macrophylla
Campanula in var.
Chelone glabra
   Lyonii
Cimicifuga racemosa
Convallaria majalis
Cymbalaria muralis
Dicentra in var.
Digitalis in var.
Dracocephalum in var.
Epimedium in var.
Eupatorium coelestinum
Gentiana Andrewsii
Geranium grandiflorum
   sanguineum
Helleborus niger
Hemerocallis in var.
Hepatica americana
Heuchera in var.
Heucherella
Hosta in var.
Iberis

Lilium canadense
   pardalinum
   regale
   speciosum and hybrids
   superbum
   tigrinum
Liriope Muscari
Lobelia cardinalis
   siphilitica
Lysimachia clethroides
Meconopsis cambrica
Mertensia virginica
Myosotis
Pachysandra terminalis
Phlox divaricata
   maculata
   paniculata vars.
Podophyllum peltatum
Polemonium in var.
Polygonatum multiflorum
Polygonum
Primula in var.
Pulmonaria in var.
Sanguinaria canadensis
Saxifraga Aizoon
   decipiens
Shortia galacifolia
Smilacina racemosa
Symphytum
Thalictrum in var.
Tradescantia virginiana in var.
Trollius in var.
Vinca minor
Viola cornuta

PERENNIALS TOLERANT OF MOIST
OR WET LOCATIONS

If you have a wet, poorly drained area and it is impractical and too expensive to install proper drainage, there are many perennial possibilities. Using plants that naturally grow in swamps and bogs or moist woodlands or meadows, the place can be made attractive and interesting. Native cinnamon, royal and sensitive ferns may be planted as well as a long list of other possibilities.

Astilbe japonica—moist
Astrantia major—moist
Chelone glabra—moist
  Lyonii—moist
Cimicifuga racemosa—moist
Doronicum plantagineum—moist
Eryngium amethystinum—moist
Eupatorium purpureum—moist
Filipendula Ulmaria—moist
Gentiana Andrewsii—moist or wet
Helenium autumnale—moist
Hibiscus palustris—moist
Iris Kaempferi—moist
  sibirica—moist
Lobelia cardinalis—moist or wet
  siphilitica

Lysimachia clethroides—moist or wet
Lythrum Salicaria—moist
Mertensia virginica—moist or wet
Myosotis scorpioides—moist or wet
Phlox maculata—moist
Physostegia virginiana—moist
Podophyllum pelatum—moist
Polemonium caeruleum—moist
Primula polyantha—moist
  elatior—moist or wet
  veris—moist or wet
  vulgaris—moist or wet
Salvia azurea var. grandiflora—moist
Sanguisorba obtusa—moist
Thalictrum aquilegifolium—moist
Trollius europaeus—not wet

PERENNIALS THAT FLOWER OVER
FAIRLY LONG SEASON

A long-flowering season counts for so much with most gardeners today that this characteristic often becomes a deciding factor in the low-maintenance garden. However, the foliage of plants such as the iris, peony, hemerocallis and penstemon (which flower for only a small part of the season) remains decorative long after the bloom is gone. They add beauty to any garden.

Achillea Ptarmica
Anthemis tinctoria vars.
Aquilegia chrysantha
Armeria maritima vars.
Aster Frikartii

Callirhoe involucrata
Campanula carpatica
Centaurea montana
Chrysanthemum cushion vars.
  maximum vars.

Coreopsis grandiflora
Coronilla varia
Delphinium grandiflorum
Dianthus latifolius vars.
  plumarius vars.
Dicentra eximia
Gaillardia aristata vars.
Galega officinalis vars.
Galium Mollugo
Gaura Lindheimeri
Geranium ibericum and vars.
  sanguineum
Geum chiloense and vars.
Gypsophila paniculata
Heliopsis scabra vars.
Heuchera sanguinea vars.
Lamium maculatum
Linum perenne
Lythrum Salicaria vars.
Malva moschata

Monarda didyma vars.
Nepeta macrantha
  Faassenii (Mussini)
Oenothera fruticosa and vars.
Papaver nudicaule vars.
Phlox paniculata vars.
Physostegia virginiana
Platycodon grandiflorum vars.
Potentilla pyrenaica
Rudbeckia speciosa
Salvia azurea var. grandiflora
Scabiosa caucasica vars.
Sidalcea Rose Queen
Tradescantia virginiana vars.
Trollius asiaticus
Tunica Saxifraga fl. pl.
Verbena canadensis
Veronica longifolia
  spicata vars.
Viola cornuta Jersey Gem

PERENNIALS WHICH REQUIRE REPLANTING
EVERY FEW YEARS
(Those starred perhaps annually)

Achillea Ptarmica vars.
Anthemis
Arabis
Aster hybridus nana*
  novae-angliae vars.
  novi-belgii vars.
Astilbe
Boltonia
Campanula
Centaurea
Cerastium
Chelone
Chrysanthemum*
Doronicum
Erigeron
Eupatorium coelestinum*
  rugosum
Gaillardia
Geum

Helenium
Helianthus
Heliopsis
Heuchera
Iris
Lysimachia
Monarda
Penstemon
Phlox
Physostegia
Polemonium
Primula polyantha vars.
Pulmonaria
Rudbeckia laciniata fl. pl.
  subtomentosa
Stokesia
Tradescantia
Veronica

PERENNIALS WHICH DO NOT NEED
FREQUENT REPLANTING
(Those starred resent it)

Although dividing perennials is not much of a chore, for a minimum-maintenance garden, choose plants that may be left undisturbed for a few or many years.

Aconitum*
Adenophora
Alstroemeria*
Amsonia
Anchusa*
Anemone
Armeria
Asclepias*
Baptisia
Bergenia
Callirhoe*
Cimicifuga
Clematis
Convallaria
Dicentra
Dictamnus*
Echinops
Eryngium*
Euphorbia
Galega
Gaura
Gentian
Geranium

Gypsophila*
Helleborus*
Hemerocallis
Hosta
Incarvillea*
Kniphofia
Lathyrus*
Liatris
Limonium*
Lupinus*
Lythrum
Mertensia*
Oenothera
Paeonia*
Papaver*
Platycodon*
Scabiosa
Sedum
Sidalcea
Thalictrum
Thermopsis
Trollius

PERENNIALS USEFUL AS SPACE FILLERS
(OF ROBUST GROWTH OR RAPID SPREAD)

Ajuga reptans vars.
Alyssum
Artemisia Stelleriana
Aster
Bergenia
Boltonia aesteroides
Centaurea
Centranthus
Cephalaria
Cerastium tomentosum
Ceratostigma
Coronilla varia

Dracocephalum
Echinops
Epilobium angustifolium
Eupatorium
Galega
Geranium
Gypsophila
Helianthemum
Helianthus vars.
Hemerocallis fulva
Inula
Kniphofia

Lamium
Ligularia
Lysimachia clethroides
Malva
Monarda didyma vars.
Papaver orientale, some vars.
Phlox subulata
Physalis
Physostegia virginiana
Polygonum
Rheum

Rudbeckia
Salvia
Saponaria
Senecio
Stachys
Symphytum
Tanacetum
Valeriana officinalis
Verbascum
Vinca

PERENNIALS OF LOW GROWTH WITH GOOD FOLIAGE
FOR GROUND COVERS

Aegopodium Podagraria variegatum
Ajuga reptans
Alyssum saxatile compactum
Cerastium tomentosum
Convallaria majalis
Coreopsis auriculata nana
Coronilla varia
Dianthus deltoides
Epimedium grandiflorum
Euphorbia Cyparissias
Galium mollugo
Hedera helix

Hosta decorata
   lancifolia
   undulata
Hypericum calycinum
Mentha Requieni
Nepeta hederacea
Pachysandra terminalis
Phlox subulata
Polygonum affine
Ranunculus repens
Sedum acre
Thymus Serpyllum
Vinca minor
Viola priceana (papilionacea)

PERENNIALS WITH FRAGRANT FLOWERS
OR FOLIAGE

Achillea Millefolium
Adenophora lilifolia
Anthemis tinctoria
Aquilegia chrysantha
   caerulea
Arabis caucasica (albida)
   alpina
Artemisia lactiflora
   Stelleriana
Asperula odorata
   orientalis
Centranthus ruber
Chrysanthemum Balsamita

Clematis heracleaefolia
   h. Davidiana
   recta
Convallaria majalis
Dianthus Caryophyllus vars.
   plumarius vars.
Dictamnus albus and vars.
Erysimum asperum
Filipendula Ulmaria
Hemerocallis citrina
   Dumortieri
   flava
Hesperis matronalis

Hosta plantaginea (subcordata)
Hyssopus officinalis
Iris germanica vars.
  pallida
Lavandula officinalis
Lilium auratum
  candidum
  regale
Lobularia maritima
Lupinus—sweet scented hybrids
Malva moschata
Monarda didyma
Nepeta Faassenii (Mussini)
Oenothera speciosa

Paeonia officinalis vars.
  tenuifolia
Phlox divaricata
  paniculata vars.
  stolonifera
Primula elatior
  Florindae
  polyantha
  veris
  vulgaris
Valeriana officinalis
Viola cornuta
  odorata

BLOOMING TIME OF PERENNIALS IN NORTHEASTERN UNITED STATES

The x months indicate major blooming times. In several cases bloom may begin the month before those given or extend to the month after. In unfavorable years with hot drying winds blooming time may be cut short to fill only a portion of the month indicated.

	March April	May	June	July	Aug.	Sept. Oct.
Achillea Millefolium			x	x	x	
Ptarmica			x	x	x	
filipendulina			x	x	x	
tomentosa			x	x	x	
Aconitum Anthora				x	x	
bicolor					x	
Carmichaelii (Fischeri)					x	x
Henryi					x	x
Vulparia (Lycoctonum)				x	x	x
Adenophora potanini			x	x		
Adonis amurensis	x					
vernalis	x	x				
Aegopodium Podograria			x			
Aethionema armenum		x	x			
grandiflorum		x	x			
pulchellum			x	x		
Ajuga genevensis		x	x			
pyramidalis		x	x			
reptans		x	x			
Allium giganteum			x			
Moly				x		
Ostrowskianum		x	x			
Alstroemeria aurantiaca				x	x	
Althaea rosea				x	x	

	March April	May	June	July	Aug.	Sept. Oct.
Alyssum alpestre	x	x				
Moellendorfianum			x			
montanum	x	x				
saxatile	x	x				
Amsonia Tabernaemontana		x				
Anaphalis margaritacea				x	x	
Anchusa azurea (italica)		x	x			
var. London Royalist			x	x		
Androsace sarmentosa			x			
Anemone blanda	x					
japonica						x
Pulsatilla	x	x				
Anthemis tinctoria			x	x	x	
Anthericum Liliago			x	x		
Aquilegia caerulea		x	x			
canadensis		x				
chrysantha			x	x		
flabellata			x	x		
vulgaris		x	x			
Arabis alpina		x				
caucasica (albida)	x	x				
procurrens	x	x				
Arenaria montana		x	x			
verna		x	x			
Armeria maritima		x	x			
Artemisia albula				x		
Schmidtiana				x		
Stelleriana					x	x
Aruncus sylvester			x	x		
Asclepias incarnata				x	x	
tuberosa				x		
Asperula odorata		x	x			
Asphodeline lutea				x		
Aster novae-angliae					x	x
Amellus				x	x	
Cushion Asters						x
Farreri			x	x		
novi-belgii					x	x
Oregon hybrids					x	x
yunnanensis		x	x			
Astilbe Arendsii hybrids			x	x		
astilboides			x	x		
chinensis			x	x		
japonica			x	x		
Astrantia major			x	x	x	
Aubrieta deltoidea	x	x				
Baptisia australis			x			
tinctoria				x		
Belamcanda chinensis				x	x	
Bellis perennis		x	x			
Bergenia cordifolia	x	x				
crassifolia	x	x				
German hybrids		x				

	March April	May	June	July	Aug.	Sept. Oct.
Boltonia asteroides					x	x
latisquama					x	x
Borago laxiflora	x	x	x	x	x	
Brunnera macrophylla		x	x			
Buddleja Davidii				x	x	x
Callirhoe involucrata				x	x	x
Campanula carpatica				x	x	x
lactiflora				x	x	
latifolia			x	x		
Medium			x	x		
persicifolia				x	x	
pyramidalis					x	x
Catananche caerulea				x	x	
Centaurea Cineraria				x	x	
dealbata			x	x		
montana			x	x	x	
Centranthus ruber				x	x	x
Cephalaria tatarica				x		
Cerastium tomentosum		x	x			
Ceratostigma plumbaginoides					x	x
Cheiranthus Cheiri		x	x			
Chelone glabra				x	x	x
Chrysanthemum (hardy)					x	x
coccineum			x	x		
maximum			x	x	x	
Cimicifuga racemosa				x	x	
simplex						x
Clematis heracleaefolia					x	x
recta				x	x	
Convallaria majalis		x	x			
Coreopsis auriculata		x	x			
grandiflora				x	x	
lanceolata				x	x	
Coronilla varia			x	x	x	
Crucianella stylosa				x		
Delphinium hybrids			x	x		
Dianthus alpinus		x				
barbatus			x	x		
Caryophyllus				x	x	x
plumarius		x	x			
Dicentra eximia		x	x	x	x	
spectabilis		x	x			
Dictamnus albus				x	x	
Digitalis grandiflora (ambigua)			x			
purpurea			x	x		
Dodecatheon Meadia		x	x			
Doronicum caucasicum		x				
plantagineum		x				
Dracocephalum Ruyschianum			x	x		
Echinacea purpurea				x	x	
Echinops Ritro				x	x	
Epilobium angustifolium				x		
Epimedium grandiflorum			x			
Youngianum	x	x				

	March April	May	June	July	Aug.	Sept. Oct.
Eremurus robustus			x			
Erigeron speciosus				x		
Erodium absinthioides var. amanum			x	x		
chamaedryoides var. roseum			x	x		
Eryngium alpinum				x	x	
amethystinum				x	x	
Erysimum asperum		x				
Eupatorium coelestinum					x	
rugosum						x
Euphorbia corollata				x	x	
Wulfenii		x				
Filipendula hexapetala			x			
Ulmaria			x			
Gaillardia aristata			x	x	x	
Galega officinalis			x			
Galium verum			x	x	x	
Gentiana Andrewsii				x		
asclepiadea				x	x	
septemfida			x	x	x	
Geranium grandiflorum		x	x			
Geum chiloense			x	x		
Gypsophila acutifolia					x	
Oldhamiana					x	x
paniculata				x	x	
repens			x	x		
Helenium autumnale					x	x
Helianthemum nummularium			x	x	x	
Helianthus decapetalus				x	x	x
salicifolius						x
Heliopsis scabra				x	x	x
Hemerocallis in variety		x	x	x	x	x
Hepatica americana	x					
Hesperis matronalis			x	x		
Heuchera sanguinea			x	x	x	
Heucherella tiarelloides				x	x	
Hibiscus palustris					x	x
Hosta Fortunei		x				
lancifolia					x	x
plantaginea					x	x
undulata				x	x	
Hypericum patulum				x	x	x
Hyssopus officinalis					x	x
Iberis sempervirens		x				
Incarvillea Delavayi			x			
Inula ensifolia					x	x
glandulosa			x	x		
Iris cristata	x	x				
germanica		x	x			
Kaempferi				x		
pumila	x	x				
sibirica			x			
Jasione perennis				x	x	
Kniphofia Uvaria				x	x	

	March / April	May	June	July	Aug.	Sept. / Oct.
Lamium Galeobdolon				x	x	
Lathyrus latifolius			x	x		
Lavandula officinalis				x	x	
Liatris punctata				x	x	
scariosa					x	x
Lilium auratum					x	
Aurelian hybrids					x	
candidum			x	x		
formosanum (early)			x			
formosanum (late)					x	
Hansoni			x	x		
Henryi					x	
Mid-century Hybrids				x		
Olympic Strain				x		
pumilum			x			
regale				x		
rubellum		x				
speciosum					x	x
tigrinum					x	
Limonium latifolium					x	x
Linum flavum			x	x		
perenne		x	x	x		
Lobelia cardinalis					x	x
siphilitica					x	
Lunaria annua		x	x			
Lupinus polyphyllus		x	x			
Lychnis chalcedonica			x	x		
Coronaria				x	x	
Flos-cuculi			x	x		
Viscaria			x			
Lysimachia clethroides				x	x	
Lythrum Salicaria				x	x	
Macleaya cordata				x	x	
Malva moschata			x	x		
Meconopsis cambrica				x	x	
Mertensia virginica	x	x				
Monarda didyma				x	x	
Myosotis alpestris	x	x				
scorpioides		x	x			
sylvatica	x					
Nepeta Faassenii (Mussini)		x	x	x		
Oenothera fruticosa			x	x		
missouriensis			x	x		
speciosa			x	x	x	
Onopordum Acanthium				x		
Opuntia compressa			x	x		
Origanum vulgare			x	x		
Paeonia hybrids			x			
lactiflora			x			
officinalis		x	x			
tenuifolia		x				
Papaver nudicaule		x	x			
orientale		x	x			

	March April	May	June	July	Aug.	Sept. Oct.
Penstemon barbatus			x	x	x	
Phlox divaricata		x				
paniculata				x	x	x
subulata	x	x				
Physalis Alkekengi						orange husks
Physostegia virginiana				x	x	x
Platycodon grandiflorum				x	x	
Podophyllum peltatum		x				
Polemonium caeruleum		x	x			
reptans	x	x				
Polygonatum commutatum		x	x			
multiflorum		x	x			
Potentialla fruticosa			x	x	x	
nepalensis				x	x	
Primula elatior	x	x				
polyantha		x				
pulverulenta			x	x		
veris	x	x				
vulgaris	x	x				
Prunella vulgaris			x	x	x	
Pulmonaria angustifolia	x	x				
Ranunculus acris			x	x		
Rudbeckia hirta hybrids					x	x
speciosa				x	x	
Sagina subulata	x	x				
Salvia azurea					x	x
farinacea				x	x	x
nutans				x		
superba				x	x	x
Sanguinaria canadensis	x					
Sanguisorba canadensis				x	x	
obtusa				x	x	
Saponaria ocymoides			x	x		
Saxifraga Aizoon			x			
lingulata			x			
umbrosa		x				
Scabiosa caucasica			x	x		
graminifolia				x		
Sedum Sieboldii					x	x
Senecio macrophyllus				x		
Shortia galacifolia	x	x				
Sidalcea malvaeflora			x	x		
Silene Schafta					x	x
Smilacina racemosa		x				
Soldanella alpina	x					
Stachys grandiflora			x	x		
Stokesia laevis				x	x	x
Teucrium Chamaedrys					x	
Thalictrum aquilegifolium			x			
dipterocarpum				x	x	
rugosum			x	x		
Thermopsis caroliniana			x	x		
Tradescantia virginiana			x	x	x	

	March April	May	June	July	Aug.	Sept. Oct.
Tritonia crocosmaeflora				x	x	
Trollius in var.		x	x			
Tunica Saxifraga			x			
Valeriana officinalis			x	x		
Verbascum hybrids			x	x		
Verbena bonariensis			x	x	x	
Veronica incana			x	x		
prostrata			x	x		
repens		x				
spicata			x	x		
Viola cornuta		x	x	x		
Yucca Smalliana					x	
Zauschneria californica					x	x

SEVEN "BACKBONE" PLANTS FOR THE SMALL GARDEN
(Listed in Order of Bloom)

Daffodils   Peonies
Tulips   Delphiniums
Iris   Perennial Phlox
            Hardy Chrysanthemums

USEFUL DEFINITIONS FOR THE
PERENNIAL GARDENER

ANNUAL—A plant that grows to maturity, sets seeds and dies within a single growing season.

AXIL—Point at which a stalk or branch diverges from the stem.

BEDDING PLANT—The term "bedding" is applied to plants grouped together for mass effect, forming a planting bed.

BIENNIAL—A plant that requires two growing seasons in which to mature, set seeds and die (complete its life).

BIGENERIC HYBRID—The result of a cross between plants belonging to different genera.

BLADE—The flat, extended part of a leaf as distinguished from its stalk.

BRACT—A modified leaf, sometimes so showy as to be called the flower. Bracts are common throughout the mallow and carrot families. Poinsettia is the classical example.

CALYX—Collective term for all the sepals of a flower; the external, usually green or leafy part of a flower. Some flowers have no corolla in which case the calyx is often colored like a corolla and replaces it as in the hepatica and anemone.

CILIA—Minute marginal hairs forming a fringe.

CLONE or CLON—Plants propagated vegetatively from one original plant. They are genetically identical.

COMPOUND FLOWER—Compound and variously branched as opposed to simple and solitary like a tulip. Like parts are united into a common whole.

COMPOUND LEAF—Composed of more than one blade or leaflet on a single leaf stalk.

COROLLA—Unit formed by petals of a flower. May be separate as in daisy or united as in bellflower.

CORYMB—A flower cluster in which the individual flower stalks elongate, cluster is flat-topped or nearly so. Blooms from the edge towards the center of the cluster.

CRENATE—Having the margin cut into rounded scallops, as a leaf.

CRESTED—The crest if often a ridge or appendage, sometimes toothed or elevated and irregular. May be on the petals as in some iris or it may modify the whole flower cluster as in the cockscomb.

CROWN—That part of the plant between the root and the stem, usually at or near the ground level.

CYME—A broad, often flat-topped, branching flower cluster that blooms from the center towards the edges, in which the main stalk is always terminated by a flower. Typical examples are many plants of the pink and gentian families.

DECOMPOUND—Said of leaves, having divisions that are compound. See Compound.

DIOECIOUS—Having male and female flowers on separate plants.

DISK—In composites, refers to the central portion of the head, composed of tubular flowers. Ageratum has disk florets but no ray flowers. Black-eyed Susan (*Rudbeckia hirta*) has purplish-brown disk florets and golden-yellow ray florets around the margin.

DISSECTED—Cut deeply into many fine lobes or divisions, sometimes almost thread-like segments, as a leaf.

DIVIDED LEAF—Parted or cut to the base or center; however deeply divided, such leaves are not compound.

ENTIRE—Whole, as without teeth, as are many leaf margins.

FERTILE—As to flowers, bearing both stamens and pistils and thus able to produce seed.

FLORET—One of the individual, and usually small flowers, that comprise the flower head in plants of the Compositae.

GLABROUS—Completely smooth, mostly applied to leaves and stems; opposite of pubescent.

GLAUCOUS—Covered with a minute whitish or grayish powder.

HEAD—Any tight, close head-like cluster of flowers. Flower clusters of the plants belonging to the huge family of Compositae.

HEEL—Basal end of a cutting, especially if there is some of the old stock taken with it.

HERB—A plant without a permanent woody stem. Commonly thought of as a plant used for medicinal purposes, fragrance and flavoring.

HERBACEOUS—Having a stem that is fleshy.

HOSE-IN-HOSE—When one flower appears to grow from within another. The cup-and-saucer Canterbury Bell is a good example.

HYBRID—The result of crossing two different plants.

INFLORESCENCE—The arrangement of flowers in a cluster. It may be simple and solitary or compound and variously branched.

LACINIATE—Cut into narrow, almost fringe-like segments.

LANCEOLATE—Much longer than broad and tapering towards a slender, pointed tip. More or less lance-shaped.

LEAF AXIL—See Axil. Many flowers are borne in leaf axils.

LEAF BLADE—The expanded or flat part of a leaf as distinguished from its petiole (leaf stalk).

LEAFLET—One of the divisions or segments of a compound leaf.

LINEAR—Narrow and long, with essentially parallel edges, as in the case of many leaves.

LIP or LIPPED—That part of an irregular corolla which resembles a protruding lip, a common feature of many flowers in the mint and figwort families and in many orchids. The snapdragon has an upper, erect 2-lobed lip and a lower, spreading 3-lobed one.

LOBE—A rounded projection or division of a petal or leaf. If the division extends more than half way to the center it is better described as divided.

MIDRIB—The main or principal vein or rib of a leaf.

NODE—The joints or swellings which occur along a plant stem where leaf and bud growth begins. The place at which leaf, bud, and branch of a flower cluster joins the stem.

OBOVATE—Having a shape like an egg but with the broad end upward.

OVATE—Egg-shaped with the broader end downward, applied mostly to leaves.

PALMATE—A compound leaf. Leaflets arranged finger-fashion, sections radiate from a common point, handlike.

PANICLE—A loose, open flower cluster which blooms from the center or bottom toward the edges or top. Adams-Needle, *Yucca Smalliana*, is a good example.

PEDUNCLE—A stalk of a solitary flower, or the main stalk of a flower cluster. Each of the flowers in a cluster may have its own individual stalk, which is then properly called a pedicel.

PERENNIAL—A plant which lives on and on under favorable conditions.

PERFECT FLOWER—One that bears both male and female organs of reproduction.

PETIOLE—A leaf stalk.

PINNATE—A compound leaf. Leaflets arranged feather-fashion.

PISTILLATE—Bearing only pistils, female reproductive parts.

PUBESCENT—Covered with soft hairs.

RACEME—An elongated flower cluster blooming from the bottom upward, with a single main stalk, from which arise the stalks of the individual flowers. Typical example is lily-of-the-valley.

RAY—The flat, marginal flower of the head in many plants of the Compositae as the aster, daisy, sunflower, etc.

RHIZOME—A thickened, fleshy, rootlike stem, occurring underground or creeping along the soil's surface.

ROSETTE—Radiating cluster of basal leaves common in plants like the houseleek and in most saxifrages. While usually basal they are sometimes terminal.

RUGOSE—Rough.

SCAPE—A flower stalk, usually leafless, that arises at the ground; often bears small scales or bracts. Tulip, bloodroot, most primroses and many others are scapose plants.

SEEDLING—A plant grown from seed.

SEPAL—One of the separate parts of the calyx. See Calyx.

SESSILE—Stalkless, attached directly at the base.

SPATULATE—Shaped like a spatula, spoon-shaped.

SPIKE—A raceme-like cluster in which individual flowers are stalkless or nearly so. (They are stalked in a raceme.) Good example is the hyssop.

SPUR—A tubular, hollow prolongation in certain flowers. Any hollow projecting spur-like appendage of a corolla or calyx, as in the columbine, larkspur, etc.

STAMINATE—Bearing only stamens, male reproductive parts.

STERILE—Unable to germinate.

STOLON—A creeping horizontal or trailing stem, from the tip of which a new plant arises.

STRIATE—Striped.

SUCCULENT—Drought-resistant plant. Having juicy tissues as most cacti.

TEETH or TOOTHED—Having marginal teeth. Notched or toothed on the edge.

TETRAPLOID—Chromosomes are cellular bodies in which the hereditary units, called genes, are located. Chromosomes are usually definite in number for any given species of plant. These numbers have been determined for hundreds of garden plants and are important to geneticists. Term tetraploid frequent in catalogues. Means plant has four times the normal number of sex or reproductive chromosomes. May or may not be superior to diploid (twice the normal number of chromosomes) although some are outstanding.

TOMENTOSE—Densely covered with matted, flat hairs giving leaves and stems a felt-like appearance.

TUBER—A swollen, mostly underground stem, which bears buds like the potato.

UMBEL—Flower cluster in which all the flower stalks arise at one point, the cluster being flat-topped or ball-like. Umbels are found in the carrot family, among the onions and in a few of the milkweeds.

WALL GARDEN With a few well-chosen evergreens and colorful perennials to soften the rock walls, this garden is never out of bounds for the casual gardener.

Opposite. GARDEN OF AN IRIS ENTHUSIAST In modern plantings, the trend is towards selecting fewer varieties, concentrating on those which require little upkeep.

Opposite. HOBBY GARDEN For the enthusiast, there can't be too much of a good thing. Specialized gardens are easily managed (irises do need splitting every few years), but are best on large properties where they can be ignored when out of bloom.

Below. COOL COMFORT A swimming pool requires maintenance (and capital outlay) but many home owners consider it a good investment in family pleasure and convenience. Here it is screened with a hedge used as a background for drifts of perennials.

RURAL SCENE In a country setting, the planting is informal, with large drifts used instead of straight borders. Forget-me-nots, ferns, clematis and arborvitae are the plants.

SPRING SETTING   By limiting the perennial border to a narrow strip against the wall, and keeping the lawn and patio large, maintenance is kept low.

Below.   RUSTIC RETREAT   Perennials thrive and grow more valuable each year if they are selected properly at the beginning. Here the emphasis is on shade plants (see page 249).

Above AN ENCHANTING DOORYARD GARDEN   This casual planting features spring-flowering bulbs and a cover of vinca for all-season good looks. A showy crab apple (upper right), complements a white lilac (left center). At left gatepost is a fragrant *Viburnum carlesi,* with pendant *Wisteria sinensis* against the roof. Aquilegia, *Campanula persicifolia* and chrysanthemums provide a palette of color from mid-August until frost.

SIMPLICITY IS THE KEY A wide lawn creates the same sense of space and distance as the ocean. The low stone wall on the right brings intimacy without blocking the water view. Paving and plants all around the border tie the area into one harmonious garden.

Photo Credits

The numbers listed refer to the pages on which the photographs appear.

American Association of Nurserymen: 178; 226, designed by Thomas D. Church, L.A., San Francisco; 227
Coonan, William: 103
Delkin, Fred L.: 22
Downward, J. E.: 77
Genereux, Paul E.: Plate I; Plate II, Mr. & Mrs. Stedman Buttrick, Concord, Mass., owners; Plate V; Plate VII; Plate IX, Mrs. Wililam H. Moore, Medford, Mass., owner; 20; 23; 30; 31; 32; 55; 65; 69; 77; 107; 115; 127; 172, Mrs. Underhill Moore, Dorset, Vermont, owner; 173, Mr. & Mrs. H. Knowlton, Auburndale, Mass., owners; 174, Mrs. Louis Phanuef, Chestnut Hill, Mass., owner; 177, Mr. & Mrs. G. S. Moore, Marblehead, Mass., owners; 180, Andover Garden Club; 183, Mr. & Mrs. Walter McGregor, Manchester, N. H., owners; 184, North Shore Garden Club; 185, Bartlett Gardens, Hamilton, Mass.; 187, Mr. & Mrs. Stedman Buttrick, Concord, Mass., owners; 188, Mrs. Karl Ohlson, Lynn, Mass., owner; 190, Mrs. Lucien Taylor, Dover, Mass., owner; 194, Mrs. Preston E. Corey, Reading, Mass., owner; 195, Mrs. E. Alan Larter, Dunstable, Mass., owner; 196, the late Mrs. Curran, Swampscott, Mass.; 197, Mrs. C. Holbrook, Brattleboro, Vt., owner; 200, Mr. & Mrs. A. L. Austin, Jr., Cotuit, Mass., owners; 204, Mrs. Howard Giles, South Woodstock, Vt., owner; 211, Mr. & Mrs. A. L. Austin, Jr., Cotuit, Mass., owners; 221; 223, Mr. & Mrs. Clifford H. Walker, Waban, Mass., owners; 224, Mrs. Irving C. Wright, Chestnut Hill, Mass., owner; 225, Frederick W. Swan, Pine Gardens, Milton, Mass.; 266; 267, Mr. & Mrs. Knowlton, Auburndale, Mass., owners; 268, Mrs. Hollis Gale, Woodstock, Vt., owner; 269, Mr. & Mrs. Knowlton, Auburndale, Mass., owners; 270, Mrs. William Warton, Groton, Mass., owner; 271, Mrs. Donald Tuttle, Middlebury, Conn., owner; 272, Dr. Allen Braily, Newton, Mass., owner; 273, Bartlett Gardens, Hamilton, Mass.; 274, Mr. Donald Kirk David, Osterville, Mass., owner.
Gleason, Herbert W.: 48, 79, 99, 124
Groffman, Nelson: jacket illustration; Plate IV, Mr. & Mrs. Robert W. Breed, Swampscott, Mass., owners
Grossman, Jeannette: 26, 68
Healy: 83, 99
Jackson & Perkins Co.: 53, 63, 64, 77, 80, 102, 112, 117, 121, 129, 131, 132
McFarland Co., J. Horace: 53, 74, 96, 115, 120, 123, 125, 126, 191, Mrs. John A. Burnham, Marblehead, Mass., owner

—INDEX—

Page Numbers in *Italic* Type Signify Principal References

277

278

279

Queen of the prairie, 73
Quilled type of chrysanthemum, 54

Rabbits, 158
Ragged robin, 99
Raised beds, 182-83
Ranunculus, *114*, 166
Rayonnante type of chrysanthemum, 54
Record keeping, 164, 233
Redesigning the garden, 226-27, 243
Red spider, 156, 238
Reflexed type of chrysanthemum, 54
Regal lily, 235, 236, 244
Resetting plants, 150
Rheum, *114-15*
Rhizomes, 242
Rhododendrons, 244
Rock base, 182
Rock-cress, 31, *39*, 115, 150, 237
Rockery, 237
Rocket, 83
Rock garden, 186, 240, 245
Rock-garden plants, 167-68, 201, 238
Rock-jasmine, 26
Rock phosphate, 159
Rock plants, 168, 232, 235
Root cuttings, 239, 241, 242
    exposure, 143, 232
    growth, 217
    lice, 157
Rooting, deep, 142
    indoor, 231
    time for, 169
Rooting cuttings, 243
Rootone, 168
Roots, 17, 215, 247
    diseased, 156
Rose, 184, 195
Rose chafer, 157
Rose mallow, 85, 192
Rosmarinus, *115*
Rosemary, 115, illus. 180
Rot, bud, 245
Rotenone, 153, 155, 156
Rudbeckia, *115*, 167, 233, illus. Plate IX
Rue, *116*
Rue-anemone, 28
Rust, 158, 245
Ruta, *116*

Sage, 116
Sagina, *116*
St. Bernard-lily, 29
St. Johnswort, 86, 126
Salvia, *116-17*, 167, 171, 233

Sand, 164, 168, 243, 245
Sandy soil, 142, 227, 234
Sandwort, 31
Sanguinaria, *117*, 226
Sanguisorba, *117-18*
Santolina, *118*, 212
Saponaria, 12, *118-19*, 233
Sapphire anemony, 26
Satin flower, 97
Satureja, *119*
Savory, 119
Saxifraga, *119-20*
Saxifrage, *119*, 186, 233, 235
Saxifrage pink, 120, *130*, 196
Scabiosa, *120-21*
Scales, 157
Scilla, 241, 244
Sea-holly, 70, 192
Sea-lavender, *95*, 121, 192, 201
Sea pink, 32, 242
Seaside garden, 189-92
Sedum, *121*, 168, 171, 192, 201, 235
seed bed, 164
    catalogs, 247
    flat, 164
    germination, 162
seeds, newly planted, 237
    ordering of, 162
    placement of, 164
    planting, 243, illus. 163
    propagation by, 160
    storing, 162, 247
    temperature for germination of, 167
Seed-sowing, 166-68
Self-sowing, 162, 239
Sempervivum, *121-22*
Senecio, *122*, 166
September, garden procedures in, 241-43
Sevin, 156, 157
Shade-growing plants, 176
Shasta daisy, *52*, 122, 139, 164, 166, 170, 171, 224, 233, 237, illus. Plate V
Shellflower, 50
Shooting star, 66
Shortia, *122-23*
Short-lived plants, 11
Shrub border, 175, 213
Sidalcea, *123*
Silene, *123*, 166
Silkweed, 34
Silver king artemisia, 33, illus. 180
Silver mound, 192
Single type of chrysanthemum, 54
Slopes and steps, plants for, 176-79
Slow-growing plants, 222